IT'S (MOSTLY) HIS FAULT

IT'S (MOSTLY) HIS FAULT

For Women Who Are Fed Up and the Men Who Love Them

ROBERT MARK ALTER

FOREWORD BY JANE ALTER

WARNER BOOKS

NEW YORK   BOSTON

Warner Books

Time Warner Book Group
1271 Avenue of the Americas, New York, NY 10020
Visit our Web site at www.twbookmark.com

Printed in the United States of America

First Edition: March 2006
10 9 8 7 6 5 4 3 2 1

Library of Congress Cataloging-in-Publication Data

Alter, Robert Mark.
    It's (mostly) his fault : for women who are fed up and the men who love them /
Robert Mark Alter. — 1st ed.
        p. cm.
    ISBN-13: 978-0-446-57777-9
    ISBN-10: 0-446-57777-4
    1. Man-woman relationships. 2. Marriage. I. Title: It's (mostly) his fault. II. Title.
    HQ801. A45 2006
    306.872'2—dc22

                                                      2005023754

Book design by Charles Sutherland

To my wife,
Jane.
Out of your great love for me
and your great respect for yourself
you have taught me all this.

_____

Then she must be your inspiration.

Gurumayi Chidvilasananda

Acknowledgments

Thank you, Gurumayi, for all the blessings in our lives. . . . Thank you to the people closest to me, my inner circle of family and friends, for their unending love and support and encouragement: our beloved daughter, Greta, and Matt and Gracie and Harper; the best mother-in-law on earth, Yvette Lebow, and Al, and River; Aunt Sally and Aunt Alberta and my cousins Mark, Kay, John, Alan, and Keith; Gail and Milt, Steven, and Lynnie and Jon and the boys; Gita and David, Lora and Steve, Mary and Michael, and Ruth and Jon; the Fruhan family, the *machetunim* one prays for. . . . Thanks to Jane for love and wisdom and beauty and the graceful and resolute editing of the book and its author. . . . Thank you to our wise and caring agent, Susan Ginsburg, who believed in the manuscript and swiftly and expertly brought it to the right editor at the right publisher, and who then quietly watched over and took care of everything. . . . Thank you to our brilliant editor at Warner Books, Amy Einhorn, who with her piercingly clear vision saw instantly and instinctively where the book needed to go, and got it there. The best thing that ever happened to this book was finding you, Amy. . . . Thanks to Jim

Schiff and Emily Griffin, Amy's assistants, and Rachel Spector and Emily Saladino, Susan Ginsburg's assistants, for all their help and goodwill. . . . Thank you to Fred Courtright, who acquired all the permissions and is the best permissions man an author could ever hope for. . . . Thanks to Kayvan Sabery for watching over my computer for the last three years and trying, with some success, to keep me calm in the process. . . . Thank you to Bill Betts, master copyeditor, who helped get the writing right. . . . A special thanks to Bob Castillo at Warner for his dedicated, patient work over many months to get the whole book right, and for being so *nice* while doing it. . . . And thank you to Chris Dao and Emi Battaglia and Jamie Raab and all the other nice people at Warner Books, Writers House, and everywhere who had a part in making *It's (Mostly) His Fault* into a book.

Contents

Foreword

You make me want to be a better man.

Jack Nicholson to Helen Hunt
in the movie As Good as It Gets

When I first read the manuscript of It's (Mostly) His Fault, my first thought upon finishing it was, "This is a revolutionary book." The ideas in this book are, in my opinion, the truth of how a man should act toward his wife. This is a truth that we wives have been trying to say to our husbands for years, but it's gone largely unheard because most men don't really listen to women. Also, we women are so used to accommodating and deferring to men that we haven't fully valued our own truth, or our worth or power. What you'll find in these pages—finally!—is a man's full validation of that truth, and an invitation and exhortation to experience your worth and your power.

This book is about the changes a man needs to make to be a good husband, written by a man who has made them. I can attest to that. He's my husband.

He wasn't always such a gem. In fact, sometimes, like many men, he was a nightmare. There was a time when he was riddled with a lot of the stuff that most men are riddled with in their relationships with women: self-centeredness, dominance, disrespect, dismissiveness, an arrogance you wouldn't believe, and communication habits from hell—stuff that really impaired him in our marriage relationship and caused me a lot of pain and anger.

We had some serious work to do.

My part of the work was to make it very clear to him which behaviors of his were okay with me and which ones weren't, and to insist that he live up to my standards of behavior and to confront him when he didn't. This took considerable strength and persistence on my part, as Robert, like many men, and especially in those days, could be unreachable to the point of impenetrable. Sometimes I just couldn't get through to him. But I stayed with it because I knew I wanted to be in this marriage, I knew what I wanted from my husband in it, and I wasn't prepared to accept less.

Robert's part of the work was to listen to me and to *change*; to get rid of everything in himself that wasn't love and respect for me; to become, in short, a good husband to me.

Which he did. He really changed. He faced what he needed to face in himself, and he fixed it. It didn't happen all at once, but little by little he became the husband I wanted him to be.

Meanwhile, down in his therapy office, Robert was listening to married people tell him about the problems in their marriages and coming to the conclusion that most of those marital problems could be solved—if the men became better husbands! This goes against the conventional concept in marital therapy that both partners in a marriage are *equally* responsible for the problems in the marriage. After a day of therapy he would come up-stairs saying, "It's *not* equal, Jane. It's the *men*. The women are sitting there basically just trying to have a decent relationship with them, but the men don't know how to do it."

Robert is not only a therapist and a writer, he's also a teacher. What follows in this book are his teachings—all he's learned about how to become a good husband, written in a man-to-man way, a kind of no-nonsense, let's-cut-the-crap, let's-just-speak-the-truth-and-get-to-the-bottom-of-this way. Men definitely feel confronted and challenged by Robert, but they also feel a camaraderie with him. They can hear what he has to say because he knows where they're coming from—he's been there!—so his message gets through to them, and the men are actually inclined to take on the task of changing. When they leave therapy with Robert, they are much better husbands, and their wives are much happier people.

This is a book about the transformation of men and women and marriages, of how we relate to each other as human beings in this world. I think Robert's whole life has been leading to the writing of this book, to the delivering of this message. As singer India Arie says of her work, "It's a true confession of a life-learned lesson I was sent here to share with y'all."

I hope you enjoy and benefit from my husband's book.

Jane Alter
June 4, 2005

IT'S (MOSTLY) HIS FAULT

What is bettre than gold?
Jaspre.
What is bettre than jaspre?
Wisedoom.
And what is bettre than wisedoom?
Womman.
And what is bettre than a good womman?
Nothyng.

Geoffrey Chaucer

Unfolded out of the folds of the woman man comes unfolded,
and is always to come unfolded . . .
Unfolded out of the friendliest woman is to come the friendliest
man . . .
Unfolded out of the folds of the woman's brain come all the folds of the
man's brain, duly obedient,
Unfolded out of the justice of the woman all justice is unfolded,
Unfolded out of the sympathy of the woman is all sympathy;
A man is a great thing upon the earth and through eternity,
but every jot of the greatness of man is unfolded out of woman;
First the man is shaped in the woman, he can then be shaped in himself.

Walt Whitman

She is your treasure; she must have a husband.

William Shakespeare

Welcome, Men and Women

I will reveal to you a love potion—without
medicine, without herbs, without magic:
If you want to be loved, then love.

Hecaton of Rhodes

This book is about love and marriage and marital connection, and it finds fault. It looks at the disconnection and unhappiness and loss of love in many marriages in our time and says that we men are primarily responsible for it.

A no-brainer if ever there was one.

It's (Mostly) His Fault is a man talking man-to-man to men. It is short, straightforward, to the point, and easy to read.

Each of the forty-four chapters is a brief explanation of a specific way we men are the ones who are (mostly) at fault for the disconnections and difficulties in our marriages, and a description of how we can get much better connected to our wives and become good husbands to them—husbands who are worthy of their respect, their love, their adoration, their sexuality, and all the other great things a woman can grace her man with when she's pleased with him.

There are chapters on talking to her, listening to her, her anger, your feelings, and your work. There are eight chapters having to do with sex. There are chapters on the greatness of manhood, service of womanhood, emotional connection, and sexual fidelity. There's a chapter called "Cheer Up!" and one called "Sober Up!" and one called "Grow Up!" Four chapters answer the questions posed in their titles: "Is There Good Sex After Marriage?" "Who's the Boss?" "What Does a Woman Want?" and "Is Your Wife a Nag?" Many chapters will describe what a real man is, and one gives the definitive answer to the timeless question, "How to Know When You're Being a Man As Opposed to When You're Being an Asshole."

All in all, the forty-four chapters are a light that suddenly gets thrown on in that doghouse we men have been living in for centuries, and finally we can come out of there and get back to our wives in the home. *It's (Mostly) His Fault* is the journey we men must take in the way we think about our wives and the way we behave to them, a journey that leads to a whole new way of relating to them. The chapters are like courses—all required, none elective!—in the curriculum of becoming a good husband to a good wife, a man who finally understands how to relate to the woman he's married to.

Each chapter begins with a quote or two—drawn from literature, scripture, film, or song—that highlights the point being made about marital connection in that chapter, and each chapter ends with a "Move" that a man can make to put into practice what he has learned in that chapter.

While this book is written to men, it is written in the knowledge that women will read it, so I have included a lengthy introduction to women and a closing message, and at the end of certain chapters there are sections written to women called "A Word to the Wives." Men, read all this too. You'll find important information about yourself, your wife, and your marriage, and you'll see what you're up against.

Man or woman, what I hope you find in this book is the way out of your marriage problems, a way to change, a way to the marriage of your dreams.

His Introduction

The best way to help women is to work on your fellow men.
That's where the real struggle is—getting enlightenment
through the concrete block known as a man's head.

Michael Moore

A million million men, or twelve men,
Must crash the barrier to the next higher form.

Jean Toomer

After thirty-five years of marriage and thirty years of being a therapist and marriage counselor, I've come to three major conclusions:

First, the notion that men and women are equally responsible for the problems in marriages is—to use one of my father's favorite expressions—a bunch of crap. Mostly it's the men. Mostly it's us husbands. Mostly it's our fault.

This is not male-bashing. Don't even *think* about going there.

That's not what this is at all. Nobody needs to get bashed, and nobody needs to be *bad* here. All we men need to do is own up to the fact that we sometimes act like jerks in our marriages, and think and say and do things that create disconnection rather than connection with our wives, and we need to change.

So just believe me: If you're having problems in your marriage, if your wife is unhappy with you, angry at you, feeling alienated from you, sexually turned off to you, it's probably your fault—mostly. Yes, our wives always have *some* work to do on themselves, and sometimes a lot of work, but when it comes to knowing how to really be in an intimate relationship, how to have true connection and true love in a marriage, we men, believe me, are a piece of work.

After thirty years of counseling married guys in my therapy office, I've also reached the conclusion that there are many great men in this world who, deep in their hearts, want to be great husbands to their wives, but they've got no idea, or a bunch of wrong ideas, about how to do that, and they need some serious help.

And third, I've learned that there are very specific ways to relate to a wife, and very specific ways *not* to relate to her, and all of that is teachable to a man who's interested. There are techniques, and there's a technology. A woman actually does come with an instruction manual, and a man can learn it.

As a marriage counselor my job is to try to convince the piece of work who's sitting in front of me that, one, it's totally great he's sitting in front of me; two, that the *reason* he's sitting in front of me is that he's done and continues to do some very *ungreat* things in his relationship with his wife, which is the major reason she's sitting over there feeling sad, lonely, and furious at him, and the children are also sad, and the family's a mess; and three, that he, the man, should just shape up and finally become a good husband to her.

You can do it, I say to the man, and the sooner you do it, the faster you'll get out of therapy.

The best way to keep a man *in* therapy, I've learned, is to tell him that if he does it right, he'll soon be *out* of therapy. Men are not big fans of therapy. I'm not either, actually. I'd much rather be shooting baskets out on the driveway or cleaning out the garage.

So I wrote this book, a man speaking pointedly and briefly to men about how to admit fault, change, and become good husbands. Based on my personal and professional experience, I believe that if we men get our act together and change, our marriages will change.

As Madden would say, "Boom!"— just like that.

We can have the wife we've always dreamed of as soon as we become the husband she's always dreamed of. No longer will we have to complain that she's never pleased with us, she's always nagging us, she won't have sex with us, she won't stop eating, she's no *fun* anymore. All we have to do is become good husbands, and that *one* change—a unilateral change that we can do on our own—will produce change all around us.

Could it really be that simple?

Yes. It really is that simple.

If we men correct the faults we have in our relationships, if we become good husbands as described in this book, if we learn to treat our wives with love and respect and give them the kinds of attention they like and deserve, and connect with them in all the different ways that women like to be connected with, I tell the men there's a huge payoff: She'll love you, *really* love you, and the love that will come back to you from her will fulfill all your dreams of love. She'll help and support and take care of you and praise and thank and appreciate you. She'll do nice things for you and say nice things to you. Because you make her feel good, she'll want to make you feel good in all the ways a woman can make a man feel good. It's in the nature of being female to be like that, to *give* like that. That's the way a woman loves—*when she feels loved.* She'll give you her whole heart—if you give her the changes she's asking of you. She'll give it *all.* I know this to be true.

In my own marriage, and in my work with married people in therapy, when the husband finally gets it, when the frog becomes a prince, and the prince kisses the princess, Sleeping Beauty awakes: "And she awaked, and opened her eyes, and looked very kindly on him. And she rose, and they went forth together . . . and gazed on each other with great eyes of wonderment . . . and they lived very happily together until their lives' end."

One couple nearing the end of their therapy with me came in for their late morning session looking very happy. I asked why.

"We had an interesting morning," said the woman. "Before our marriage hit the skids and our sex life went south a few years ago, James and I had this running joke between us: Whenever he did something for me that was really nice, that really pleased me, I'd hold up one finger, meaning, 'That gets you sex with me, fella.' And then we started having our problems, and he basically stopped doing nice things for me or being there for me in any way, and I wasn't holding up any fingers, I'll tell you that.

"But now things are getting better between us. Instead of blaming *me* for being angry at him and insisting that he change—like it was somehow *my* fault that I was unhappy with him!—he's able to look at himself, own his part in it, and change. Now he's doing all kinds of things for me—he's really taking this good-husband thing seriously—so at eight this morning I come out the front door on my way to do food shopping and he's standing by the side of the car holding the door open, and my car is all vacuumed and washed! He's looking cute as a button, my heart melts, and I hold up *two* fingers! We both burst out laughing, and I never did quite make it to shopping."

As a married man myself I have undergone a thirty-five-year personal training in how to be a good husband from a woman with immense self-respect and great inner strength and beauty who wasn't kidding around and who's totally worth it. Looking back on our marriage, I now realize that I *was* (mostly) at fault for the problems in it all those years. I don't have a hard time saying that—because it's true. I'm proud that I finally became a good husband to her, not proud that it took me more than a quarter of a century to do it, and sorry that she had to stay on my case for such a long time.

The first step in becoming a good husband is to admit you're a case. I'm a case. Most men are a case. If you're reading this book right now because your wife gave it to you with an imploring kind of look in her eye, take that as a probable sign that you're a case, and possibly a hard case.

A couple of things you should know about becoming a good husband:

- It involves some time. There's a lot of stuff to unlearn and a lot of stuff to learn, some bad habits to break, and sometimes some hard feelings from the past kicking around the marriage—and it takes some time to go through all of that.
- It involves work. Some of it's easy, some of it's not so easy, and some of it's heavy lifting. The heavy lifting part is the looking inside yourself, seeing the mental and emotional machinery

in there, when and where it got installed, what parts are noble and good and honorable and admirable in you, and how incredibly screwed-up the rest of you is.

- It involves changing ourselves. To get us men to change ourselves—even to think that we *need* to change ourselves—is the very definition of heavy lifting.

- But it's doable. If a dolt like me can do it, anybody can do it. And it won't take you thirty-five years like it took me. The trail's blazed, and it's mostly common sense anyway.

And besides, we have no choice. It's our manly *duty* to become good husbands. It's our duty to our wives, to our children, and to the world. The very essence of manhood is the doing of one's duty. The New York City firemen and policemen who ran *into* the World Trade Center towers on September 11—and billions of other men who are just quietly doing their jobs every day—can tell you about duty.

This book was conceived on September 11. I think that was the day I finally grew up as a man. I was so in awe of the heroism of those men that, in a kind of revelatory moment, I finally understood what male duty and male maturity and male heroism really are—what the greatness of *manhood* really is: It is when a man assumes 100 percent of the responsibility in a situation to serve the needs of that situation. Inspired by the example of those men, I decided to apply that model to my own situation of being a husband. What would it be like to do my marriage as a mature man, as an actual grown-up? I made the decision to take 100 percent of the responsibility for the behavioral and attitudinal changes needed in my marriage; and from that day forward I would see my marriage, including the changes my wife wanted me to make in it, as a giving of myself to her in the same way that the heroes of September 11 gave themselves to their fellow human beings, in the spirit of loving service.

I also began to apply that model in my marital counseling. More and more I found myself saying to the men, "Hey, guys, she's *not* crazy for feeling the way she does in this marriage. Given the way you act toward her, the way you talk to her and actually think it's *okay* to talk to her like that, the fact that you *don't* talk to her most of the time, and don't listen to her, and don't seem to have a shred of interest in what's actually going on inside her, and think that getting sexually inside her is your God-given right as opposed to a privilege you have to earn by the way you relate to her—given all that, no wonder she's pissed off at you. Who wouldn't be? You're the one who's (mostly) at fault here in this relationship. You don't know how to do relationship. If you want to change the way she feels about you, just change in the ways she's asking you to change, and don't use anything about her or anything at all as an excuse not to change. Just change"—and I was amazed by the results.

Most of the men took it. Most of them could hear it. Even the "it's (mostly) your fault" part they were man enough to hear. Talked to in this way, most of the men rose to the challenge, copped to their responsibility for what was wrong in their marriages, began to look inside themselves in a way they had never done before, and started to change. And the women, seeing their husbands becoming changed men, started liking them again and relaxing into the relationship; and the love and respect and care-taking and service that the men were now offering their wives became reciprocal; and the marriages became friendly and happy places for both of them. Couples who had come in on the first day looking totally shut down to each other, with years of hurt and conflict and anger and loneliness behind them, estranged, hardly speaking, left on the last day smiling and feeling good with each other, friends and lovers, all because the husband was man enough to hear what was being said to him—that the diffi-culties in the marriage were primarily because *he* was difficult—and decided to do this good-husband work, to learn how to *really* connect with his wife, and *changed*.

Then I got it: When a man is mature enough to accept fault where fault is due, and is willing to change where change is needed, it will create change all around him. He can change his marriage, his family, his whole world—when he changes. Maybe it wasn't only me who grew up on September 11. Maybe all us men did—or were supposed to.

And so this book came to be.

As a marriage therapist I will do whatever it takes to help a man become a good husband to his wife. I'll explain that this good-husband thing is a journey, a trip, and I'll explain the whole trip and every step of the trip as many times as I have to. I will teach, coach, exhort, correct, confront, judge, joke around, and argue with a guy. I'll talk over him and around him. When he's being an asshole, I'll tell him he's being an asshole. When I have to, I'll yell at him. I'll take the guy on. You *have* to take guys on. Like when we grew up as kids. On the football field, on the bas-ketball court, on the hockey rink, pitcher and batter, you go one-on-one with each other. Man-on-man. Toe-to-toe. It was fun. Therapy is a place where me and the guy go one-on-one with each other, week after week, for years sometimes . . . until I win. But when I win, he wins. It's a total win-win. The guys who sit in my office get that, though they'll fight me most of the way on it. One guy in the process of getting it said to me recently, "Robert, you're absolutely right, and I know you're right, and I hate the fact that you're right." Another guy, a lawyer, really got it: Nearing the end of his therapy with me, reflecting on his experience, he said, "You have a very interesting job, Robert. It's a tightrope. You have to both inspire your clients to greatness . . . and *defeat* them."

I coulda kissed the guy.

Maybe not all of what I say here about your faults and your need to change applies to every man. Probably more than you think, so consider it all, and if the shoe fits, wear it. And it may be that what I say here applies to you sometimes, but not at other times. Of course. Many of us are pretty good guys a lot of the time and are driving our wives crazy only here and there. And if it sometimes seems that I'm just taking potshots at you, giving you a hard time for the sake of giving you a hard time, I'm not. I wouldn't do that. I'm just being tough on you the same way that I'm tough on myself in these husbandly matters, and for the same reason: to get good at what we do, to become *great* at it.

Aren't we *supposed* to become great at what we do? I think we are.

And besides, I always figure men can take it.

Here's why you should want to read this book, face your faults in how you relate—or don't relate—to your wife, get your act together, and become a good husband to her:

Because it's the manly thing to do and the greatness of a man.

To look deep inside yourself—to see what needs to be seen in there and to change what needs to be changed—takes guts (see Chapter 42, "Look at You!"). It's an exploit, a quest for who you really are inside there. You're like an astronaut, going not into outer space but inner space. If you've been looking for a test of your manliness, you've got one right before your eyes.

We men like to take something that isn't working and fix it. We fix cars and computers and furniture and a million other things around the house, and we love to do it, and we feel a great sense of accomplishment when we do. And here, in this good-husband work, is the biggest fix-it opportunity of them all—we can fix our marriages and families! You want power? *That's* power. So don't get confused here, don't be stupid and think that fixing your faults and becoming a good husband to your wife is about disempowering and emasculating you and cutting your balls off. It's the opposite of that. It puts tremendous power into your hands because now you can make something work—like, your life!—that, if you're honest with yourself, is not really working right now.

If you're into sports, if that's manliness to you, I'm with you. I've been playing and watching sports my whole life, and for me, as for all true sports lovers, there is no greater pleasure than being or watching a great athlete who plays his position like it's supposed to be played. To watch a great third baseman take a hard shot down the line, come up, and rifle a throw to first is a beautiful thing. Nothing better. And there is nothing better than for you to realize that being a husband to your wife is a position you're playing on a major league field called marriage, and you're supposed to play that position well. That means you stop making errors in the relationship with her, and you become a good husband to her. It's an athletic thing. It's a great play.

Any man who wants to call himself a man always wants to just *do his job*. Doing your job and doing it well are the essence of manliness, I think. Your job as a husband is to treat your wife with the love and respect she deserves, to take care of her in the ways she wants, to behave well toward her. That's your *job*. In your life, it's job one. With the help of this book, you can learn it well and do it well. *Then* you can call yourself a man.

Read all the chapters in this book. They're short. They're interesting. Some of them are funny. Take it all in. Think about it. At the end of each chapter, there's something called "The Move," which is an action to do, a new behavior to try, words to say—in sports terminology, the *move* to make—to begin to practice in your marriage the point being made in that chapter. They're great moves. Walter Payton, Barry Sanders kind of moves. Orr and Gretzky kind of moves. Jordan or Bird or Magic or LeBron kind of moves. The kind of moves that bring you cheering to your feet in a stadium. And bring you and your wife close together in your marriage.

Some of the Moves may seem unnatural to you—like, "That's not me, that's just not me." Some of them may seem strange—like, "Are you kidding?" But I'm not kidding. Remember that when you change behaviors you've been doing your whole life, the new behaviors are going to seem strange and you may even feel a little silly doing them, but I guarantee that your wife won't think they're strange and silly—she'll love these Moves and love you for making them. Trust me here. Just start off slowly, stretch a little into these Moves the way you stretch your muscles before you go for a run. If you feel a little uncomfortable, it's because you're stretching. In time and with practice as you progress through the book, the Moves will start to feel more natural until one day they'll feel totally natural and comfortable—like, "This *is* me. This is the way I've always wanted to act toward her, I just didn't know it till I did it!"—and on that day your wife and everybody stands up cheering.

So make the Moves. Put all this into practice. Do the program. It works. I swear to you, it works.

I hope you take the book seriously, and I hope you enjoy it. It's really great you're reading it.

And *you're* really great for reading it. As you read, remember that no matter what I'm saying to you, no matter how hard a time I'm giving you, no matter what tone I'm talking to you in, I'm always talking to your greatness.

You're a man. You're a gem, a diamond in the rough. You already are—inside, in that great male heart of yours—what you're trying to become. You already *are* what she wants you to be.

That's why she married you, dummy. That's what she saw in you. She saw your *real* manhood. Now it's just a question of becoming the man you already are.

It takes some work, some changes, but we can do it.

I was born, raised, and live in Boston, and if the 2004 Boston Red Sox can come back from down 0–3 to the New York Yankees and—in the greatest sports story EVER—beat the damn Yankees four straight to win the American League pennant and then go on to beat the St. Louis Cardinals four straight to win the World Series for the first time in eighty-six years, if they can do that—and they *did*—we can do this.

Hey, we're *men*. We can do anything.

Her Introduction

In my view the hardest work in changing habitual patterns in marriage must be done by men. But many of us must be jolted, confronted, or in some way awakened to the need to do our part of that work. And this is a job that still falls predominantly to women.

Augustus Y. Napier

The thing women have got to learn is that nobody gives you power. You just take it.

Roseanne Barr

I. Provincetown, Either Way

Here in Massachusetts, if you're traveling on Route 6 on Cape Cod heading for Provincetown, there's a spot in Truro, the town just south of Provincetown, where 6A splits off from 6, and there used to be a big sign there at the fork that always made me smile. It said,

PROVINCETOWN
EITHER WAY

Maybe you and your husband read this book and he corrects his faults and becomes the dreamboat you've always wanted in a husband and the two of you live happily ever after. I know that's possible, and I hope it happens. But maybe that doesn't happen, and he remains the disappointing guy or total jerk he's always been, and you decide what you're going to do from there.

Empowerment, either way.

Empowerment is knowing that you have the right and you *are* right to set the highest standards of behavior for your husband in your marriage, and to hold him to those standards until he meets them. Empowerment is deciding what *you* want to do if he doesn't meet them. No matter what, you will benefit from reading this book because if you read it in the spirit in which it was written, you will feel a sense of empowerment when you're done.

Empowerment, all ways.

I was explaining the philosophy of It's (Mostly) His Fault to a new female client the other day—that her husband is primarily responsible for the problems in their marriage and that if he changed, she'd rather easily make the changes *she* needed to make in the marriage, and then the whole marriage would change—and she burst out laughing and said, "You know, a lot of women are going to like this idea!"

Hello, women. Welcome to It's (Mostly) His Fault.

I purposely wrote this book to men—because they're the ones who are (mostly) at fault for marital unhappiness and who need to change most, and they're the ones who need to be spoken to in the way I speak to them here—but I knew that you, the wives, would be the first readers, before your husbands. It doesn't take a genius to know that. Men on their own don't typically read relationship books like this. The dozen or so who do are scattered around the country and won't admit it.

So here's what to do.

When you're done reading *It's (Mostly) His Fault*, casually hand it to your husband and in an indirect, roundabout way, ever so gently hint that he read it—as in, **"READ THIS BOOK, LEON! OH DEAR GOD! *PLEASE* READ THIS BOOK!"**—and then maybe he'll read it, and like it, and *get* it, and *change*, and then things'll get a lot better in your marriage.

Here's the thing you've got to remember about us men:

You women are approximately ten light-years ahead of us in figuring yourselves out psychologically and twenty light-years ahead of us in wanting to—and knowing how to—create connection and mutually fulfilling relationship with another human being. You do it beautifully with other women all the time, and most of you have tried to do it with your husbands.

So how come it doesn't turn out so beautifully with us? Why do you have to work so hard and so long at it?

"Talking with a man is like trying to saddle a cow," says one woman. "You work like hell, but what's the point?"

How come that is?

Because women are all about connection and men are not. Because a man has a ton of work to do on himself to even *want* to come into a relationship and then another ton to know what the hell to *do* in it once he's there.

You know that. Your whole marriage has been about that.

That's why we men need so much help from you women—because we've got to overcome so much in ourselves to want to be relational with you.

A lot of us men, for example, are quite shy, uncomfortable in company, preferring to be alone. That's why we have offices and dens and garages and newspapers and televisions to retreat to: to get away from people, to be alone, where we feel most comfortable.

And most of us men have fully downloaded our gender training. The entire gender training curriculum for a man in our culture is to be the strong, silent, independent type. The loner. The John Wayne thing. The man who doesn't have any feelings to speak of and wouldn't speak of a feeling even if by some miracle he realized he was having one. The gender-conditioned man in our culture is a man for whom it is effeminate and weak to have any needs, including the need to relate to anyone.

I'm fine alone, so leave me alone.

That in a nutshell is our gender training.

Try overcoming *that* one, ladies.

For a man, there's also the one about doing and accomplishing and working and being responsible. Using time productively. Doing my list of things to do. Sitting down with my wife and talking with her? Spending time just hanging out with her? Being with her for the sake of being with her? Excuse me? I don't see *that* on my list.

And then there's your husband's family-of-origin one. Many of us men (like you women) come from families where the relational space—the family circle that was supposed to be warm and welcoming and rewarding and safe—wasn't that way. There was rejection in it, criticism, ridicule and humiliation, outright abuse for some of us, all kinds of weird stuff—so, intelligently, we stepped out of the relational space, mainly by shutting down. We shut down our faces, our feelings, our words, our needs—and disappeared, see ya later. Some of us disappeared into sports, into the streets, into school, into work, into television, into alcohol or drugs or pornography or a million other addictions, and very few of us have reappeared.

But guess what?

Later has arrived! It's *now*. It's time for us men to appear in the marriage with you, to come back into the relational space with our wives. I'm going to tell your husband this point-blank in the very first chapter of this book, "Hey! You're in a Relationship!"

I know what I know about men because I am one, and I know what I know about difficult men because I've been one, and I've been working with them in individual and couples therapy for many years. Being a man, I don't know you wives as well, but I do know you're having a hard time in your marriages to these difficult men, and you need help. Based on my experience sitting and talking with you in my therapy office for three decades— sometimes with your husbands present in couples therapy, sometimes individually—and based on my thirty-five years of living with one of you, my wife, Jane, here's what else I know about you:

I know that you're women married to difficult men in all fifty states of the Union and in all countries around the world. I know that you're different colors and cultures and religions and political persuasions and hairstyles and generations and ages, and I know that you've lived in all generations and ages since the beginning of human history.

I know you're a woman who's not as happy as you'd like to be in your marriage. I know you're married to a man who needs to become a better husband to you. Not only can he be difficult, he can sometimes be very difficult. Some of you have been married to this man for a few months, some for many years. Most of you are still in love with your husbands, in some of you the love is be-ginning to wane, and some of you are hanging on by the skin of your teeth. Some of you are married to dominating, controlling jerks who don't respect you at all and treat you very badly, even abusively; and some of you are married to pretty good guys who do respect you and who are nice enough but just don't seem to know all that much about how to actually *relate* to you. Some of you are hopeful because you're married to men who you know have a lot of potential; some of you are depressed because you're married to slugs. There's a wide spectrum of husbands here, but all these men—the good, the bad, and the clueless—share one thing: They all need instruction on how to relate to you better.

That's what this book is. It's an instruction to your husband on how to relate to you better: *like you're a human being of great importance and worth who deserves the greatest respect and love from him.*

Suzanne, a thirty-nine-year-old account manager at an insur-ance company, explained it to me this way in her first session with her husband, Carl: "I don't understand him," she said. "Here he's got the best wife a man could ever want—I really love him, and I still find him attractive, I'm a great mother and a hard worker, and all I want is to be in a happy marriage with him, to have a real relationship with him where we feel close and con-nected, like friends and companions. But he doesn't seem to want that, or maybe he doesn't know how to do it—I don't know. All I know is I don't like the way he treats me, I feel neglected by him and adrift from him, like there's nothing but the car pool schedule holding us together, like we completely *miss* each other, like our marriage, which is supposed to be 'the tie that binds,' isn't a bond anymore. I've tried to explain all this to him so many times. I don't know what to do anymore."

"What do you think of what Suzanne is saying, Carl?" I asked.

"I know she's unhappy," he said. "She's certainly said it often enough. She tells me I don't really hear her, but how can I *not* hear her? I don't know what I'm supposed to be hearing. I don't know what to do anymore either."

"I do," I said. "Stay here in this therapy for a while, and hear what she has to say, and hear what I have to say, and make a big change in the way you relate to her."

He looked at me blankly for a moment. "Are you saying it's all my fault?"

"I'm saying it's mostly your fault. Can you handle that?"

"If it's true."

"It's true."

"How do you know? We've been here for all of twenty minutes."

"I've been here for thirty years, sitting in this chair listening to wives tell me the same thing over and over—that they're trying to have a good relationship with their husbands but the husbands don't know how to do it. And week after week I see it happening right before my eyes—women reaching out to their husbands, trying to talk to us, work things out with us, be nice to us, make things better, and we sit over there being defensive and mad and shut down and unreachable—so I've come to believe the women. And that's why you're here, Carl: to listen to what Suzanne is trying to tell you about your shortcomings in this relationship, to believe her, to *trust* her, and to do whatever it is you have to do to change into the husband she wants you to be. Then watch what happens."

"I always thought marriage was a two-way street," he said. "Doesn't it go both ways? Doesn't she need to change too?"

"Yes, she needs to change, but it's not within ten galaxies of how much *you* need to change. And yes, marriage is a two-way street, but a lot of the women are so frustrated and fed up with us after years of trying unsuccessfully to have a decent relationship with us that they've walked *off* the damn street, so we men need to show up on the street and walk toward them to try to get them to come back on it. All you need to do, Carl, is accept that, change yourself, change *first,* and *then* it's a *two-*way street."

A lot of what I say in this book about us men admitting our deficiencies as partners to you women and becoming good husbands to you will come as a totally new way of thinking for your husband—a whole new way of understanding husbanding and marriage. It may seem new to you too, but less so, I think, since much of what I'm going to tell him here is what you've been trying to tell him since day one. New or not, this book may be coming as just the support and validation and *ally* you need right now to finally get through to him and have the good husband you've always wanted.

That's the hope of this book.

As you can already see, I use the term "a good husband" a lot in this book—because the ultimate goal of this book is for your husband to correct all his faults and become one—so here's what I think a good husband is:

He's a man who's smart enough to believe in the principle of cause and effect; mature enough to see that your unhappiness in this marriage and your anger at him are the *effect* of which he and his lousy behavior to you have been the *cause;* and strong and dedicated and *brave* enough to change his behavior and cause you to feel good in your marriage.

Then he becomes a good husband—a man who always treats his wife with love and respect. Who respects what's important to you, like listening to you when you want to talk with him, and talking to you when you ask him a question about himself. Who'll turn off the TV and take a walk with you because you asked him to take a walk with you and because he knows you like taking walks together. Who respects your time and *requests* your company or your help instead of expecting and assuming it. Who says kind, complimentary things to you because he sees all that you do for him and the family and because he always wants you to feel good about yourself. Who takes care of you in all the ways that you like being taken care of—who sometimes makes you lunch to take to work, gets up with the kids on the weekends so you can sleep in, talks to your parents on the phone when you don't feel like it, comes up behind you and rubs your neck and shoulders when you've had a long day, takes you to movies *you* want to see. A good husband is attuned to you and attentive to you and frequently inquires how you're doing, how you're feeling, how come you seem kind of sad tonight. He's totally devoted to you, still head over heels in love with you, and still relates to you like when he was courting you because his understanding of marriage is that he'll *always* be courting you.

A good husband is a man who remembers he's *married* to you and is therefore in an actual *relationship* with you; who has decided not to be, except on very rare occasions, an immature asshole anymore in this relationship; who *likes* the marital connection with you, knows how to maintain that connection by communication with you, and knows how to reconnect with you after there's been a disconnection; who doesn't outmaneuver and outmuscle and scare the wits out of you with his anger anymore; who doesn't call you a nag or a bitch or a ballbuster anymore because now he knows what you really are: a strong, self-respecting woman who rightfully wants her husband to always treat her with respect. A good husband is sexually attracted to you throughout your marriage and understands and respects the way your female sexuality actually works, and so is a great lover to you. He is totally faithful to you: He doesn't touch, flirt with, or look at other women. He's a gentle man and a gentleman. He appreciates everything you do and are. He reveres you. Out of his great love and great respect for you, he's basically just nice to you all the time.

If this seems like an impossible ideal to you, it's not. It *is* an ideal, but it's not impossible, because this ideal already exists in your husband. It's the ideal husband that deep in his heart he wants to be to you, and it's the same ideal that exists in *your* heart as the husband you want and the one you know he has it in him to be.

In other words, women, he's in there somewhere.

That's the faith of this book.

It's your husband's duty to dig through all the less-than-husbandly stuff inside him to find the good husband in his heart, and to become him, and then to be him for the rest of your days together. No exceptions, no excuses. This transformation into a good husband is his *job*. His labor of love. You can think of this book as the job description. By the time you're done reading it, you'll know exactly what you want from this guy, and you'll feel totally right for wanting it, and empowered to get it. By the time *he's* done reading it, he'll know exactly what to do to be a good husband to you, and he'll have been told in no uncertain terms to do it.

All of this means that to whatever degree you've been alone in trying to get through to your husband, to get him to see his failings and faults in the marriage, to get him to *change*, you're not alone anymore.

II. Paradigm Shift

It's about time we men admitted our faults and became good husbands to our wives.

As a matter of fact, it is precisely the time.

We are living in a time of major transformation on this earth. There's a paradigm shift going on here, a balancing of worth, power, and prerogative between men and women, a major change in the way women and men relate. This paradigm shift is happening in world society and in your marriage.

Under the old paradigm we men related to you women however we wanted to relate to you, thank you very much. We were attracted to you, we adored you and wooed you and had sex with you and married you and had more sex with you and had kids by you and were sometimes nice to you and sometimes not so nice, and some of us have been really mean to you, spoken unkindly to you, yelled at you, been violent with you, neglected and ignored you, taken you for granted, spent long periods of time withdrawn from you, not even talking to you—and still we want more sex with you!

We're amazing like that.

No wonder many of you women spend long periods of time frustrated, lonely, anxious, and unhappy in your marriages: They aren't happy places. No wonder many of you are so relationship-starved that you're having a long series of clandestine love affairs with various high-end pastries and leaf-strewn sexual fantasies about the gardener. Communication is difficult or nonexistent with your husband. Talking to him is like talking to a wall. There are repeated arguments and fights with him, cold silences that last for days, and times when he seems so angry at you that you walk around scared of him. The sex is infrequent and short—

thank God, because it's so mediocre for you. The family isn't doing all that well either. The children are bravely doing the best they can with their parents' marital problems, as children do, but inside they're having a hard time, and you know it. Many of you aren't doing so well inside either, but are enduring it with grace, as women do, living your lives, performing your daily duties, enjoying your kids and your friends, with episodic paroxysms of, "I can't stand this anymore! What the hell is *wrong* with you?!" which everybody, including you, blames on your hormones.

Under the new paradigm, all this changes, because he, your husband, finally gets it. I mean, once and for all he gets it, he *changes*, he changes the way he thinks about you and feels about you and relates to you, and he—finally!—becomes a good husband to you.

And the reason this paradigm shift is happening now, in world society and in your marriage?

I don't know.

But I know its time has come.

You say you want a revolution?

We're all living in the middle of one.

III. Women's Work: 14 Things to Remember or Do to Have a Good Husband

You women have your work cut out for you. You know that. We men are not easy. You definitely know that. Some of us are a little bit challenging, with a few small but significant adjustments to be made in our thinking and behavior toward you; and some of us are completely off the wall, impossible and impenetrable, with so much wrong in our thinking and behavior toward you that you're totally fed up with us, at the end of your rope.

Most of us are somewhere in the middle, but none of us are easy. With all of us there've been times you've wanted to string us up with that rope.

Hold off on that awhile. We have some work to do.

So do you.

When a wife asks me in therapy what *her* work in this transformation of her husband into a good husband is, what *she* is supposed to be doing during the course of it—especially when I'm sitting there the first session and almost all the sessions telling her husband that it's (mostly) his fault, that he is the primary cause of the problems in this marriage, that he behaves wrongly and sometimes outrageously to his wife, and that he should just cut it out and grow up and become a good husband to her—when she turns to me at some point, like my client Robin, and says skeptically, "You seem to be saying that it's all *his* work. Don't *I* have any work to do? What's *my* part?" I tell her that her part is huge.

"Actually," I say, "you play the most important part. You're the leading lady. You're the one who with the eye of clear perception and a voice filled with conviction tells your husband where he needs to change, grow, and improve; you're the one who drives his transformation into a good husband. There are many things for you to remember and do in his transformation, and they're all really about your power. Your part in this is to experience the power within you and then to assert that power with your husband for the purpose of changing him, the marriage, and the family. This work is all about self-empowerment for you. His work is to move from a place where the problems in the relationship are (mostly) his fault to a place where they're not his fault, and nobody's fault, because there aren't really any more problems in the relationship—*and the road to this transformation goes through your power*."

Here are fourteen things for you to remember or do in this work:

1. It Is Very Difficult to Deal with a Difficult Man

The making of your husband into a good husband is one of the most difficult things you'll ever do in your life. Complicated. Laborious. Tricky all the way. Tiring. Hard.

How, for example, do you take on an ego—the male ego—that is simultaneously so weak and fragile that any attempt to oppose it is perceived by it as mortal threat and met with massive resistance, and so domineering and arrogant and wrong that sometimes it needs to be stopped dead in its tracks?

How do you get a man to respect the power and authority and sovereignty of a woman without making him think he's less of a man . . . having his balls cut off . . . *losing* to a woman . . . being controlled by a controlling woman . . . pussy-whipped?

How do you get a man to hear you when you're angry at him for some wrong thing that he does without him completely dismissing what you're saying even as you're saying it because now you're a bitch who's nagging him to death?

How do you get a man to realize that 85 percent of his behavior in his marriage and family is being driven by a self-centeredness and a sense of entitlement so huge and monolithic that he can't even come close to seeing it?

How do you get Leroy over there to turn off the TV where he's ogling euphoric young nymphomaniacs in beer commercials, and turn to you and say, "Hi, honey. Whatcha wanna do this afternoon?"

How the hell do you get a man to *change*? How do you get him to change behaviors he's totally convinced are right and proper? How do you get him to change behaviors that he's been locked into since he was fourteen?

With most men it's probably going to be very, very, very difficult, and you should have great respect for yourself, and compassion and patience with yourself, and be acknowledging yourself every step of the way for the really hard thing you're trying to do here.

2. Hold the Bar High

The good-husband work sets for a husband the highest standard of marital behavior toward his wife, and says to you wives, "Hold him to it." Bob Dylan once sang, "I got nothin', Ma, to live up to," but now we men do have something to live up to: We live up to *you*. We live up to the ideal that you hold for us, to what you want and expect and demand of us as your husbands and partners and lovers. That high bar.

- "I want you to treat me with respect."
- "I want you to stop talking to me in that tone of voice. I don't ever want to hear it again."
- "I want you to stop all violence or threat of violence in this household."
- "I want you to stop always criticizing and correcting me."
- "I want you to learn how to have a real conversation with me."
- "I don't want you looking at other women anymore."
- "I don't want you always pawing me. I want you to learn what I like sexually and what I don't like."
- "I want you to stop using the fact that you make more money than me as a way to feel more important than me."

- "I want you to stop treating me like a servant."
- "I want you to once and for all understand that there really is a *me* over here, that I'm a real person leading a real life, a full and challenging life, and I have thoughts and feelings about it all that should be of extreme interest and importance to you. I'm tired of being invisible to you. I want you to get that I *exist*."

That high bar.

It is inherent to mature manhood that if a man knows where he's trying to get to, if he knows where *there* is, a good and strong man will get there. It'll take him some effort and it might take him a while, but he'll get there. We men call that rising to the challenge, stepping up to the plate, aspiring to be the best we can be, getting the job done—and it's what mature manhood loves to do. In the case of marriage we step up to *you*, our wife, we rise to *your* challenge and try to be the best husband we can be.

So hold that bar high for us. However high you're holding it is where it's supposed to be. What you want in your marriage is what you're supposed to be wanting and should be getting. You set the standard. You. You *are* the standard. Remember that his becoming a good husband to you is the true fulfillment of his manhood.

3. It's a Journey and It Takes Time

The making of a good husband is a journey, and that journey takes time. I know it's already been a long time for some of you, and some of you are just about out of time, but my advice is to give it more time—at least *one* more time—because this is the first time there's been this book as your ally and tool.

Sometimes a woman will come into therapy in despair.

"We've *been* to therapists," she says. "We spent a year with one therapist, and nothing changed. I don't think it's ever going to change. I don't think *he's* ever going to change."

"Yeah, but you've never been *here* before," I say. "He's never had to deal with *me* before. He's never been spoken to the way I'm going to speak to him."

You will have to practice patience while the idea that it's (mostly) his fault sinks into your husband's resistant brain, so keep remembering that your husband is a total product of his family, his gender, and his social conditioning (the major message of which is that *nothing* is his fault, it's all *your* fault!) and therefore has much to look at in himself, and question, and throw out of himself, and much to learn about how he's really supposed to relate to you . . . and all that takes time.

In my own case, fresh from twenty-four years of Alter-family training and thousands of years of male gender conditioning, I arrived in 1970 in the relationship with Jane knowing next to nothing about relationship with anybody, least of all a woman. I actually thought it was okay to tell her exactly how I wanted the kitchen kept, and then expected her to keep it that way, *exactly*, and if she didn't, I'd get mad at her, and I thought this was okay. I spent an hour one evening telling her about all the places on her body I thought she could stand to lose a little weight. Believe me, I was a *project*.

A long project.

Way more than she bargained for.

Most men are.

But some of us are worth it.

To whatever degree you women are impatient with us at this point, that's okay, you should be, so take your impatience along with you on this trip; but also take some patience, and hang in there with us while we do this last, great piece of work on ourselves.

4. You're Totally Right!

There'll be times on this journey when you think that you're being selfish, that you're asking too much of him, that you're being the nag, witch, bitch, and ballbuster that you've always been told you are and said you'd never be, but that's not true, you're none of those. You're *supposed* to be asking for what you're asking for.

In other words, you're *right*.

Did you hear that? You are *right* to want what you want from him.

There'll be times in this work that you get worn down and you waver and start to doubt yourself, and you say to yourself or a friend or a therapist, like women say all the time to me in therapy, "Am I crazy to want these things from him? Am I expecting too much of him? Am I being unreasonable?"

"No, you're being totally reasonable," I say. "Because look what you're asking for. You're asking for respect, to be treated by your husband with respect. You're asking that he respect your privacy when you want privacy, your body when you don't want him climbing all over it, and your right to a peaceful home free of anger, violence, and fear. You're asking that he respect your desires and wishes, and your needs for attention and connection, and your personality and idiosyncrasies. A husband is *supposed* to treat his wife with respect, isn't he? What else is husbanding? So how can you be crazy to want that from him? The only way you're crazy is thinking you're crazy for wanting it, and you're very crazy there. Don't be crazy anymore. *You are right to want what you want from him.*"

5. Trust Your Anger

Trust your dissatisfaction with your husband and trust your anger at him. They are reliable guides to what he still needs to change. Your dissatisfaction tells you that he isn't yet the good husband you want him to be. Your anger tells you when you've been wronged or hurt by him in the relationship. If you're unsure about your dissatisfaction and anger, if to any degree you've bought the false concepts "She's always complaining, she's an angry bitch, she's a nag, it's impossible to please her," pay particular attention to Chapters 9, 10, 17, and 18 and the "Closing Message to Women Readers" and learn not only how to trust your dissatisfaction and anger but how to use them for the purpose of making him face his faults and become a better husband.

Remember that every woman who has ever been disrespectfully treated by her husband, or by any man, is, inside, angry. She may bury her anger under all kinds of things—motherhood, medication, food, alcohol, television, makeup, meekness, cutesywootsy sexiness, all of it wrapped in a shroud of silence—but it's there, inside, seething, and it's supposed to be there.

And sometimes it's supposed to come out.

At him. At the right time and in the right way.

And while you're at it, completely drop the idea that you're "just an angry bitch." You're not an angry bitch, you're an angry woman, a woman who's anywhere from mildly annoyed to absolutely furious at her husband because he doesn't treat her the way he should.

6. You're in a Fight and You're Supposed to Win

A woman said it in my office the other day: "What I keep learning in all this is, it's a fight, and I need total tenacity with him. *Total* tenacity. If I'm not fighting as hard as he is, I'm a goner."

I know that's not the best news you've heard today, because fights aren't pleasant, and I know it's a weird way to talk about an intimate relationship like marriage, but it's true: You're in a fight, a real fight, the fight of your life.

Remember that it's not a fight against your husband but against his many faults in this relationship with you, against whatever he thinks and feels about you and says and does to you that isn't loving, respectful, attentive, supportive, and caretaking of you. It's a fight against the belligerent way he talks to you sometimes and the demeaning way he sometimes treats you. It's a fight against his pornography and his infidelity and all the other stupid things he does that hurt and betray you and scare you and piss you off. It's a fight against his thinking it's okay to watch nine hours of football on Sunday while you and the kids are wanting to have family time with him. It's a fight against his thinking it's ever okay to yell at you and the kids. It's a fight against his thinking it's okay not to talk to you except to say, "What's for dinner?" It's a fight against his unskillfulness as a sexual lover to you and then blaming you for not enjoying it, and against all the other forms of his mind-boggling ignorance and colossal arrogance.

It's a long and hard fight, so if you lose some battles along the way, which you will, don't worry about it . . . but make sure you win the fight.

If you're opposed to fighting because it's associated in your mind with violence and killing and cruelty and atrocity, remember that there is a kind of fighting that is not about that, but about truth opposing untruth and right overcoming wrong and a new and good way of behaving that replaces an old and bad way.

That's "the good fight" the Bible talks about and commands us to engage in.

That's what this fight is.

That's why you're supposed to win it.

Here's a story about how to win a fight:

In ancient days, a woman once inadvertently offended a cruel warrior, who said he was going to kill her the next day in the town square unless she could defeat him in a fight. The woman had never fought any kind of fight before, so she sought out a great swordmaster and asked for help.

The swordmaster told her, "I am going to teach you one stroke of the sword. It is a powerful stroke that cannot be defended against, and if you use it tomorrow, you will defeat this man."

"But I don't even know how to hold a sword, never mind use one," the woman said. "How is any stroke of mine going to have the power to defeat him?"

The master said, "Today I will teach you to use a sword and to make that stroke. Tomorrow when you go to the town square, put the point of the sword in the ground and draw a circle around you. This is your circle of power. During the fight, if you keep your foot in the middle of the circle, as you stand there a tremendous power will surge through you when you make the stroke, and you will defeat this man."

The next day the woman went to the town square and met the warrior there. She stuck the point of her sword in the ground and drew her circle of power around her. The fight began. The man attacked her. With her foot planted firmly in the circle, the woman picked just the right moment and lunged forward with a mighty stroke and sent the man reeling to the ground.

In this fight that you're in against your husband's wrong understanding of how to behave to you and how to speak to you and how to relate to you, always keep your foot firmly planted in your circle because that's where your power is.

Your circle of power is your absolute conviction that you're right, and your adamant insistence that he change.

I'll say it again:

Your circle of power is your absolute conviction that you're right, and your adamant insistence that he change.

When we men see that certainty in you—when you're so strong that we have no choice anymore, when being less than a good husband is just not an option anymore, when we see *that* power coming at us—many of us men will get our act together, which means you've won the fight.

7. Be Strategic

The way to win a long fight against a formidable foe is to be strategic at every turn.

In everything you do with your husband, in everything you say to him and the way you say it, in everything you give him or refuse to give him, be strategic. Outthink him. Outflank him. Especially outtalk him. Men like to talk competitively and combatively, to argue—and they're good at it—so you have to outargue him. The way to outargue a man is by *not* arguing with him, by not allowing him to draw you into the argument he wants to have with you, but by standing firm and immovable in your own truth and responding to whatever he says from that place of truth. From that place always have an answer back to him. Yes, talk back to him. Always trump his statement with a truer and stronger statement of your own. Find that place of truth within yourself and give voice to it. It's a voice men listen to. It's the *only* voice we'll listen to.

If he says derisively, "What's come over you, Harriet? You're always talking about what I'm doing wrong in this marriage now. All I ever hear now is good husband this, good husband that. What the hell's come over you?" say back matter-of-factly, "What's come over me is a new way of thinking about how you're supposed to relate to me, Dave."

If he says, "I can't be the husband you want me to be," say back, "That's ridiculous. Of course you can."

If he says, "There's a double standard here. I'm being asked to do things that you're not being asked to do," say back, "That's very perceptive, Sidney."

If he says, in anger and disbelief, "What?! You expect me to be perfect?!" say back, in calmness and confidence, "Not immediately and not completely, but eventually and mostly, yes, and the sooner the better, Reggie."

In the 1998 movie *Pleasantville*, there's a moment toward the end when the husband, George, says sternly to his wife, Betty, "Now you listen to me. You're coming to this meeting. You're going to put on some makeup. You're going to be home at six o'clock every night, and you're going to have dinner ready on this table," and Betty smiles at him pleasantly and says matter-of-factly, "No, I'm not, sweetie."

That's the kind of power I'm talking about.

Go, Betty.

Let the power within you speak from you. In reply to what he thinks, say what you think and then say you know you're right. You know your husband well enough at this point to know most of his moves—what he's going to do behaviorally or verbally to try to defeat you—so have a response ready for all his moves. Make better moves. Stronger moves. Cagey moves. Head him off at every pass. Beat him at his own game when you can, but more important, make him play your game. Or, as we say in the sports world, don't let him take the game to you, you take the game to him.

It's mostly a word game. Words and names. No longer let *his* name for something be *the* name for it. Reclaim the power of naming, and correctly name what he's misnaming.

Here are examples from my therapy practice of women taking back the power of naming:

- "No, Stanley, looking at other women is not 'just what men do;' it's what I hate, and most women hate, and I don't want you doing it anymore." (See Chapter 30, "Fidelity!")
- "This is not 'nagging,' Seth. This is me having to repeat myself because you didn't get it the first or the millionth time I told you." (See Chapter 10, "Is Your Wife a Nag?")
- "My feelings are not 'ridiculous,' Jeff; they are my feelings, and you should never put them down, and you should learn how to talk to me about them." (See Chapter 12, "How to Talk with Her.")
- "What do you mean you 'asked' me to get the car washed? You didn't *ask* me, you *told* me, and I've already told you I don't like that." (See Chapter 37, "Respect.")
- "It's not that I want you to stop drinking because I'm so 'controlling,' Glenn, it's that I want you to stop drinking because your drinking is out of control and it's making a mess of our lives." (See Chapter 21, "Sober Up!")
- "No, this is *not* 'you can't talk to me because I'm going crazy'; this is I'm going crazy because you never listen to me when I'm talking to you!" (See Chapter 13, "Listen to Her.")
- "What you call my sexual unresponsiveness, Walter, is what I call, 'Do you actually think that touching me like that is

going to turn me on?'" (See Chapters 26 and 27, "Her Sexuality" and "All Women Have Curves.")

You are involved in a long fight to change your husband. Your
words, and the truth of them, and your strategic use of them, and
your moment-to-moment courage to actually say them and then
stand behind them are your main weapons in this fight.

8. Teach Him

The good-husband work is all about how a man is supposed to
treat the woman he's in intimate relationship with, so remember
that when it comes to relationship and connection and true intimacy, you, being a woman, know a million gazillion times more
than your husband about these matters . . . which means you're
his teacher.

So teach your husband well.

This book will teach you how to teach him. Teach him how
to relate to you. Teach him that when he drives fast and reck-
lessly, it scares you, and scaring you is definitely not the way to
relate to you. Teach him that no, you don't like having sex with
him when he's all sweaty and whiskery and smelling like an ex-
haust pipe. Teach him the best way to relate to you, which is with
consistently kind attentions. Teach him that.

"The whole secret of the teacher's force," says Ralph Waldo
Emerson, "lies in the conviction that men are convertible. And
they are. They want awakening."

Believe that your husband wants this great teaching of yours,
wants this awakening. He may not know that he does, or think
that he does, but he does. In his heart he does. The whole secret
of the wife's force lies in her conviction that what she's teaching
her husband is what her husband in his heart wants to learn.

9. Are You a Feminist?

Don't get hung up on whether this is "feminism" or you're a "feminist" or not. The words have been kidnapped and corrupted in our society, so it's hard to use them meaningfully these days. Much has been written, said, and debated on the subject of feminism. The English novelist Rebecca West said, "I myself have never been able to find out precisely what feminism is. I only know that people call me a feminist whenever I express sentiments that differentiate me from a doormat or a prostitute"; and the American writer Sally Kempton said, "I became a feminist as an alternative to becoming a masochist."

That completes our discussion of feminism.

If you call yourself a feminist, more power to you. If you don't call yourself a feminist, more power to you. If you wouldn't be caught dead calling yourself a feminist, more power to you.

Whatever.

He's *still* supposed to become a good husband to you.

10. Get the Help You Need

Ask for as much help and support as you need on this journey toward a good husband. People to listen to you, comfort and commiserate with you, advise you, support you, inspire you. As much as possible, try not to be alone in all this. Getting the help you need is a courageous and wise act.

There's help and support with your women friends; from marriage counselors and therapists and clergy; in women's groups; in programs like Al-Anon; on TV shows like *Oprah* or *Dr.Phil;* in magazine articles and books; and, of course, from God. The Sufi poet Jalaluddin Rumi says, "You need more help than you know."

Do not go to the kids for help. Leave them out of it. This is your show.

11. Hold Him Accountable

Let your husband know that there are actual consequences to his good or bad behavior toward you.

When you're pleased with him, smile at him, be nice to him, hug and kiss and touch him, sit down and watch a few minutes of the game with him, and commend, praise, and appreciate him like it was going out of style.

Men love that stuff.

When you're displeased with him, withhold all that good stuff. Walk around the house looking busy and righteous. Don't even talk to him. Don't go get the dry cleaning for him. Forget about sex.

Speaking of sex, tell your husband that only by facing how he's (mostly) at fault for the problems in this relationship, only by becoming a good husband to you, by learning how to relate to you and connect with you, will he ever get the good sex he wants from you. Read Chapters 25 through 32 on that one, the sexual one. Tell your husband that a man does not get the great sex from a woman, the one where she *really* opens herself up to him, until he really starts opening up to *her*.

Let your husband know that his bad or good behavior toward you has certain effects and that these effects are going to affect *him*. Teach that lesson. It's the same lesson we teach our children. It's called accountability.

My wife holds me completely accountable for my behavior toward her. Every big and little interaction with her, everything I say to her and the tone of my voice when I say it, every single time I get even slightly annoyed with her, she brings it up as something we have to talk about.

"Robert, there's something we have to talk about."

I'm a guy, so that sounds about as much fun to me as a colonoscopy, so I'll do anything to avoid it. Genius that I am, it has only taken me about three decades to figure out that the best way to avoid it is to stop doing and saying things that make her say it.

So I do.

(Mostly.)

So stay on his case.

12. He Has to Sail the Three Cs

Stay on his case and persevere. To persevere is to make effort through time. His becoming a good husband is going to take some time because he has to sail across the three Cs to get there: consciousness, conduct, and character.

First, in *consciousness*, he's getting the idea—because you're telling him—that to whatever degree there is disconnection and alienation in your marriage, it is (mostly) his fault and he has to learn to connect with you better, that he has to majorly change his ways with you. He starts to become conscious—because *you're* making him conscious—of how he's supposed to change, what the new things are he's supposed to be doing and saying, and what the old things are he's not supposed to be doing or saying. You're telling him to stop always leaving his dishes in the sink for you to do, and to start helping out getting everyone off to school and work in the morning. You're telling him to stop belching so loud when you and the kids are in the car with him. You're telling him to not always be thinking about himself but about what *you're* feeling or needing in a particular moment. You're telling him to *talk to you*. Remember that these are novel ideas to him, and they need time to sink in. He thinks about them; they're downloading into his consciousness; he's getting the idea; that's good.

Because then it moves from consciousness to *conduct*. He starts to *behave* differently with you. He stops old behaviors and tries new ones. He makes the Moves given at the end of each chapter in this book. He actually tries to start a conversation with you one day in the family room. In the beginning he feels awkward and forced and phony, and he *looks* awkward and forced and phony, but over time, with practice, he gets the hang of it, and before long he's genuinely and sincerely relating to you better. Now the change is in his conduct, in his behavior; one by one he is correcting his faults, getting his act together, and behaving and speaking differently toward you; that's good.

Because then his change moves into *character*. It becomes not just what he's thinking or what he's doing or saying, but who he *is*. He's just a good husband to you now, period. When his change moves into character, it becomes transformation. He is now, literally, a changed man, a good husband, as close to a no-fault guy as a man can get short of sainthood, and you feel good in your marriage.

The three Cs: consciousness, conduct, and character. That's how change happens.

So, as you watch your husband sail his boat out on the high seas of change, remember that you might be watching for a while before he lands on your shore.

13. Acknowledge, Appreciate, and Admire Him . . . a Lot!

My advice as he sails the three Cs is to find things to acknowledge and appreciate him for every inch of the way. You can acknowledge and appreciate him verbally, in passing in the kitchen, or with little notes that you leave in his lunch box or briefcase, or with e-mails, voice mails, or whatever. Doesn't matter. Just do it, and do it a lot.

Appreciate all indications that your message has arrived in his consciousness, like when he tells you he thought about calling you during the day to see how you're doing, but blew it, plumb forgot . . . appreciate him for that. Say, "Thanks for thinking of me. That was nice. I'm glad you're starting to understand that I like it when you connect with me during the day." If he tells you he's thinking about coming to your yoga class that you've been inviting him to for about a decade, say, "I'm so glad you're thinking about it, Luis. The fact that you're even thinking about it is a change in you, and it makes me feel good." Any sign that he's being thoughtful, that there's change going on in his consciousness, acknowledge and appreciate it.

And then when he starts to behave differently to you, when the change is showing up in his conduct, also acknowledge and appreciate him.

Big changes, small changes, teensy-weensy changes, even the awkward ones and the forced and phony ones, even the ones that don't quite work, *all* his attempts to change his conduct toward you, appreciate each and every one of them. When he comes home a half hour early from work and helps you prepare dinner, or asks you about your recent visit to the dentist—which this time, God bless him, he actually remembered you went to—or gives you a back massage without trying to get your breasts involved, say, "Thank you! I really appreciate how you've taken this to heart and are giving me all this nice attention."

Behavior rewarded is behavior repeated. Positive reinforcement. With us men, when we do something good, getting appreciated by you feels so good that we want to do it again. Inside every guy, even the tough guys, there's a little boy who loves to hear various forms of "Good boy" and "Atta boy!" a lot. This is true whether we say so or not. It's not manly to admit that we love appreciation from our wives, but trust me, we do, so don't worry about what we *do* with your appreciations, whether we scowl or smirk or pooh-pooh them or not, just realize that way down deep in your husband, underneath his show of independence from you, he is totally dependent on your opinion of him to make him feel either good or bad about himself. I'll tell you a secret about your husband: Deep inside him, how he is seen in your eyes is how he sees himself. The other day in my office I saw a man's face actually start glowing when his wife was appreciating him for helping her find her gloves that morning. What all this means is that you hold considerable power over your husband, so it's important to acknowledge, appreciate, compliment, commend, acclaim, extol, and sing the praises of him as he makes his long effort to overcome his ignorance, correct his faults, and become a good husband to you.

As one woman client recently told me, a woman who cheerfully calls the good-husband work "chipping away at el capitán": "I'm taking your advice on trying to notice and appreciate and mention to him his little tiny ways of trying. It's hard, because they're quite tiny and he can still be such a big jerk sometimes, but I can tell it works. I can tell it encourages him to keep trying. I think when I say, 'Nice going,' it helps him *keep* going."

And when we men get there, when we've really changed and it all moves into our character as transformation, let your appreciation of us take the form of admiration and adoration of us . . . because . . . hey, we earned it!

One last point, which I'll try to make delicately: If your appreciation and adoration of us ever happens to take the form of giving us unbelievable, drive-him-out-of-his-mind, send-this-guy-to-heaven sex, that works very well for us. We'll take that over a new polo shirt *any* day.

14. His Journey to You Is a Journey to His Best Self

And last, tell your husband that you're the way out for him. Tell him that his ability to admit and correct his faults in this marriage, to mend his ways with you and become a good husband to you, truly and totally connected to you, is the way out of his immaturity, his isolation and loneliness, feelings of failure, and many other bad feelings he may have about himself. Tell him you're his exit from all that and his entrance into a *great* feeling about himself, a feeling that all men love to feel: being a success. He will be able to say, "I have become a good husband to my wife. I have become successful at my most important job in life: being a husband." As Richard Gere says to his wife, Susan Sarandon, at the end of the movie *Shall We Dance*, "The one thing I am proudest of in the whole world is that you are happy with me." In other words, by becoming your good husband, by learning to love and respect you, by taking the journey to you, he gets *saved*. From time to time, remind him of that, and believe it yourself: His journey to you is a pilgrimage, and you are his salvation.

This, by the way, is totally true.

IV. Everyone's Work: The Relational Space

If you want your husband to be connective and relational with you, be relational with him. That means you're going to have to do your own work of psychological and spiritual self-inquiry. Remember: It's only *mostly* his fault; you've got some faults to correct too.

So figure out what your work is . . . and do it. Your work might be to emerge out of that mousy servility you've lived in all your life—that silence you scurry around in, that fear—and to find your voice and your power; or it might be to find the soft little girl inside you, the one who was getting abused all those years in your family, so you sent her away to a place down deep inside yourself and built so many defenses around her that nobody, including your husband, can get to you anymore.

I don't know what your work is. You may not either. Your husband might. You could ask him.

You could say to him, "I know what *your* work is, Mike—it's to look at the unbelievable entitlement you grew up in with your parents and to stop acting it out in this marriage. And I'd also like to know what you think *I'm* supposed to do to make this a better marriage." Tell your husband that you are committed to learning the work you need to do on yourself and that you'll definitely do it and you'll completely do it . . . on the condition that he starts doing his.

That's the deal. Guarantee it. Stand firm on the condition.

If you've already done a lot of your psychological and spiritual work, good going. Most women I know have done a lot of work on themselves. They've read the books and articles, gone to the workshops, and sat for years in therapists' offices and meditation groups to come to know themselves. You're definitely the leaders of us men into the inner world of the human psyche and heart, and you're drawing the whole culture into it. All hats are off to you.

If you think you're finished with your psychological and spiritual self-inquiry, however, if you think your work is done, you're wrong. I don't know anyone whose work is done.

Every time, every single time, that a wife in couples therapy with me thinks she has *no* work to do on herself, that her husband is *entirely* at fault and all the work is his—and won't let me correct her thinking on that—the therapy has blown up at some point. I'll tell you the point. It's the point, a month or a year or two into the therapy, when I turn my attention away from her husband and over to the wife and mention something wrong I think she's doing in the relationship:

- "Uh, Gladys, telling Ira he 'shouldn't feel hurt' by your drunkenly asking that young man to dance with you at your nephew's bar mitzvah last Saturday—after you just told Ira a minute ago that you want him to share his feelings with you more—is probably not the way to go here. If you want him to open up to you, you've got to listen to what he feels even if you don't like what you're hearing."
- "There's a way that you talk to him, Peggy, which is so belittling, such an assassination of his character, that if my wife talked to me like that, I'd walk out of the room. You should ask Thomas what it's like for him to listen to it."
- "Yeah, Tina, I do think there'd be more sex in this relationship if you pulled yourself together physically."
- "You're such a defensive person, Ann Marie, that Vince stands about zero chance of ever getting you to look at something about yourself and correct it. There's a way in which he's completely powerless in this relationship."

Some women bolt at that point.

I hate when that happens.

The work that I do with a married couple in my therapy office is to invite both of them into what I call the relational space that exists between them. This "space" exists between all people in relationships, but it particularly and most intensely exists between married people. The relational space is the visual and auditory field where action and reaction are constantly happening between the couple. It's the place where all the transactions occur, the "he said, then she said, then he said" place, the place where, in a therapy session, for example, he says his thing in that particular condescending tone of voice that she knows and hates, and then she says her thing with that suspicious, defensive look in her eye, and then he says his next thing with his angry little smirk, and she reacts by starting to yell at him, her eyes lit with rage, and he hates that look in her eye so he interrupts her and starts to yell back at her, louder, and then they're both off to the races, back and forth, action and reaction, the two of them putting absolute crap into the relational space, while I'm sitting there aghast, with thoughts of suicide flitting through my head.

The relational space is where all the "meetings" take place between a married couple, the nuances of words and subtleties of tone when they speak to each other, the fleeting expressions in their eyes and faces, the little and big things they do to and for each other during the course of a day. It's the place where she says, "I don't think anyone really understands what it's like for me to work all day and then have to come home and cook a meal for this family," and he nods, like he gets it, and there's a sympathetic look in his eye, and she sees all that and relaxes, softens. It's the place where the husband and wife are both so tense talking to each other that the conversation isn't really a conversation at all, it's just two Gatling guns spitting at each other at a rapid rate and nobody's hearing anything except the *ra-ta-tat-tat*. It's the place where he leaves a note on the dashboard of her car saying, "Have a nice day at work, honey. See ya later. I'll make dinner," and when she comes home from work and sees him standing with a spatula at the stove, she smiles and gives him a big hug and kiss. That place.

"Put things into the relational space that are easy for your partner to connect with," I tell couples. "Put gratitude in, and appreciation, and agreement, and courtesy and sweetness, and endless interest in each other's life, thoughts, and feelings. Put words and tones of voice and facial expressions into the relational space that make your partner feel good and put in behaviors and actions that please. Don't put accusation and criticism and impatience and sarcasm in there. They're disconnective. When you have to put a critique or correction in—a negative—be very careful, and try to wrap it in a positive package that your partner might actually stand a chance of hearing. In general, put in good stuff that creates safety and gives pleasure to your partner and makes him want to keep coming back in. If he tells you that he emptied the kitty litter this morning, don't say, 'I *know* you emptied the litter box, Henry. I do it every morning. You want me to bow at your feet?' That's going nowhere. Say, 'Thank you, Henry. That was nice. It'd be great for me if we could do that a little more often, dear.' That'll keep him in the relational space and might actually work."

Try to make the entire relational space a place of pleasure for both of you. It's the same thing we're trying to do with each other in sex: just make it all feel good. Ultimately in marriage we're trying to just make it all feel good.

Remember that under all that maleness and muteness of your husband, under all that aloneness and aversion to relationship, he's just a human being who—like all human beings—is extremely sensitive to all the bad things that can happen in the relational space: rejection, blame, put-down and insult, accusation and attack. We men feel all that, and we get hurt, mad, shamed, and scared—just like you—but unlike you, we don't say one single word about any of it because we're men and . . . well, we just don't.

So if you or some genius therapist can ever get your husband to talk about how he feels in the relational space with you—the disconnections *you* create, the ways *you're* difficult to talk to, the stuff *you* put into that space that drives him out of it—listen hard and long to your husband, believe every word he's saying, thank him for telling you what he feels about you, and change accordingly. Even though you'll probably be hearing things you won't like hearing, do not—I repeat, *do not*—debate, deny, or dismiss his feelings or get angry at him for having them, because then you'll be defeating your own purpose, which is to get your husband to open up to you, to come into the relational space with you and talk about intimate things, like his feelings.

So say to yourself, *I know he's not always coming from the right place inside himself when he talks to me, and I know he's not always speaking the right language to me, but what language am I speaking to him and where am I coming from? My own wounds? My own meshugas? My own ignorance of how to have a conversation and stay connected with him? Or am I coming from a good place inside myself, a mature place, the place that wants to sit down in the kitchen with him and try to solve some of our marital problems and talk in a way that keeps him at the table?*

You should know where you're coming from inside so you'll know what you're putting into the relational space. You should know where you're coming from inside so you'll know what language you're speaking. That means you're going to have to look inside.

That's the self-inquiry piece.

That self-inquiry is your work, and everyone's work.

V. A Tale of Two Women

Do not be this woman . . .

Twenty-nine-year-old woman, paralegal, no children yet, six

years married and one year into marital counseling with her husband. For most of that year, as so often happens in my therapy, I'd been working on the husband, an essentially good and decent guy, hardworking manager for a cable company, who knew literally nothing about relating and connecting to his wife. Spent a lot of his time working at his office in Boston, and when he was at home, he was on the computer or in front of the TV or down in the basement with his baseball card collection. Barely talked to his wife, hardly ever *saw* her, thought he could do the marriage the way he had done everything in his life, which was alone.

Nope.

Praise be to her, she brought him into marriage counseling, and praise be to him, he came each week and sat there for a solid year of me telling him, in all the ways I know how to tell men, that he was basically an idiot when it came to knowing how to be married, and he had to look at himself and change himself in this marriage and learn how to connect with his wife. Talk with her. Be with her. Be her friend. Be in *relationship* with her. I turned most of my therapeutic attention on him for a full year ("Brian, you've got to talk to her" . . . "Brian, you can't just go to bed without saying good night to her" . . . "Brian, tell her how you feel about that" . . . "Brian, try to look at her when she's talking to you" . . . "Brian, she just asked you a question. That shrug won't do as an answer. Use words" . . . "Brian, the reason she doesn't want to have sex with you is because she doesn't feel connected to you" . . . "Brian, be as attentive to her now as when you were dating her. The relating to her doesn't stop once you marry her, for God's sake! It's not like now that you're married to her, you've permanently *won* her and you *possess* her and you can forget her for the rest of your life" . . . "Brian, don't do your stupid

baseball cards tonight, take your wife to a goddamn movie!")
while she sat over there in her chair, not saying much, carefully
eyeing him to see if he was getting any of this. For all the therapeutic focus I was giving her, she could have spent that year over
there *knitting*.

And then a funny thing happened.

As we entered our second year of therapy, he started to get it.
He started relating to her more in their daily lives, doing things
for her, talking to her more, taking her out to dinner; and in sessions, with my encouragement, he started to talk about his feelings more, including his feelings about how hard—in his word,
"unrewarding"—it sometimes was to talk to her.

"Sometimes she can be so self-righteous," he said. "Like she
always has to be right. If I have a different way of doing something, or a different opinion about something, or if what I want
to do is different than what she wants me to do, she can squash
me like a bug. She always takes the moral high ground, and I end
up feeling like an asshole, and after a while I just give up and shut
up."

At that point she started getting angry at him. *Really* angry.

"What do you mean it's not 'rewarding' to talk to me?! You
never talk to me! You're never *with* me! You're always in that
goddamn basement of yours with your goddamn baseball cards
or . . ."

She was yelling at this point, and he was disappearing way inside himself, dissociating, leaving his body there as a kind of
husk—in a few seconds he wouldn't be there at all—so I stepped
in.

"Let's look at what's happening here. First of all, Lauren,
you're totally right. Every word you're saying about Brian was
true for six years, and it's still somewhat true, so you're right to be

angry about it. It's been six long years of this, and I don't blame you one bit for not being able to stand it any longer.

"But can you see that you're doing right now—in *this* moment—exactly what he's saying you do at home when he tries to talk to you: taking the higher ground, denying his experience of you, and shutting him down? He just put something pretty good into the relational space—a feeling he's had about you for a long time—and he said it pretty vulnerably and with no intention to hurt you, I think, just to explain a way that he feels. You've been asking him to tell you how he feels your whole marriage, and now that he's doing it, look what you're doing, look what you're putting into the relational space in response. Anger and attack. No one in his right mind wants to hang around for that. Is this what you really want to be doing?"

She turned her anger on me now.

"What?! I can't get angry at him?! You won't let me have my anger?! It's been *six years* of no relationship in this marriage! I'm so pissed at him I could scream!"

"I am in complete support of your anger at him. And it's not that you can't have it—you *should* have it—but the way you're expressing it right now, as a response to him beginning to tell you how he feels, isn't going to work. Look at him. It's exactly as he says: He's sitting over there scared to death of you right now, scared to even open his mouth again. All he's saying is you're a difficult person to talk to sometimes. From my observation I think he's right. Maybe you should listen to him on this one and be grateful that he's sharing his feelings with you."

Her eyes leveled at me. "Don't you tell me what I should or shouldn't do," she said, and she walked out of the office.

I never saw her, or them, again.

Don't be that woman.

No matter how angry and how deservedly angry you are at him and how much looking at himself he needs to do, *you* still have to look at *yourself*. There's a certain level of marital work where—as I tell him in Chapter 9, "The Five Big Lies That Keep You from Changing"—it's *all* looking at *our*selves, man or woman, young or old; it's all about *us, our* work, learning to come from the right place inside ourselves so that we're putting the right stuff into the relational space.

So don't be that woman. She wasn't able to do that. Be this other woman:

I had been seeing this other couple for three years. The wife was forty-four, a teacher, homemaker, and mother of two teenage kids. The husband, a producer for a local television station, was a nice guy but a mess, addicted to sports gambling, marijuana, and pornography on the computer. They had been married for nineteen years and came into therapy after she had found out about an extramarital affair he had five years before. It had been a very rocky therapy. Fueled by her fury, the marriage had teetered on the edge of dissolution several times; but partly due to their love for their kids and partly because I kept telling her I thought this guy was redeemable, they managed to hold it together. As I'd done with the other couple, I spent a great deal of my therapeutic attention on the husband, trying to help him feel and create real connection with his wife.

One session—after a bad week between them—she was berating him for his not having called her from work that day, really laying into him, while he tried to explain why he hadn't made the call. She wasn't having any of it, though, and continued her tirade.

I interrupted and turned to him.

"Max, you must understand that, given what you've done in

your marriage and the huge disconnection from Elizabeth you've acted out, any fraying of the connective cord between the two of you—like not making one short phone call that you said you would—is a major deal with her, bringing up all her feelings about your infidelity, and you simply have to be more careful about keeping that connective cord strong and taut at all times."

"I get that," he said. "I understand. I know that I've wreaked havoc in my marriage, and I have to rebuild the whole relationship with everything I do. I just blew it today."

And then I turned to Elizabeth.

"We know that Max has a really hard time with connection. Given the family he's coming from, we know why. We also know that he has caused a horrible rupture in the marital connection with you. And we know that this therapy and his whole life journey are about repairing that connection with you and then learning to connect with you in the total way a husband is supposed to connect with his wife—and I will never let him forget that in here. I think you know that, Elizabeth. He must emerge out of all his addictions—all that isolation he lives in—and fully connect with you in this marriage. But here's the thing, Elizabeth . . ."

She braced. She knew something was coming.

"That energy that you just put out to Max? The tongue-lashing? The berating of him? Who the hell wants to connect with *that*?"

She looked daggers at me for a moment, but she didn't say anything, and in a few minutes the session was over. When they came for their next session the following week, they both looked relaxed, and reported they had had a good week where they had just been basically friendly and loving to each other. Then Elizabeth said to me, "I was so angry with you last week when you made that crack at the end about 'Who the hell wants to connect with *that?*' And I left angry and stayed angry for a couple of days. But then Max asked if I wanted to talk about it all, and I said yes, and we talked—for a couple of hours!—and I think I'm finally beginning to understand what Max has been trying to tell me about a way I can get—implacable and punishing—that makes it really hard for him to want to relate to me." She paused. "So it's been ringing in my ears—'Who the hell wants to connect with *that?*'—and it's actually been very useful. Not easy to hear, especially with what he's done, but useful."

Be *that* woman.

VI. The Inner Place

If you want your husband to connect with you in that marital relational space where so many wonderful things can happen all your life, here's what to do:

Through whatever means you have at your disposal for self-inquiry—reading, talking with friends, therapy, meditation, prayer, intuition—learn to distinguish between the part of yourself that is disconnective, that says and does wrong things that break connection with your partner, and the part of yourself that is connective and knows the exact right thing to say or do that maintains connection.

Try to come from the connective place within you. I'll try to describe it.

This place is always aware of what's needed in the moment to maintain connection with your partner (and everybody!) and is skillful in doing it. This place always considers the effect that your words and actions will have on your partner before you say or do them. Will these words I'm about to say bring us closer? Will the situation get better? Is there benefit here? Or will they cause disconnection and distance and make the situation worse? When your husband says to you, "I wish you had more sexual desire for me," don't come from the place that would say, "Well, that's too bad, Barney, because I don't!" That snaps the connection in two and stops the relationship dead in its tracks. Come from the place that says, "Of course you wish that, Barney. So do I. The thing is I'm post-menopausal now, and it's kind of different with me these days. We need to change some of the things we do sexually. Let's talk about it, okay?"

That has benefit. That has a future. That's the place you want to be coming from.

The place inside you that says things like that, that stays in connection, that speaks a language that brings people together—that's the place you're looking for, and your work is to find it. It's your inner work, your outer work, all our work on this earth, I think. That's what we're doing here. It's all about learning how to be in relationship with each other, how to connect us all up. There's a place inside us, a place of great wisdom and power and love, that knows how to do that. It's in every one of us. It's built in. All we have to do, as husbands and wives trying to get along in our marriages, as human beings trying to get along on this planet, is find that place inside. No one, neither man nor woman, is exempt from the responsibility to find that inner place.

And now to the ones who are (mostly) at fault for the problems in their marriages: the men. At the end of the forty-four chapters addressed to your husbands, you'll find a "Closing Message to Women Readers." We'll talk more there.

MAN-TO-MAN

CHAPTER 1

Hey! You're in a Relationship!

Part of me loves and respects men so desperately, and part of me thinks they are so embarrassingly incompetent at life and in love. You have to teach them the very basics of emotional literacy. You have to teach them how to be there for you.

Anne Lamott

Marriage is a relationship . . . You're no longer this one alone; your identity is in a relationship.

Joseph Campbell

Let's face it, we men don't know squat about relationships. We don't really *do* relationships. We do work, we do sports, we do cars, we do wars, and we do sex (which is what often passes for relationship with some of us), but we don't really do relationships.

"His idea of a relationship," said Margo of her husband, Paul, in their first session, "is he comes home from a three-day business trip, tired and cranky, says a perfunctory hi to me, who's standing there at the door to greet him, stoops down to hug the kids for a few seconds, then makes a beeline upstairs to shower, change his clothes, and come down a half hour later. He sits down with us at the table where he gobbles down his favorite meal, which I've spent two hours preparing for him, hardly says a word to us, not a word of thanks to me, then gets up and goes into the den and turns on the TV and falls asleep. If I question him about it, like, 'Is this your idea of a relationship, Paul?' he either looks at me like I have two heads, or he gets mad at me. I really don't think he knows what I'm talking about. I'm not even sure he knows what the word 'relationship' means."

What we men mostly do is alone. "I am a rock, I am an island" . . . "Jo-Jo was a man who thought he was a loner" . . . "Desperado, you've been out ridin' fences" . . . that sort of thing. Even relationships we're in—like our marriages—we do them alone, or try to.

This drives women completely nuts.

Because women do relationships. They *like* relationships. They find their very *identity* in relationships and connections. In the same way that it is the nature of water to be wet, it is the nature of women to be relational.

This is somewhere between quite surprising and totally incomprehensible to most of us men.

But it makes sense, when you think about it.

Because women are totally biologically built for relationship. In pregnancy they carry another human being inside their bodies for nine months, which is about as relational as it gets. In the early years of their mothering they're nursing that baby night and day, which is also about as relational as it gets. In lovemaking they open up their beings and their very bodies to another human being, which is also about as relational as it gets.

Women, it is clear, are relational.

And you went and married one!

What were you thinking?

You probably weren't thinking, but if you had been, here's what you could have been thinking:

I'm a guy. I don't know squat about relationships. If you want to know the truth, I'm scared to death of relationships, the reason being that there's a secret little part of me that so needs a relationship, that's so dependent on a relationship—with a woman, with this woman who I married—that if I ever admitted it, especially to myself, the sheer power this woman has over me, I'm a goner.

So this dependency thing—I'll repress it, forget it, deny it, make fun of it, get mad at it, do everything but own it as a part of myself. In this way I will present the image of myself as an independent loner type, a mature man, a manly man, a regular John Wayne, off by myself, out ridin' fences . . .

If I don't get honest with myself here, I'll spend the next fifty years of my marriage off by myself ridin' fences, moving from one self-constructed isolation booth to another—work, TV, sports, pornography—silence, alcohol, depression, pornography, work—while my wife's over there lip-synching Roy Orbison's "Only the Lonely" and looking in the yellow pages under "Divorce Lawyers."

Hey, guys, the women are lonely!

You can diagnose them with depression and pump 'em full of Prozac, but they're really just lonely.

Did you hear me? Our wives are *lonely*.

So let's get honest with ourselves here.

I started getting honest with myself in 1969. Twenty-four years old. Two years out of Cornell, in graduate school in Boston.

Rooming with a fellow graduate student in a house by a pond in a suburb of Boston. Jane, twenty-one, a senior at Cornell, visiting me from Ithaca. Our first weekend together. A cold, snowy Sunday afternoon in late December. A walk through the woods. Snow crunching under our feet. Talking. Getting to know each other. Talking about ourselves.

"I'm quite happy by myself," I was saying. "I don't need anybody."

I'd been saying it for years—to girls, to myself, to everybody: *I don't need anybody.* It was my mantra. Coming from the family I came from, where we all lived in a kind of silent seclusion from each other, no wonder I said it and completely believed it.

I don't need anybody.

It was total bullshit. The opposite was true.

"I don't need anybody," I was saying to Jane, the two of us walking up a wooded hill, our boots breaking through the snow, her mittened hand in mine. "I really don't. I'm happy alone. I don't need *anybody.*"

She stopped, turned to me, took my forearms in her mittens, held me still, looked up into my face. Her light blue eyes were sparkling in the falling snow.

"Yes, you do, Robert," she said. "You need *me.*" And broke out into a big, beautiful smile.

In getting honest with yourself it helps if you meet a woman who sees right through you from the beginning of time.

All over the earth, since ancient times, women have been carrying the message of connection and relationship to us men. In bringing that message they also bring the messages of kindness and caring and communication, of human cooperation, of tending and befriending, of trust and love and peace.

Women know the way: It's the way of relationships. Of

human connections. Of getting together and talking and listening to each other. Of liking and helping and having a good time with each other.

Of *love*.

Don't you get it?

Your wife is trying to teach you *love*.

It's like Dylan says to a woman in one of his songs:

> *Love is so simple, to quote a phrase*
> *You've known it all the time, I'm learnin' it these days.*

Women *are* love.

"You need *me*," said the woman who loves me.

What you need is your wife.

What the world needs now . . . are the women!

And as soon as possible 'cause things are gettin' kind of scary here on the planet.

THE MOVE

Hey! You're married to a woman! You're in a relationship! With *her*!

That means you're supposed to stay connected to her. Here are three simple things you can do today to stay connected to her. Do one or two or all three of them.

1. Right now go find your wife wherever she is in the house and ask her how her day went. Like if she's in the kitchen fixing a snack for the kids, go in there and sit up on the

counter and say, "How'd your day go today?" or "Tell me about your day today" or something like that. And then listen.

2. When you leave the house today for work or to do errands or to go outside and do yard work, leave a little note on the kitchen counter: "See ya, honey. Love ya. You look pretty today."

3. When the two of you are watching TV together tonight, instead of sitting in your armchair, go sit next to her on the couch and put your arm around her. When the commercials come on, mute them and tell her little tidbits from your day.

These little daily connections are the stuff of relationship. You're in one. The fact that you're married to a woman means you're up to your ears in one.

A WORD TO THE WIVES

All the Moves at the end of all these chapters are designed to bring your husband into closer relationship with you. Most of them will be new and unfamiliar behaviors for him, and he'll be stretching outside his comfort zone to try them.

So when he tries them, try to make him feel as comfortable as possible by welcoming him when he approaches you and responding positively when he does the new behavior. Tell him that you see and appreciate what he's trying to do with these Moves and that you hope he keeps making them as he reads through the book. Give him a hug and a kiss, and tell him you're proud of him for doing what he's doing. Remember that we're men, which means that your welcome of us is huge positive reinforcement for us all the way through.

CHAPTER 2

What Does a Woman Want?

> The great question that has never been answered
> and which I have not been able to answer, despite
> my thirty years of research into the feminine
> soul, is, "What does a woman want?"
>
> Sigmund Freud

> If you treat me fairly, I'll give you all my goods
> Treat you like a real woman should . . .
>
> Alicia Keys

A good husband wants to know the answer to Freud's famous question.

So let's ask it.

What does a woman want?

I came across the following story many years ago:

A man is walking along a California beach and stumbles across an old lamp. He picks it up and rubs it, and out pops a genie.

The genie says, "Okay, okay, you released me from the lamp. This is the ninth time in two centuries, and I'm getting a little sick of everybody's wishes, so you can forget about having three of them. You only get one."

The man excitedly says, "Hey, I've always wanted to go to Hawaii, but I'm afraid to fly, and I get very seasick. How about building me my own bridge to Hawaii so I can drive over there whenever I want?"

The genie laughs and says, "Come on now, you didn't give this any real thought, did you? How could I possibly do that? Think of how big it'd have to be and the problems of building it. Like how would the supports ever reach the bottom of the Pacific? How high would it have to be to let all the ships out there pass under it? Do you know how much concrete it'd take? And steel? This time think *carefully* of your one wish."

The man says, "Okay," and sits down for a long time to come up with a better wish.

Finally he says, "I've got it! I've been married and divorced three times. My wives always said that I didn't care about them and that I'm insensitive and ignorant. So I wish that I could understand women, know how they feel inside and what they're thinking, know why they're crying, know why they're angry at me, know what they really want, know how to make them truly happy—"

The genie interrupts and says, "You want that bridge two lanes or four?"

What does a woman want?
That's the question.
Here's the answer, contained in a legend from King Arthur's time, the legend of Dame Ragnell:

King Arthur is out hunting deer one day in a forest. Ordering his attendants to stay behind, he goes alone deeper into the forest. Suddenly Sir Gromer Somer Joure, "a knight full strong and of great might," in black armor, with an old grievance against the king, accosts Arthur and threatens to kill him unless Arthur finds the answer to the knight's riddle. The knight's riddle is: "What does a woman want most?" He gives Arthur one year to come up with the answer and rides off.

Arthur returns to his court at Carlisle and tells the noble knight Sir Gawain of his encounter with the dark knight. They agree to spend the next twelve months riding through the kingdom asking every man and woman, "What does a woman want most?" Which they do, for a whole year, and collect a whole book of answers, but they know in their hearts that none of the answers is the true one.

As the deadline approaches, King Arthur rides forth one last time into the forest and meets there a hideously ugly old hag, Dame Ragnell. She is hunchbacked and covered with warts, and her face is red and splotchy, with bulging, bleary eyes. Her yellow teeth protrude out of her lips, her hair is snarled and clotted, her nose is "snotted withal." She tells Arthur that she has the correct answer to the dark knight's question and will give it to him on one condition: that he give her the hand of the noble Sir Gawain in marriage. Otherwise, says Dame Ragnell, Arthur will surely die at the hand of the dark knight.

Arthur tells Dame Ragnell that he must first ask for Gawain's consent. Dame Ragnell agrees, and Arthur rides back to Carlisle and explains the situation to Gawain. Gawain immediately agrees.

"I will wed her at what time you will set," he says to his king. "For love of you I will not hesitate."

Arthur rides back into the forest and tells Dame Ragnell of Gawain's consent. Dame Ragnell then gives Arthur the answer:

"Some people say that women most desire to be beautiful, or to have lust in bed with many men, or to be always fresh and young, but the truth is what women most want is 'sovereyntee,' the power to choose for themselves, the right to have their own way."

King Arthur thanks Dame Ragnell, then rides off to meet Sir Gromer and gives him the answer:

"What women most want is the power to choose for themselves," says Arthur. "Sovereyntee."

Sir Gromer concedes defeat and rides away.

King Arthur then rides back to court with Dame Ragnell, and she and Sir Gawain are married, while Queen Guinevere and the other ladies of the court stand there weeping at his pitiful plight.

After the wedding Sir Gawain takes Dame Ragnell to the bridal chamber, and she asks for a kiss from him. As their lips meet, Dame Ragnell is miraculously transformed from an ugly old hag to a stunningly beautiful young woman, "the fairest creature that ever he saw without measure."

"I had been under a curse," she explains, "transformed by necromancy into a hunchbacked old crone until a courteous knight like you married me and kissed me."

Sir Gawain is, of course, delighted, and the young couple "made mirth in the bedroom all night."

In the morning Dame Ragnell thanks Gawain for lifting the curse.

"But it is not *fully* lifted," she says. "Because of you, I am now free to be my true beautiful self . . . but only for half the day! My beauty will not hold. So I must ask you, dear husband, which do you choose? To have me beautiful by day and ugly in the nights, or beautiful by night and ugly in the days? Choose, choose, Sir Knight."

"Alas," says Gawain, "the choice is hard."

If he chooses her to be beautiful at night, he will have to look at her all day. But if he chooses her to be beautiful only during the day, he will have the ugly hag in his marriage bed.

"I don't know what to do," he says. "Choose what *you* think best, dear lady. The choice I put into your hand. Do as you want."

"Thank you, dear husband," says Dame Ragnell. "Now you have lifted the whole curse. Because you gave me the choice, you shall have me beautiful both day and night, always fair and bright. Because you gave me the power to choose what *I* want instead of what *you* want, you've freed me to be my beautiful self always."

What does a woman want?

She wants what she wants.

She wants her say. She wants the choice.

Your wife wants the power to choose.

And the good husband that you are wants to give her that because, according to the legend of Dame Ragnell, look what happens when you do.

THE MOVE

For the next week, do what your wife wants to do. Surrender to that.

Keep saying to her things like, "You choose" . . . "It's up to you" . . . "Whatever you want" . . . "Whatever you like" . . . "I just want to do what you want to do."

Watch the TV shows *she* wants to watch and then turn it off when *she* wants. Sit down and talk with her because *she* wants to sit down and talk with you. Plan the vacation *she* wants to take. Drive at the speed *she* wants to drive at. Have sex the way *she* likes it. Treat her like *she* wants to be treated.

Keep reminding her, "This is about what *you* want, not me."

For one week.

Little surrenders.

Just one week.

After the week is over, chances are that the two of you will be happier than you've ever been, getting along better than you ever have. She'll be gazing at you fondly—or is that amorously?—from across the living room, and not only hasn't this Move been hard for you, it's been interesting, novel, and kind of fun.

CHAPTER 3

Excuse Me? Did I Hear You Say "Surrender"?

> *You surrender not because you are weak;*
> *you surrender because you are strong.*
>
> A sage

Surrender?

Excuse me?

I don't think so.

I'm a man, and what surrender means to me is 1954 in Cabot Park in Newton, Massachusetts, and Frankie Morrison is sitting on top of my chest with his hands pinning my arms to the ground and his pukey, pimply face right down in mine, screaming, *"Give, Alter?! You GIVE?!"*

I'm a man, and what surrender means to me is one of those biblical cities that surrender and everybody in them—man, woman, and child—gets put to the edge of the sword and slaughtered.

Surrender is defeat. Humiliation. Weakness. Failure. For losers!

And surrender to my *wife?* To a *woman? Excuse me?*

It doesn't *get* any weaker than that.

But here's the thing: It's not weakness when you surrender to a woman—it's not losing—because women, as far as I can figure out, aren't into winning. They don't want to overpower and dominate and humiliate us, they just want to *connect* with us. They don't want us to say, *"Uncle!"*; they want us to say, *"Wife!"* They want us to say, *"I love you!"* They want us to say, *"Let's be together today! Let's go have lunch at the mall!"*

Surrendering to your wife in this way is not weakness. It's strength. It's mature manhood. It's a true giving of yourself to someone you love. Because you've now attained a solid and secure sense of self, you can give yourself to your wife with no loss of self, in the same way that the sun can give its light with no loss of light—it's that strong, that full of light.

What does it mean to give yourself to your wife?

It means many, many things over the course of your marriage. Here's what it mostly means to me these days:

It means that at this moment as I'm sitting here in the living room writing this book and Jane is in the bedroom lifting weights, her experience is as important to me as my experience. We're *married*, so her experience is the other half of my experience. I live inside her experience of life, as she lives inside mine. You see, we're *married*. Whatever I'm doing or thinking about doing in my life, the effect of my actions on her life and feelings is primary in my thinking. You see, we're *married:* Her life and feelings and my life and feelings have merged.

Some people get all hot and bothered at this point and start shouting, "Codependence! That's codependence!" . . . "You're codependent on her" . . . "You two are in a codependent relationship."

If they want to call it codependence, so be it, but I think it's just marriage. A state of union with another human being. God's intention for marriage. "And the two shall become one flesh, so then they are no longer two, but one flesh," says the gospel of Mark.

"Marriage," says mythologist Joseph Campbell, "means that the two are one, the two become one flesh. If the marriage lasts long enough, and if you are acquiescing constantly to it instead of to individual personal whim, you come to see that that is true—the two really are one."

And a spiritual master from India says, "An ideal spiritual union is one in which the husband and wife have become so absorbed in each other that when the husband eats, the wife is satisfied, and when the wife eats, the husband is satisfied . . . The two people should be one. The wife should become the husband's soul, and the husband should become the wife's soul . . . This is an ideal spiritual marriage."

That takes codependence to a whole new level. To the level of union, spiritual union. A surrender of both of you to each other, of both of you to the marriage.

Here's more of what my surrender to Jane feels like:

- It feels like I never want to hurt her, never want to cause her harm or pain by anything I say or do. "Be careful not to make a woman weep," says the Talmud, "as God keeps count of her tears."

- It feels like I never want to do anything to cause her anxiety or fear. I do not want my wife living in fear of any kind, and certainly not in fear of me. I want to be a safe and gentle man for her so she always feels safe and secure with me.
- It feels like I want to be with her a lot, to spend time with her and walk and talk with her and laugh with her and love with her and just basically hang out together. There's a young teenagey part of us that likes just hanging out together.
- It feels like I want to help her a lot. In everything. With everything. Help her if she's feeling out of sorts or stressed, help her figure out what that strange new noise in her car is, help her when she needs something heavy to be lifted, help her when *she* needs to be lifted.
- It feels like consulting her in every major decision of my life, going to her for wisdom I do not always have and encouragement and inspiration I always need. "Hey, Jane, say something that'll keep me going with this book. I'm bogged down. I'm losin' heart here." . . . "You *are* this book, Robert, and you're the man to write it. Just write from your experience. All the words'll be there."
- It feels like the quiet pleasure I take inside when she is having pleasure.
- It feels like absolute and total loyalty to her. Whatever happens to her in her life, I will take her part.
- It feels like modeling myself on her: her kindness, her indomitable cheerfulness, her courage, her discipline, her devotion to love and truth.
- It feels like continually trying to fathom the depth of her love for me, although, from the looks of it, I'll never be able to fully grasp it. It feels like spending my whole life trying to return it.

- If that's surrender, if that's giving in, it feels like a good giving in. It's giving in to the fact that I want my wife to be happy. I'm her husband: Of course I want her to be happy. And I act accordingly.
- It feels like immense gratitude. In her great song "Kind and Generous," Natalie Merchant sings to someone she loves, "I want to thank you, show my gratitude, my love and my respect for you, " and ends the song repeating "Thank you" over and over and over, as if, when you get to the deepest place in the heart, the truly surrendered place, that's all you *can* say to someone you love—*Thank you.*

Thank you, Jane. For being so kind and generous to me. For being the amazing woman that you are. Thank you, God, for the amazing grace of her.

Did you hear me say "surrender"?
Yes, you did.
And it's a sweet, sweet surrender, let me tell you.

THE MOVE

Think about this surrender thing.

What are your associations with the idea of surrender? Do you understand the difference between surrender as defeat and surrender as love? Do you feel a resistance inside to giving yourself to your wife in the ways I've described? How come? Is that "losing" to you? Are you such a loser that you interpret that as losing? If you can ever get your act together and give yourself to her in the ways I'm describing, what do you think you'll get back? Do you think she'll give you *any*thing back? Do you think you might get the same gift from her that you've given her? Do you think she might surrender to you in the same way that you've surrendered to her? Do you think that maybe both of you will finally get what you've always wanted from each other? Hello? Anyone home?

Think about this.

Now go ask your wife if there's something you do around the house that she doesn't like and wants you to stop—like when you summon her from another room and expect her to drop whatever she's doing and come to you, or when you hurry her off the phone with her friends or leave the toilet seat up.

When she tells you what it is, say quickly, "I won't do that anymore."

And surrender to that. Don't do it anymore.

CHAPTER 4

How to Know When You're Being a Man As Opposed to When You're Being an Asshole

You're gonna have to serve somebody.

Bob Dylan

*I understand the large hearts of heroes,
the courage of present times and all times.*

Walt Whitman

M en are heroic. Our role in the evolution of the species has been heroic. We've been providers and protectors and warriors— hunting, building, fixing, defending, working our asses off to make this sometimes dangerous and hostile planet a safer and more comfortable place to live. This is rooted very deep in us. It's the way we love.

That's why, every single day, we get up and go to work. We'll work as much as we have to, and we're not afraid of it. We *are* afraid of danger, but we'll walk right into the teeth of it if necessary to defend and protect our loved ones. We'll do whatever we have to do to provide for them. We take on our protector and provider service with the fervor of a knight and the endurance of a mule.

Men, in other words, are great. We're heroes in selfless service to those we love. We really are. We're really wonderful.

Except when we're not.

Except when we're assholes.

Because we can also be flaming assholes.

We're assholes when we're in heroic service not to our loved ones, but to our own self, our own puffed-up horrid little ego, the little *pisher* in there who's always trying to prove how big and strong and important he is by controlling and intimidating and dominating others and putting himself at the center of everything.

The spoiled-rotten brat.

The jerk.

The schmuck.

The biggest asshole I ever met in my therapy practice was a guy named Chet who fancied himself a spiritual kind of guy, but who was really the most self-centered, entitled, condescending, arrogant bastard that ever walked into my office, and treated his wife, Cindy—one of the nicest people I ever met—like shit. This was a guy who expected his wife to have sex with him after he'd just gotten through yelling at her for forgetting to get the car inspected. He blamed Cindy for his daily immersion in computer pornography—"because she doesn't put out anymore for me." He threw a tantrum one morning when someone else in the family finished the orange juice and there was none left for him. If he was taking a nap in the living room, which he did often, every-body else in the house was expected to tiptoe around like ghosts and not even talk to each other. His wife would cook dinner for him and the kids, and after dinner Chet would go into his "read-ing room" and close the door while Cindy, who was by this time of day completely exhausted, cleaned up. He blamed everything that was wrong in the marriage on Cindy and, with his little smattering of psychological knowledge, was convinced—and was trying to convince her—that the real problem in the marriage was that she was manic-depressive and should go to a psychiatrist to get medication for it.

"I don't think that's the diagnosis, Chet," I told him one ses-sion. "What you call her manic episodes are, in my opinion, when she is simultaneously so scared of you and so ripshit at you that she doesn't know what to do with herself, and what you call her depression is the dejection bordering on hopelessness that any sane person would feel being married to you. It's like that movie *Gaslight*, Chet, where Charles Boyer is trying to make his wife, Ingrid Bergman, whom he is basically holding captive in their house, believe that she's crazy, when all the time it's him who's crazy—until Joseph Cotten shows up and tells Bergman, 'You're not going out of your mind. You're slowly and systemati-cally being driven out of your mind.' That's what's going on in this marriage, and many marriages like yours. I don't think Cindy is manic-depressive at all; I think that's an incorrect diagnosis; I think the correct diagnosis is you're an asshole."

As I said all this to him, he sat there with a stupid smirk on his face and glanced at his watch. I felt like killing him. I had the thought that what this marriage really needed, therapeutically speaking, was for Cindy to punch the friggin' guy out. He stayed for about five sessions and then never came back. I wasn't surprised—some assholes are such assholes that all you can do is wonder why the women married them in the first place and then stayed with them.

When we men are being assholes, our behavior, especially our treatment of others, and especially our treatment of our wives, gets horrible. Appalling. We treat them like servants and expect their obedience. When we get what we want from them, we can be nice enough, but if we don't, watch out, girls. We'll get silent, sullen, angry, pushy, loud, violent, and mean. We sulk and we stew, like babies. We close down completely and there's no getting through to us. We have no attention for anyone but ourselves. We don't even care about anyone but ourselves.

This is not manhood. It's the opposite of manhood. It's narcissism, which is the *really* asshole thing we men can be.

No offense, guys. Just trying to distinguish between a man and an asshole.

Since, in order to be good husbands, we've got to stop being assholes and start being men, start being heroes, it's an important distinction.

It all comes down to who we're trying to serve.

THE MOVE

In your daily interactions with your wife this week, and especially in any disagreements you may have about how to use time, energy, or resources, stop and ask yourself the following question:

"Who am I trying to serve here?"

If the answer comes back "Me," that means you're being

an asshole, so stop being an asshole and start being a man by serving her.

For example, you're lying in bed with your wife before sleep. She's reading, and you're watching a totally stupid movie with sex and violence in it. It's really disturbing her—in fact, she hates movies like that—and she asks you to turn it off so she can have some peace and quiet. You're into the movie and don't want to turn it off, so you're a little peeved at her even asking. A moment goes by. A decision is called for.

Base your decision on who it is you're trying to serve: you or her.

Make it her.

Turn it off, asshole.

That feeling you feel after you turn it off is called manhood.

CHAPTER 5

Remember You're Great

And I turned to myself, and said to myself,
Who art thou? and I answered, A Man!

St. Augustine

How beautiful maleness is, if it finds its right expression.

D. H. Lawrence

Yes, you can sometimes be an asshole—and worse. Yes, you need to change—big-time. And yes, I'm giving you a very hard time in this book, and yes, you deserve it, and yes, you should remember it.

But here's another thing you should remember:

You're great.

I'm not trying to flatter you, and I'm not kidding. I mean it. *You are great.*

The only reason I give us men a hard time is because we need to shape up. Once we've pulled ourselves together, once we're operating from who we *truly* are in our heart of hearts, from our *real* manhood instead of from the shriveled little macho travesty that goes by the name of manhood in this culture, the world will be astonished by us.

Are we (mostly) at fault for the problems in our marriages and the unhappiness of our wives? Yes. Are we (mostly) at fault for the distress in our families and the discord and danger in the world? Yes. But we're going to work on all that; we're going to work on ourselves and fix all that. In the meantime the sages say there is no greater fault than considering oneself bad, low, ordinary. Have the highest respect for yourself, they say. Remember that you're great.

Men are great.

We are strong, giving, helpful, kind.

We love to use our brains, our brawn, and our lion hearts to help and serve people. We'll take on any challenge. We're rescuers and savers of lives. We can design, engineer, build, and fix *any*thing. Our deepest desire is to serve. At our best we will devote our lives, risk our lives, and give our lives in service to those whom we love.

"Greater love hath no man than this, that a man lay down his life for his friends," says the Bible, and we men are doing that every day of the year all over the world.

We work. Boy, can we work (as you'll see in the next chapter). If we have to, we'll work past strength, past exhaustion, past health. We do our jobs and provide. Our providership is our service to the world, and we are performing that service, doing our duty, every day.

We're something to look at! Handsome, strong, muscular,

sexy. In some of us the strength isn't so much physical but an inner strength of mind, of resolve and spirit.

We play. We *love* to play. All those sports we're watching? It's all play—a bunch of boys filled with so much exuberance and life energy that they have no idea what to do with it all except run around and randomly bang into each other and fall down. And then get up and run around again and randomly bang into each other again and fall down again. That's *fun* for us. It's what we live for. Play. Give us any moment in time when there's nothing else to do and we'll invent a game for it and fill it with play.

Those are only a few of the ways in which men are wonderful. If you want to see others, look around you. Or look in the mirror.

We are all the good men and true who have ever lived. We are every good and upstanding husband, father, son, and brother who is doing his duty and meeting his responsibilities all over the world. There are billions of us, and we are worthy of the world's respect, gratitude, admiration, and love.

The other day I was driving on the highway and saw a car broken down, its hood up, on the side of the road. It was raining. A woman holding an umbrella was standing by the passenger door with her two young children at her legs. Two men were leaning over the hood, their sleeves rolled up and their arms down in the engine. They had stopped their pickup truck to help. Up my back came a little chill of reverence for those guys and for all guys.

That was the essence of manhood.

Helpfulness. Service. Skill. Teamwork. Plain old niceness.

That's *you*.

You're a good guy. You're a good guy as you already are, and you're a good guy for wanting to become a better guy.

Why else do you think you're reading this book?

Think about it.

Yes, you need to change, but you can't change if you think you're an asshole—because if you think you're an asshole, then you'll just go ahead and act like an asshole. So think that you're a good person. Know that you're a worthy person, a great person, a noble man. Then you'll want to act nobly. Then you'll want to do good deeds. Then you'll want to be the good husband that in your heart you already are.

We're talking about potential here. Potential means power. The full power of the entire oak tree is already there in the acorn. The butterfly is in the chrysalis. You already are what you want to become!

It's like I told one guy in couples therapy who was feeling bad about himself: "Zach, you are not the screwup that your father always told you you were. That's just an old, dried-up thought in your mind. All those feelings that you're bad, they're all bullshit. Deborah doesn't think you're bad. She adores you. So do your kids. You're a great guy. *I* think you're a great guy. Who else but a great guy would sit through this therapy week after week and be willing to look at himself at this depth? If you weren't a great guy, why would Deborah be sitting over there right now with love in her eyes for you?"

Take my point here, guys. It's really important. We men step into our greatness from the platform of our recognition of our greatness. It's really simple: All we have to do is become the great men we already are.

THE MOVE

Go ask your wife to tell you all the ways she thinks you're a good man and a wonderful husband. No qualifiers on her part, no objections or demurring on yours. Just be quiet and write them down.

Then take the list and for the next few days read and reread it. Let it sink into your mind, past all your disbelief and doubt.

If disbelief and doubt do come up, go back to your wife and ask her to repeat it—all the ways she thinks you're a good man and a wonderful husband—while you sit there nodding.

And then, whenever you do something good, make it a point to acknowledge yourself. Stop for a moment and acknowledge yourself whenever you come through on something, or perform an action that benefits others, or do something hard, or behave well, or accomplish a goal, or try a new and improved behavior with your wife.

Take a moment and thank yourself for all the wonderful things that you do and the worthy man that you are.

- "I did my job today. I did my duty. I went to work, worked hard, and provided for my family."

- "I love my kids and spend lots of time with them. They love it that I coach their soccer team."

- "I let that woman come in front of me in traffic today."

- "I called my sister last night for no particular reason, just to say hello. I could tell she liked that."

- "I'm a good guy. It's not easy doing what I have to do in my life, but I just do it."

Acknowledge yourself. Appreciate yourself. Thank yourself.

Take this Move really seriously.

CHAPTER 6

Men at Work

*You know, I work all day
to get you money to buy you things.*

The Beatles

And the men did the work faithfully.

2 Chronicles 34:12

Here's a hard one. It's the work one.

On the one hand, we men *have* to work. Unless we're really wealthy, we have to earn our living by the sweat of our brow to feed, clothe, and house our families. We do this eight or ten or twelve hours a day, five or six or seven days a week, fifty weeks a year, for forty or fifty years. That's a lot of work. Some of us like our work, some of us don't, but it doesn't matter, we have no choice, we just do it.

We're *men*. When we have to do something, we *just do it*.

So we work hard and long. Our work serves our families and the world. It's a form of sacrifice. "Work is love made visible," says Kahlil Gibran.

On the one hand.

On the other hand, for many of us our work goes beyond service and beyond love and becomes workaholism, that compulsive, fear-driven, often greed-driven thing we do *instead* of loving, an addiction we have that few of us know we have because almost all of us have it.

On the one hand, our work serves our wives, and they deeply appreciate us for the major contribution we're making to the marriage and the family.

On the other hand, our work is a major—sometimes *the* major—problem in the marriage, and it doesn't serve our wives but abandons them, angers and depresses them, and they don't deeply appreciate it but give us a major hard time about it.

Here's something that happens in my therapy office all the time:

A couple comes in because they're really mad at each other—particularly she at him—and really distant and unhappy; and one of the problems, it turns out, is that the man is never available to her and the kids because he's always working. The wife reports that he's never home, and not really part of the family even when he is home, because he's usually so tired.

At that point the man gets really pissed off and says that he has no *choice* in any of this! . . . he has to *work*! . . . and his work *demands* this! . . . and it's his *work* that allows her to shop at *Bloomingdale's*! . . . And on and on.

The woman sits there glazing over and looking around for an oven to stick her head into, then turns to me plaintively and says, "We can't talk about this. You see what happens. We're really stuck here. We need help."

So I take a deep breath and tell them about the time zone we all live in.

"We live in a time zone—Male Standard Time—in which the main purpose of time on this planet is the endless accumulation of money through work. Its chief operating arm is a global economic system called corporate capitalism that makes using time in this way imperative. In Male Standard Time almost all time is claimed directly or indirectly for the man's work. He's at work a lot, and even when he's home from work, he's preparing for work, doing extra work, comatose in front of the TV destressing from work, or on the golf course getting away from it all.

"In Male Standard Time," I say to the husband, "your wife and your children never get to do what *they* want to do with time, which is to be with *you*, so they're lonely. So are you, but you don't know it because you're completely seduced, brainwashed, and trapped by the system, and so used to it."

Usually the husband is not too spectacularly happy with me at this point, but then I tell him that I myself am still hung up by this work stuff—even as I sit here in my *tenth* therapy session of the day—and am still trying to get a handle on it, at which point he relaxes a little.

So I go on.

What to do?

You've got to figure it out, the work one, each man for himself, each couple for itself, and somehow make it work in your marriage and family. It's hard, because the system has us all trapped inside it, but you've got to try.

You've got to honestly ask yourself, *What am I doing? Does my work serve the connection between me and my wife—is it my rightful contribution to the relationship?—or is it just another form of discon-nection in me, another one of the isolation booths I hide in to get away from the relationship?*

Or both?

You've got to figure it out.

It's not easy, but it's a little easier if you remember that the goal here is to be a good husband—to serve, love, and please your wife—which means that if your wife gets to drive around town in a spiffy new Lexus because of all the hard work you do, good! But if she's planning to drive the spiffy new Lexus *into* you because she feels so disconnected from you and so pissed off at you, not so good.

Check that out with her.

Remember: Women are really into being connected with their husbands.

And while you're at it, remember that the *real* work of a man—his *real* service to both his family and the world—is to cre-ate a strong, close, happy, healthy family in a world that needs a lot of those families to get back on its feet.

If you're into providership—and you should be, you're a *man*—that's the *true* providership: providing *yourself* to your wife and children and providing the world with a model of a happy family.

As the *I Ching,* an ancient Chinese book of prophecy and wisdom, says, "When the father is a father and the mother a mother . . . a husband a husband and a wife a wife, then the house is set in order. When the house is set in order, the whole world is set in order."

A good husband doesn't disappear into his work, off on his own, away from his family. Hard as it is, he does his level best to make his work truly work for his family, and so sets his house and his world in order.

THE MOVE

Sit down with your wife and ask her about this work stuff.

Given the socioeconomic system we're living in, it's a hard one to figure out on your own, and a hard one to change even when you do figure it out, so assume you need help and go get it from your wife.

Actually say to her, "I need your help with this work one."

If she gives you a glib, unhelpful answer like, "Well, just work less!" say you don't feel at all helped by that and keep the conversation going.

Tell her it feels like a conundrum to you, a real predicament, how to make your work life more harmonious with your family life. Tell her the truth, which is that you feel trapped by it all. Caught between a rock and a hard place.

Keep the conversation going. In fact, make it an ongoing conversation and keep telling her you need her help in figuring it out. Particularly ask her for suggestions of things you might do to better balance work and family.

For example, I used to see therapy clients every week from Monday morning at seven to Saturday at noon. Some time ago Jane suggested that I end my work week Friday at noon. I hemmed and hawed about that for a few months— no, I think it was actually nine years—but eventually did it, and both of us are the happier for it. Friday nights are a lot more fun now, we go out to dinners and movies, and Saturday mornings we do other things. I could never have done that without Jane's suggestion and encouragement. Not in a million years.

You, too, are going to need help with this work thing. Go to your wife and ask her for help. And then the two of you can figure it out together.

A WORD TO THE WIVES

It is almost impossible to overestimate the pressure a man in our society feels to work and make money. His family's well-being and survival, his self-esteem, his very manhood, are tied to his ability and willingness to work, earn, provide, and succeed. It's how he measures himself, and it's why he loses himself—and you lose him—to work. We men feel really trapped in this, and there's no obvious way out for us, no easy solution.

So be patient with us on this work one. Balance your requests for more time and connection with him with your appreciation for what he has to do and what he contributes. Say, like Debra says to Ray in an episode of *Everybody Loves Raymond,* "You're trying and you care and you work hard and yeah, your job takes you away a lot, but it's because of your job that we were able to pay the doctor today." We're all caught in an economic system that is bigger than us, and most of us—men and women—are pedaling as fast as we can in it, so let your desire for more of him be balanced with your gratitude toward him.

CHAPTER 7

Are You Being Served?

And Jacob served seven years for Rachel; and they seemed unto him but a few days, for the love he had to her.

Genesis 29:20

A good husband, by definition, lives in a state of service to his wife—as opposed to where many men live, which is in a state of *being served by* their wives, and if they're not being served by their wives, something is seriously wrong with the marriage—namely, the wife.

The thing that's wrong with this marriage is *you*, buddy. It really is (mostly) your fault. And the thing that's wrong with you is you think the marriage is *about* you. And you think that your wife's central purpose for existing on this earth is to please and serve you.

You think she has nothing all that important to do in her day, and nothing better to do with her time than drop your dry cleaning off and pick you up at the airport.

You think she should handle all the babysitting arrangements, and the social arrangements, and the holiday arrangements, and the delivery of the new couch.

You think she should know what you want, and she should anticipate what you want, and she should give you what you want, and you think it's okay to bark at her when she doesn't do what you want.

Be there for me . . . Understand me . . . Support me . . . Assist me . . . Listen to me . . . Get food for me . . . Get sexy for me . . .

Notice how often you use the word "me"?

You're so at the center of things that you don't even know you're there.

But you are, completely, so start watching it in yourself.

Here's how to do that:

In every interaction with your wife, watch for every time you're thinking *in the direction of you*—like: What's coming to *you* from *her?* How much attention (or understanding, care, assistance, sympathy, or sex) are *you* getting from *her?* How is she acting toward *you?* What is she giving *you?* And so on.

Do this when she brings you your grilled cheese sandwich as you sit watching East Podunk State play the University of Nowhere in the first round of the Midwest regional NCAA basketball tournament, and do it when you're wanting sex.

And every time you catch yourself thinking in the direction of you, say, "Good catch!" Say it like you really mean it—the same way my best friend, Jonny Berenson, really meant it when he said it from third after I snagged that liner at short—"Good catch, Alts!"—because it really *is* a good catch, and not many men can make it because they're so busy making themselves the center of things.

Once you catch yourself thinking in the direction of you, change the direction of your thinking. Throw it into reverse. Think in her direction.

If you need a model for this, you can use St. Francis, whose famous prayer is one of the world's purest expressions of thinking in the other person's direction:

> *Grant that I may not seek to be consoled but to console*
> *Not so much to be understood as to understand*
> *Not so much to be loved as to love . . .*

Now let's apply it to your relationship with your wife.

What mood or emotion is going from you to her? How are you behaving toward her? How are you treating her? What face are you showing her? What tone of voice are you speaking to her in? Are you giving attention to her? Understanding? A helping hand? A friendly smile? What *are* you giving to her?

Are you *serving* her?

This is revolutionary.

Here's how to know if you're serving her:

Have you tuned in to her exactly as she is right now in this moment? How's she feeling? What's her mood? Has she had a long day? Tough day? Tough time with *you* lately, by any chance? How's her life going? What's happening for her at work? Why has she been so quiet lately? Where is she in her menstrual cycle? Why did she come into the room where you are right now and try to engage you in conversation? What's she wanting from you right now? What's she needing from you in this very moment?

Figure it out. It's not rocket science.

It's called tuning in to your wife.

It's called figuring out what she wants in this moment and then trying to give it to her. And then in the next moment it's called tuning in to her again and figuring out what she wants and trying to give it to her again.

You ride that wave of her. It's a beautiful wave.

And guess what? It's the wave that takes you to that *other* beautiful wave of her that you love to ride. That's not rocket science either. We'll talk more about that later.

Just serve her. Think of her as a divine female being, a goddess, who has, by your great good fortune, miraculously appeared in your life to live with you, love you, and save your sorry ass— WHICH SHE IS!—and serve her.

As Dylan says, you're gonna have to serve *some*body.

Here's the revolutionary thing:

It's supposed to be *her*.

THE MOVE

Do the following three-step process today:

First, observe your wife in a particular moment and figure out what she might want or need from you in that moment. If you're having trouble figuring it out, ask her.

Second, remind yourself that she is a great, great woman whose presence in your life is a total miracle in the life of a schnook like you, and she therefore deserves your complete devotion.

Third, let your devotion take the form of devoted service to her, and serve her what she wants or needs from you right now. Like when you finish reading this chapter, close the book, go to your wife wherever she is in the house, and ask her if there's anything you can do for her right now. Since this might be a new behavior on your part, she might wonder why you're asking. She might even seem suspicious. Tell her it's because you were just thinking about her and how much she has on her plate every day, and you just wanted to see if you could help her with anything.

Since this is a very new behavior on your part, she might look at you like you're nuts, and you might feel so awkward doing it that you do feel like you're nuts, but stay with it and say again, "I was just thinking about you, Joanna, and how much you have to do every day, and I just wanted to see if I can help you with anything."

She might ask you to do something at that point, like take out the garbage, help the kids find their sneakers, or rub her shoulders for a second.

Do what she asks you to do.

Repeat this kind of behavior a few times over the week, get in the habit of it, and both of you will start to accept it as normal behavior from a husband to a wife—which it is—and both of you will feel really good about it and really good about each other.

Chapter 8

Grow Up!

The great majority of men seem to be minors.

Ralph Waldo Emerson

A good husband is a grown-up.

You're not a grown-up because you're over twenty-one or because your body, biceps, portfolio, or penis is big. Size really doesn't matter here.

What matters is you facing the fact that you sometimes act so immaturely in your family that you're like having another kid around the house—but worse, because you're bigger, louder, and scarier. Believe me, your wife is totally fed up with your infantile behavior and has been wanting to say something to you for years, but won't because the last time she tried it, you went into a ridiculous snit that ruined her entire week.

What she's been wanting to say to you for years is, "Grow up!"

Some wives would phrase it a little differently. They'd say, "For God's sake, Eddie, grow up, will ya!"

Either way, don't take offense, please. You're in good company. The company of men who haven't grown up. Who are little babies inside those big bodies. It's an international company, with headquarters in your house.

So grow up.

Listen. Here're twenty points of information that might help you grow up:

Point one. You're not the center of the universe.

Points two through nine. You're not the center of the universe.

Point ten. Your wife has a life independent of yours. There are things she likes to do and things she has to do that, believe it or not, have nothing to do with you.

Eleven. You're not fourteen, for heaven's sakes! Stop giggling and sniggling about sex all the time! Making love to your wife is not "hiding the salami" or "getting some nookie tonight"!

Twelve. Her breasts aren't boobs, bombs, knobs, knockers, balloons, jugs, tits, or hooters, they're *breasts*, and they don't exist so you can be grabbing at them every single time you see them.

Thirteen. Get control of your eyes, for God's sake, and stop staring at other women's breasts!

Fourteen. Stop pouting when you don't get your way. And when you're stressed or depressed, stop stomping around the house like a big baboon, criticizing and lecturing and insulting everybody and ordering everybody around and scaring the hell out of everybody. What gives you the right to make your whole family run for cover just because you're in one of your crappy moods?

Your majesty, the baby!

Get off it!

Fifteen. Yes, you work hard—but stop expecting everybody to feel sorry for you forever for that. And for heaven's sakes, stop thinking it means you never have to do anything else around the house.

Sixteen. Please try to understand the female response to your coming home two and a half hours after you said you would.

Seventeen. Life does not come to a screeching halt for everybody because you want to Watch The Game. Don't you get it yet? There's *always* a game, and you're always watching it. Get off the couch and go be a husband and father with them. Get a life. *They* are your life.

Eighteen. Your wife's woman friends are important to her, so stop making fun of them and stop giving her grief when she wants to spend time with them. She's not your *possession*, you know.

Nineteen. Stop saying no to your wife all the time. Stop this stupid *fight* with her. When she asks you to do something, when she makes a request, when she needs your help, when she wants to stay longer at the party than you want to stay, try saying yes. You can't get to adulthood on that "no" to her.

Twenty. Practice not acting like a petulant twit when it's perfectly clear that you're totally wrong about something. You're often wrong about things. Most of what's wrong in your marriage is (mostly) your fault. Be a man, admit it, and move on.

I could go on and on, but you get the point.

The point is we've got to grow up.

THE MOVE

Ask your wife to make a comprehensive list of all the ways she thinks you're immature.

When she presents it to you, take it from her hand and thank her for her time and effort.

In her presence silently read down the list, saying "Hmmm" at each item.

Then give it back to her and ask her to read it out loud, saying "Hmmm" after each item again, but this time *loudly,* like you're having a string of epiphanies.

When she's done, thank her again, take back the list, and go somewhere to look at it.

For each item that she's put on the list, write down the *opposite* behavior. For example, if she's written, "When you don't get your way in something, you go off and sulk like a seven-year-old and bum the whole family out!" write down, "When I don't get my way in something, I'll understand that that's the way it sometimes is in relationships, and I'll stay with the family and be nice to everyone." If she's written, "I hate your stupid sexual innuendos!" write down, "No more stupid sexual innuendos! When I want sex, I'll maturely suggest it, request it, or create other kinds of intimate connection with her—like talking to her, being with her—that I now understand lead to intimate sexual connection with her."

Go down the list of your immature behaviors and write down the opposite behaviors.

You now have a list of mature behaviors.

Start practicing them with her.

CHAPTER 9

The Five Big Lies That Keep You from Changing

Self-responsibility is the key factor if any growth or transformation is to take place. Until we recognize and accept that change is up to us, we are stuck.

Elinor Dickson and Marion Woodman

Some people claim that there's a woman to blame But I know it's my own damn fault.

Jimmy Buffett

To be a good husband, you have to change yourself, and to change yourself, you have to quit telling yourself the lies that keep you from changing yourself. These are the five big lies we men tell ourselves so we don't have to change. They come up early on in therapy, and repeatedly and strongly, so I have to correct them—early on, repeatedly and strongly.

- **The first big lie is,** *"I don't need to change."*

Yes, you do. Or your wife wouldn't be telling you to read this book. Don't be a moron. Next.

- **The second big lie is,** "She's *the one who needs to change. There's something wrong with* her. *She's always angry . . . She's hypercritical . . . She's oversensitive . . . She's too emotional . . . She's too needy . . ."*

Actually, if you want to know the truth, she *doesn't* need to change, not really; she's okay. The only thing she needs to change is *you*. To whatever degree she's *not* okay—to whatever degree she's feeling dissatisfied, angry, critical, and unhappy in the relationship with you—it's because the relationship with you is so far from okay it isn't even funny.

And besides, to whatever degree she does need to change, it's not within three galaxies of the amount that *you* need to change, so don't try that one anymore, please.

Don't try it because it's not true, and it's not *manly* either. A man doesn't spend his life putting the cause of his problems *outside* himself. It's a form of cowardice, of passing the buck, a big excuse.

Harry Truman, who had a sign on his desk that said, "The Buck Stops Here," would be ashamed of you.

She's the one who needs to change?

Oh, please. Stop hiding behind her skirts.

Here's what's true and what's manly:

All the responsibility for all the change needed in your marriage rests on you. That's right, *you*. And *only* you. There's no one *but* you. It's not only (mostly) your fault, it's all your fault. You are 100 percent responsible for the whole damn thing.

Stay with me here. This is important.

The instant we think that there's another on whom the responsibility for change rests, we become victims, and power starts draining out of us like oil out of a leaky engine. The very thought that it's up to her to make a change weakens our resolve to change ourselves. It gives us an out. It's an excuse. It's a cop-out. A whine. No muscle in it. No balls.

She's not the one who needs to change. Don't go there. If you let yourself hide behind that one once, you'll hide behind it forever, and your marriage will stay stuck forever. It's a lie. "See it to be a lie, and you have already dealt it its mortal blow," says Emerson.

"The test of a first-rate intelligence," says F. Scott Fitzgerald, "is the ability to hold two opposed ideas in the mind at the same time, and still retain the ability to function." In other words, can your mind deal with paradox? Good, because here's one: Of course your wife needs to change—we all need to change—but she doesn't need to change, you need to change, so change, and when you do, I guarantee you, *everything* will change.

- **The third big lie is,** *"I'll change when she changes."*

Nope. That's not the way it works. *You* have to change *first.* Here's why:

Because we've blown it with the women, guys. For thousands of years we've been awful to them—disrespectful, irresponsible, demeaning, abusive. We've lied to them, cheated on them, scorned and ignored them, completely bungled the relationship with them. All of us men have our own version of that, and the women are pissed. We've broken faith with them, so they've lost faith in us. They don't trust us anymore, and we have to win back their trust by changing into the true and trustworthy men we told them we were when we pledged our troth to them. We broke our pledge, you see, and broke their hearts, and now we have to win back their hearts by proving ourselves to be men worthy of them.

It's like in olden times. The true man, the knight, must win the lady by doing whatever it is he has to do, whatever it is she requires him to do, to win her. If he has to slay dragons, he slays dragons. If he has to cross moats and scale castle walls to get to her up in that lighted window, he crosses moats and scales walls. That was the way it worked back then, and that's the way it works now.

And the requirement here, in our time, is for us men to *change*. Change *ourselves* and change *first*. Slay our *own* dragons. Prove our manhood to them. Restore their trust in us. Renew their faith in us. *Earn* it.

* **The fourth big lie is,** *"I'll never be able to change enough for her, so what's the point of trying? Nothing is ever good enough for her. She always wants more from me. She's always angry at me. She's impossible to please."*

Not even close to true, but it's understandable that you may think it.

Because the truth is she hasn't been too deliriously happy with you for a long time. And she gives you a major hard time about the way you are in the marriage and family. And she's always wanting you to change something about yourself, change more and be different and be better.

True. All true.

But that's not because you'll *never* change enough for her, it's because you *haven't* changed enough for her . . . yet. The reason she wants more change from you is that you need to change more.

Duh.

If you're shooting baskets and you hit the rim five times in a row, you don't say, "I'll never get one in" or "It's impossible to get one in" or "The reason I haven't gotten one in is there's something wrong with the basket." No, you realize that you have to shoot *better* to get one in. So you do, and they start going in.

If you're trying to get into a building by hitting the right code on the numeric keypad by the door, and if the code is 971, you don't get in if you hit 425, or even if you hit 972 or 917. It's not that the door will never open or is impossible to open or doesn't want to open, it's just that you haven't hit the right code yet, but when you do, the door clicks open, and in you go.

It's called getting it right. In marriage it's called getting yourself right.

So stop hiding behind "This is impossible, She's impossible to please, I can't get it perfect, She's just a demanding bitch." I had a guy try that one in therapy this morning. Over the previous weekend he had flown down to Jacksonville, Florida, to see the Super Bowl between the New England Patriots and the Philadelphia Eagles. He flew back Monday and got in around midnight. His wife, who had been sick with a cold over the weekend, had waited up for him in bed, but when he got into bed, he was so tired that he just grunted hello to her and fell asleep immediately. The next morning she was cold toward him and didn't speak to him on their car ride into work. It was now Friday, and he came into therapy still really angry at her.

"I can never do anything *right* with her! No matter what I do, she's always pissed at me. She just *likes* being pissed at me, I think! I'm not perfect, and I'll never be perfect, and unless I'm perfect, she'll never be pleased."

"Not true, Gordon," I said. "It was simple to please her Monday night. All you had to do was spend a few minutes reconnecting with her after being away all weekend, like getting into bed and hugging for a few minutes and asking her how her weekend went, telling her a little about your weekend, asking how she was feeling, whatever, just reconnecting with her, and then the two of you would have gone to sleep and she'd be fine with you— not pissed, but pleased. In football, if you call the wrong play, you don't gain any yards. You called the wrong play Monday night. This was an easy play: Just always remember that Marti likes to reconnect with you after she's been away from you. Women are weird like that: They're into connection."

So don't try that one anymore. It's a big lie. It's not only possible to please your wife, it's not all that hard. Just learn the plays and keep trying to make them. Like one client said recently: "I feel like I'm fooling myself when I say I have to be perfect to please her, to give her what she needs. I don't. I just have to be *trying*."

Your wife is not an angry bitch who demands perfection and is impossible to please; she's just a woman who wants you to keep trying to change into a man who knows how to connect with her, how to have a relationship with her, how to love her. So keep trying to change into that man and keep changing, and keep getting better in all the ways she wants you to get better, and I guarantee you, when you do, when you finally cross that goal line and become the good and loving husband she wants, she'll be waiting there smiling with open arms, totally pleased with you, and you can spike the ball!

• **The fifth big lie is,** *"I can't change. I've always been like this. This is me. This is just who I am."*

First of all, if that's true, God help us.

Second of all, only God gets to say that: "I AM THAT I AM." Or maybe Popeye: "I yam what I yam." Not you!

Third of all, it's not true. That's not the way it works.

All that stuff you think is you isn't really you. It's who you believe you are, who you've been told you are, who you would swear
on a stack of Bibles you are, but it's not who you are.

I hate to be the one to have to tell you this, but most of the
stuff you think is you is stuff that's been conditioned into you by
your family or society or religion or gender. Most of the ideas that
you hold so sacred aren't your ideas at all, but somebody else's
ideas that've wormed their way into your noggin and now swarm
around in there like so many fruit flies. Those things that you do,
those ways that you have, that impregnable fortress of delusion
and denial that you somewhat euphemistically call your personality, that's not you!

Are you kidding?

Your short temper, your adolescent sexuality, your compul-
siveness, your bossiness, your moodiness—all that stuff that
makes you so difficult to deal with and impossible to live with—
are not *you*. Not the *real* you. They *cover* the real you.

The real you is love and kindness and service and devotion
and sensitivity to her. The real you is a treasure. Buried treasure.
Buried under all the other stuff you've always thought was you.
All you've got to do now is dig through that stuff and get to the
real you.

This is not a difficult concept.

It's called separating the good from the bad in you, and it sep-
arates the men from the boys. (See Chapter 42, "Look at You!")

Confucius says, "In the archer there is a resemblance to the
mature man. When he misses the bull's-eye, he turns and seeks
the reason for his failure in himself."

Come on. Don't tell yourself lies anymore. Be a mature man
and knuckle down and get to work on changing yourself.

THE MOVE

Every time one of the five big lies comes up in your mind, absolutely refuse to believe it.

- "I don't need to change."

- "She's the one who needs to change."

- "I'll change when she changes."

- "I'll never be able to change enough to please her."

- "I can't change. This is just who I am."

Bullshit.
Bullshit.
Bullshit.
Bullshit.
Bullshit.

Now tell yourself the truth: "*I* need to change, and I *can* change, and I *will* change."

Now choose one piece of your behavior that your wife has been complaining about forever—like the fact that you never put your dishes in the dishwasher, or you play the TV too loud, or you flirt with other women, or you drive too fast—and change it.

Just change it.

The first thing you'll notice is that she stops complaining about it. The second thing you'll notice is that she seems happier with you. The third thing you'll notice is that she's nicer to you. By changing yourself, by always changing yourself, you change the way she talks to you, thinks of you, and relates to you.

This will happen, and it's within your power to make it happen, if you stop lying to yourself.

CHAPTER 10

Is Your Wife a Nag?

Women have had the power of naming stolen from us.

Mary Daly

Nagging is the repetition of unpalatable truths.

Baroness Edith Summerskill

Is your wife a nag? No. That's another big lie you tell yourself. Like my client Kevin, who told himself that lie throughout his marriage and told it to me pretty much every session.

"She's such a nag," he would say, "always hammering me, hammering me, hammering me."

"That's what you have to do to get a nail into a block of hardwood, Kevin," I said. "You hammer it and hammer it and hammer it. That's what it's like for her to try to get a new idea into your head."

A good husband doesn't think of his wife as a nag, doesn't call her one, and doesn't create the conditions in his marriage where she has to become one.

What, after all, is a nag but a misogynistic term for a woman who wants something from a man who's so disdainful and dismissive of her that he simply doesn't listen to her, so she's forced—*forced!*—to repeat herself a trillion times to try to get through to him?

And we men call that nagging!

What gall!

Yeah, maybe we can shut her up by making up a bad name for what she's reasonably and rightfully asking for from us, and then calling her that.

Nag! . . . Shrew! . . . Battle-ax! . . . Harpy! . . . Witch! . . . Bitch! . . . Ballbuster!

"You're always on my case!" we yell. *"Get off my case!"*

Hey! The only reason she's on our case is because we're such a goddamn case!

An adult woman who wants something from a man, usually a change in his consciousness, conduct, or character, and says it, and repeats it, is not a nag. She's an adult woman who wants something from a man and has the self-respect and the strength and the courage to say it—and the tenacity to repeat it—until he friggin' gets it.

A good husband gets it, and gets it fast, so his wife doesn't have to repeat it.

And if he doesn't get it fast and she does have to repeat it, he doesn't call her a nag, he calls her a strong, tenacious woman, and himself a nitwit.

THE MOVE

Expunge the word "nag" from your vocabulary.

Never call her that again—to her face, or behind her back, or in your mind.

Sometime in the next few days, go to her and ask her if there's anything she's been wanting you to do, change, or look at in yourself, for a long time, that you still haven't done or changed or looked at:

- "I want you to stop making insulting little jokes about me when we're with our friends."

- "I want you to clean up after yourself in the kitchen."

- "I want you to stop getting that predatory look in your eye when you see an attractive woman."

- "I want you to fix the faucet in the downstairs bathroom that's been leaking for the past six months."

- "I want you to call when you're going to be more than twenty minutes late from work."

- "I want you to appreciate me more."

When she tells you, do it, change it.

And I promise you—you'll never hear about it again.

A WORD TO THE WIVES

Expunge the word "nag" from your vocabulary too. Never call yourself that again—with your husband, with anybody else, or in your mind.

While you're at it, you can also lose "bitch" and "ball-buster" and all the other bad names women are called in our society. All of them are misogynistic, and none of them are true.

What's true is that you're a woman who's dissatisfied with the way things are in your marriage, and you have a right to be, and you want things to change, and you're saying so.

That doesn't make you a nag; it makes you a woman of power, a force to be reckoned with.

By taking back the power of naming yourself, you are taking back the power.

CHAPTER 11

Talk to Her

I would rather get into a serious fistfight with any guy on the street than have an intimate conversation with a woman.

A former client

A woman wants you to like her and talk to her.

D. H. Lawrence

Don't kid yourself. This husband-and-wife thing is a talk thing. There's no way out of that one.

Because women *like* to talk. I think it's actually *fun* for them. A nice way to spend time. And they're *good* at it.

You're married to her, so you've got to talk to her. You've got to talk to her when she talks to you—that's called *being responsive*—and you've even got to talk to her *before* she talks to you. That's called *initiating a conversation*.

By conversation I don't mean you say, "Did you call my

mother?" and she says, "Yes," and then you say, "Thanks," and pop off to Home Depot.

And I don't mean you say, "Let's go upstairs and have sex," and she says, "Not now," and you say, "Why not?" and she says, "Because you never talk to me."

And I don't mean you launching into one of your endless monologues about the difficulties of your work or the state of the world or the kids' misbehavior while she pretends to listen, using most of the small muscles in her forehead trying to keep her eyes from rolling.

That's not the talking I'm talking about.

The talking I'm talking about is you spending time with your wife for the purpose of exchanging friendly words with her.

Just that.

It's like playing catch with her—not with a baseball or football, but with words. It can be in the car, on a walk, on the phone, across the kitchen table, in the living room on the couch, or in the bedroom in the dark, the two of you lying next to each other, feet entangled, holding hands, drifting off to sleep.

Women really like that sort of thing.

The talking I'm talking about is the two of you talking for the sake of talking, talking for the sake of connecting and relating and growing closer to each other. The talking I'm talking about is pleasant and relaxed and often meanders from subject to subject. There's the news to talk about, the neighbors, the kids, the eternal verities of the universe, and retiling the kitchen floor. The talking I'm talking about is a long, interesting conversation conducted over the course of a lifetime between two people who really like each other and who like talking with each other.

Nietzsche knew this one: "When marrying, ask yourself the question: Do you believe that you will be able to converse with this person into your old age? Everything else in marriage is transitory."

Converse. Conversation. The talking I'm talking about is a conversation. Etymologically, the word "conversation" means "a turning with," the thoughts and feelings of one person being turned over in words to the other person, who then re-turns her thoughts and feelings in words, and so on back and forth, back and forth, each one taking their turn.

It's exactly like playing catch.

Women are world-class experts at this.

Recently at a beach club I saw two women turned toward each other on chaise lounges talk like this for two hours straight, without so much as a pause. I couldn't hear their words, but each woman seemed totally interested in what the other was saying, and they looked like they were having a grand time. I was amazed and impressed. Two men couldn't have done it for two minutes.

In a therapy session last week a woman trying to explain to her husband what it was like talking with her woman friends said with a delighted laugh, "The more we talk, the more there is to talk about!" while the husband looked at her trying to blink himself into some comprehension of that statement.

Women can *talk*, man, and we men who are married to women must learn to talk.

And don't get me wrong here. I'm not a talker by nature. When it comes to talking, I'd rather not, so when I talk about not talking, I know what I'm talking about.

(And for God's sake, don't ask me how I came to be a therapist, which is *all* talk. I don't want to talk about it.)

The thing you've got to understand is that for your wife all forms of marital connection (including the sexual connection) are dependent on the talking connection. That's the way women are, and it's not going to change. The connection thing, the sexual thing, the husband-and-wife thing, the married-for-life thing—it's all a talk thing for them.

If I'm lyin', I'm dyin'. You've got to talk to her.

THE MOVE

So talk to her.

When you find yourself in the same room with her, or in the car, or anywhere, try saying something. Anything. Words. That come out your mouth. About anything at all. About nothing. It doesn't matter. Just start a conversation.

If it feels awkward, it feels awkward. So what? When you first learned to ride a bicycle, it felt very awkward, and you zigzagged all over the place, but you kept at it until you got the hang of it.

So right now talk to her. If words start coming out your mouth that are completely inane, don't worry about it. Just talk. Keep the conversation going, no matter what.

Think of it as playing catch with her. You throw her some of your words, which she catches, then she throws you back some of her words, which you catch, and you throw back more of your words.

And so on. Like that. About any subject under the sun.

It's a conversation. A turning with her. A game of catch. Get into it.

CHAPTER 12

How to Talk with Her

> *You have the power to make me feel appreciated,*
> *valued, loved, seen—all you have to do is speak*
> *the words. It's all how you talk to me.*
>
> A client to her husband

Now that you know you *have* to talk with her, here are fifteen suggestions about how to talk with her.

• **Listen.** When you're talking with your wife, listen when *she's* talking. Everybody loves being listened to, but especially women by men, since it's such a rare occurrence in their lives. So listen a lot and give her your undivided and undistracted attention. You can start by turning off the TV and actually turn your body, face, and eyes to her. This'll be hard, since it makes us men feel we've gotten ourselves into something—i.e., an actual conversation—that we'll never get out of, but do it anyway. Turning to her says, "I'm here, I'm really here." This will be so shocking to her that it may render her momentarily speechless, but she'll recover in a jiffy, her speech will start to flow, and chances are you will actually find yourself in a conversation.

- **Nod.** Nod a lot when she's talking. Nodding is a powerful signal that says, "I'm with you . . . I understand . . . I get it . . . Keep talking . . ." When you don't get it, crane your head forward like you're trying to get it, and nod tentatively.

- **Go "mm-hmm."** Make that little "mm-hmm" sound in your throat from time to time when she's talking. It's pretty effortless—you don't even have to move your lips—but it lets her know you're following along, you're really with her.

- **Be *with* her.** Remember: What your wife mainly wants from you is for you to be *with* her. With women it's always the "withness" that counts. So when you're talking with her, do everything you can think of to communicate to her that you're *with* her.

- **Ask questions.** Questions are forms of talking that lead directly to listening. Ask real questions, honest questions, questions that show interest in her, questions that want to know her better—the experiences she's having in life, her thoughts and feelings—questions with real question marks at the end of them. Toward the end of the 1995 movie *Don Juan DeMarco*, the psychologist Marlon Brando, having learned from his patient Don Juan DeMarco how to be a great lover, starts to ask his wife, Faye Dunaway, about her life. "I want to know what your hopes and dreams are," he says. "They got lost along the way when I was thinking about myself." Faye Dunaway immediately bursts out crying and laughing at the same time and says, "I thought you'd never ask!"

• **Make her feel good.** When you're talking with your wife, say a lot of things to her that make her feel good. Especially if she's feeling bad about herself, but even if she's not. If at any given moment you're at a loss how to make her feel good with your words, think of something to appreciate, admire, or thank her for—and appreciate, admire, or thank her. Tell her you love her a lot. Say to your wife that she's the greatest thing since sliced bread (which she is) and the best thing that ever happened to you (which she definitely is). See Chapter 34, "Getting All As," for more on this way of talking to her.

• **Don't go on and on.** Some men go on and on. Don't lecture her. Don't harangue her. Don't go off on one of your famous rants. It's boring. At best when you're going on and on, she feels like running out of the room screaming, at worst like killing herself. Or you. So have a heart: Talk to her, yes, but every once in a while *stop* talking to her and let her talk to you.

• **Defer.** When you and your wife are talking, if one of those moments occurs when the two of you start to speak at the same time, you back off, let *her* speak, you listen. What you were about to say is nowhere near as important as the respect you show her by deferring to her and letting her speak.

• **Watch your tones.** I have a theory that after the first six or so months of marriage, couples don't really hear each other's words anymore, they're just hearing *tones of voice*, so be careful with your tones. Basically there are two tones of voice: nice and not nice. Nice is gentle, patient, sweet, respectful, agreeable, quiet, loving, humble. Not nice is sharp, impatient, annoyed, argumentative, belligerent, condescending, sarcastic, mocking, mean. Talk to your wife in nice tones, tones that keep the kids and the dog in the room.

- **Listen to her feelings.** When your wife is sharing a feeling with you—if she's upset, depressed, anxious about something, mad about something, hating the carpeting, hating herself, feeling sad, feeling ornery, feeling *anything* and talking to you about it, do not—I repeat, *do not*—try to argue her out of her feeling, reason her out of it, joke her out of it, try to solve it, minimize it, or do anything to it except listen to it, nod, and basically say different variations of, "I'm really glad you're telling me how you feel, honey." This'll probably be difficult for you, since it's nowhere near true, but it's doable with discipline, and truer than you think, so just sit there, look kind, and listen to your wife's feelings.

In order to do this, you'll have to remember that there is a huge aversion to feelings inside us men—they're slithery, messy, insistent little things that threaten our male sense of control—so when your wife starts to share any of her feelings with you, there'll be a huge impulse in you to dismiss them almost as fast as they're coming out her mouth. She'll say, "I'm so sad that my friend Charlotte has to deal with her mother having Alzheimer's" and you, thinking you're just trying to be helpful (which you are) but also hoping to save yourself from the agony of listening to someone having feelings, say something like, "Why be sad? Parents get Alzheimer's, and their children have to deal with it. It goes with the territory. And besides, she's in the best facility in the state," fully expecting that your wife's sadness will instantly dissolve in the face of this supernal wisdom and she'll return to her normal state of serviceable cheerfulness that you know and love.

Nope. Don't go there. Just say, "Oh yeah, that's sad," and look at her sympathetically while she tells you more.

- **Share *your* feelings.** Go for broke and talk about *your* feelings too. When I say "your feelings," I don't mean your angry feelings or your critical feelings or your horny feelings—she's heard plenty about *those* feelings for the last few thousand years, thank you very much—but tell her about your *sad* feelings and your *scared* feelings and your *insecure* feelings and your *hurt* feelings. Tell her your boss not only didn't appreciate all the work you did on that project that's been consuming you for two months, he called you into his office today and said it was second-rate, and you felt hurt and discouraged. When it comes to your feelings, think *vulnerable*. Women *like* vulnerable (think *vulva*) and feel soft and safe and in love with you—and sexually attracted to you (think *vulva!*)—when you're being vulnerable. Trust me on this one. There's an episode of *Everybody Loves Raymond* where Debra and Ray are sitting up in bed talking about Ray's childhood, and Ray says something poignant. Debra, touched, melts, her eyes shine with love of him, and she leans over and gives him a deep sexy kiss. When she pulls back to look at his face, Ray is sitting there stunned.

"What the hell was that?" he says.

Debra smiles. "I just can't believe how adorable you are," she says. "I never knew you had all these *feelings*."

Ray sits there still dumbfounded for a moment, but then he gets it—*somehow there's a connection between him sharing his feelings and Debra's sexy kiss*—and a sly smile plays on his face.

"Don't tell anybody," he says, "but yes, I'm *full* of feelings!"

- **Speak as her equal.** Do not speak from on high to her, holding forth the way you do in pronouncements, denouncements, demands, commands, and judgments. Speak like the two of you are totally equal to each other, totally on the same level, which you are. Do not say, "The Johnsons are two of the most insufferably boring people I have ever met, and we're not going on any weekend trips with them ever again." That's on high. Cut it out. Say instead, "I almost shot myself that day we had to spend five hours with the Johnsons. Do you find them as unbearable as I do?" That's on the level.

• **Watch your face.** When you're talking with her, remember to take off your male facial mask of seriousness and sternness and try putting some expressions on your face. Make your face mobile and fluid, letting it travel along with what she's saying, looking interested, empathic, amused, supportive, as the moment requires. If you want to learn how to do this, watch two women talking. Their words and faces are bouncing off each other, back and forth, like reflections in mirrors, like a swing dance of expressions they're doing with each other, and the name of the dance is, "Yes, I get it, I'm with you." When in doubt as to what to do with your face, make it look gentle and sweet. Women like sweet, as in, "He's such a sweet guy" or "That was really sweet of you." Smiling is always good. Look at her softly. Women really like softly.

• **Don't argue!** And for heaven's sakes, stop arguing with her. It's a thing we guys do—a power thing, a competitive, combative thing, a really, really stupid thing. Women hate it. For them, talking is about connecting. Arguing is about *disconnect-ing*, trying to prove your own dopey point at the expense of somebody else's point. She hates it when you do that and gets tired and depressed. Arguing—also called debating—is a disease of egocentricity, carried and transmitted mainly by men. Give it up as a way of talking to her. If you can't help yourself and you find yourself arguing with your wife, stop on a dime, come to your senses, wake up, and return to real talking. Real talking is not argumentative, but collaborative, cooperative, and connective, even when there's difference and disagreement between you.

For example, if she says, "The best time for me to make love is in the morning, when I have energy, not at night when I'm exhausted," do not say, "That doesn't work for me at all. There's no time in the morning, and you're just trying to avoid it anyway." Argumentative. Instead, say, "That makes sense. I like it in the morning too. Sometimes I like it at night, though—it helps me relax and get to sleep. Any possibility of working that in once in a while?" Collaborative and connective.

- **Keep the conversation going.** Women like conversations that keep going. The trick to keeping a conversation going is to look for a link, a thing she just said that you can hook onto to say the thing you're going to say to keep the conversation going. The way to do this is to pay close attention to what your wife is saying, and then say or ask something that connects with some piece of it. For example, if she says, "I spoke to my friend Judy today, who told me they may be moving to Minneapolis because Ron's been offered a position there," you could link with "my friend Judy" by saying, "I didn't realize the two of you still spoke regularly on the phone. How's your friendship going with her?" You could link with "Ron" by saying, "I've always liked that guy. Do you remember when he helped our daughter with that science project?" You could link with your wife emotionally by asking, "If they do move, will that be a big loss to you? Will that make you sad? What *will* you feel?" Or you could link with the information she's just offered by asking for more: "Minneapolis? That's a long way away. Do you know what kind of job he's been offered?" Or you could get philosophical and say, "It's amazing to me how you actually enjoy talking on the phone with people. What *is* that?" Or you could throw her a little curveball and surprise her by linking with her need—and every human being's need—to feel good about herself, by saying, "With all you have to do in a day, it's really great that you make time to speak with your friends. You're a good friend to people." All of these responses (and there are dozens more) are better than what you probably usually do—not replying at all, or changing the subject. All of them function as links to keep the conversation going—which is your goal here. Once you get the hang of this, you will be able to keep a conversation going for a decent amount of time and, theoretically, forever.

Isn't *that* good news?

In Hinduism, the goddess of speech is named Vak. That's where our English words "voice" and "vocal" come from. In the Vedas Vak is described as "bountiful with good energy."

How does a good husband talk to his wife?

Frequently. Bountifully.

With good energy.

THE MOVE

Reread this chapter a few times until its major points are pretty much committed to memory and usable.

Then go to your wife and say, "I'd like to talk with you."

If she says, "About what?" say, "Nothing in particular. Just to talk."

She'll look anywhere from pleasantly surprised to totally flabbergasted. Take this as encouragement to go on.

Now go on. Take a deep breath and begin talking with her.

Use all these techniques, and any others you can think of, to keep the conversation going as long as you can.

Minimum, ten minutes. Ideally a half hour.

When the conversation is over, before you leave, say, "I like talking with you," and give her a kiss.

CHAPTER 13

Listen to Her

*What would happen if one woman told the
truth about her life?
The world would split open.*

Muriel Rukeyser

*I tried everything. Except really listening.
Really listening. And that's how I left her alone.*

Andy Garcia, playing Michael Green
in the movie *When a Man Loves a Woman*

The way I figure it, for the last ten thousand years, most of the talking that people have paid attention to on this earth has been done by men. *Our* thoughts and ideas and philosophies, *our* wants and needs, *our* perspective on things, *our* experience of life. It's a man's world, and in that world it's been men's voices that have been mostly heard, and women's voices have been mostly silent.

A poem of the Ute Indians reads:

> *I am the woman who holds up the sky.*
> *The rainbow runs through my eyes.*
> *The sun makes a path to my womb.*
> *My thoughts are in the shape of clouds.*
> *But my words are yet to come.*

The way I see it, the women's words are coming now. *Their* thoughts and ideas and philosophies, *their* wants and needs, *their* perspective on things, *their* experience of life. Their feelings. Their story. Their *way*. It's all coming, in words, from women's mouths, from my own wife's mouth, and I'm trying to listen to it.

A good husband listens when his wife talks to him.

He manfully resists all the negative impulses that arise when she does—like turn on the TV, start thinking about other things that have nothing to do with what she's talking about, fall asleep, run the car into a bridge abutment, or stop her in her tracks by saying something like, "Do we have to talk about this *now?*"

He also watches all the negative words he uses to describe her talking, like "chatting," "gabbing," "babbling," "yakking," "gossiping," and "woman talk," all of which are misogynistic and demeaning, and completely miss the point.

The point is that women are great talkers, interesting talkers, and like to talk, and love to talk to *us*, their husbands.

The other point is that we men have been deeply conditioned to dismiss their talking—and them—pretty much the moment they start. Let's face it, guys: We barely listen to them. That's no big news to anybody, but it's good to finally come out with it: Inside us, when they're talking to us, we're barely listening.

If they're talking to us because they want something from us, we dismiss them as "nags." If they're talking to us because they're angry at us, we dismiss them as "bitches." If they're talking to us because we've hurt them, we dismiss them as "too emotional" and "oversensitive." If they're talking to us because they're sad and lonely, we dismiss them as "needy" or "clingy." And if they're talking to us about their opinions or suggestions or firmly held beliefs, we dismiss them as "pushy" and their thoughts as trivial.

Go ahead. Admit it. The moment we hear it's a *woman's* voice, that *high* sound, our attention drops like a shot.

I've seen this again and again in my therapy practice, the man not listening to the woman. I saw it last night with Paula and Leigh, a new couple in their first month of therapy.

Leigh was explaining to me his experience of a fight they had over the weekend. Paula sat very still, looking at Leigh, listening. When he was done, I asked Paula to tell me her side of the story. As she drew in her first breath to begin talking, Leigh, who had been leaning forward while he talked, leaned back in his chair, crossed his legs, and placed his arm in his lap in such a way that if he looked down he could see his watch—which he did, frequently, as Paula told her story. His eyes did not look at her once. The few times he looked up, he looked at me, as if to say, "Will this be over soon?"

"Paula," I interrupted, "how's your peripheral vision?"

"Why do you ask?"

"While you're talking to me, can you see that Leigh isn't listening to you, that his attention isn't on you at all, that he's basically waiting for it to be over?"

A wave of anger crossed Leigh's face.

"I wasn't noticing it now, but that's the way he is all the time at home, so I guess I'm just used to it. I don't even expect him to listen to me anymore. He's got a touch of ADD, and—"

"He may have a touch of ADD," I said, "but that's not what this is. This is NLW—Not Listening to Wife when she's talking—and it's epidemic among men, and Leigh has a particularly virulent strain of it."

I turned to Leigh.

"Leigh, do four things. While Paula continues telling her side of the story, take your arm off your lap so you can't see your watch, uncross your legs, sit up straight and alert and lean slightly forward toward Paula, and be looking right at her face as she talks so that if she glances over at you or sees you peripherally, she's going to see her husband who's listening to her."

Here I have to make a confession.

There was a time—a long, long time ago, in a galaxy far away—that the instant my wife started to talk to me—about anything—I immediately started to contract inside—actually dissociate—and I had to make an actual effort to come back, stay present, focus on what she was saying, and listen to her. It didn't happen because I didn't love her or because I wanted to insult or ignore her, it just happened, and so fast and automatically it amazed me.

So I trained myself to listen. *Really* listen. As if the thing she was saying to me in that moment was the most significant event happening in the universe at that moment. It's interesting to listen to your wife like that—as if the thing she's saying in the moment is tremendously important.

I think, for a husband, it is.

Because his wife is saying it.

And—surprise, surprise—I'm actually learning to like listening when my wife talks to me. For one, I get to hear how the other half of the human race experiences life. It's really different from us, and it's really interesting.

Another reason I like listening to her is that it's helpful. To be honest, like most men, half the time in my life I have no idea what the hell I'm doing, and my wife is a very wise woman who can advise and guide me, and explain things to me that I can't figure out on my own, and correct me when I'm off course, which is a lot. She's amazing that way.

Just like *your* wife.

I also like listening to my wife because it's pretty easy. All I basically have to do is shut up, pay attention, ask interested questions, and enjoy the connection with her as she talks. And I do enjoy it. Whether she's sharing her wisdom with me, or a feeling, or a memory, or a dream she had last night, or telling a story from her day, or setting me straight on the latest lamebrain thing I did in our marriage, or just talking to be talking with me, it feels like love.

When you learn to listen—*really* listen—to your wife, it feels like love to her, so she's falling ever more deeply in love with you. There are rewards when a woman falls in love like that with a man. Here are three:

- The thing you call nagging or bitching completely stops because now she doesn't have to repeat herself because now she trusts that you're really listening to her.
- You find yourself feeling better and more lighthearted about life because now you're connecting with someone who loves you and you're not so sad and solitary anymore.
- Since listening to your wife makes her feel closer to you, she'll want to actually *get* closer to you, including physically closer.

One last thing about listening, guys.

Here's the Chinese character, *ting*, for the verb "to listen":

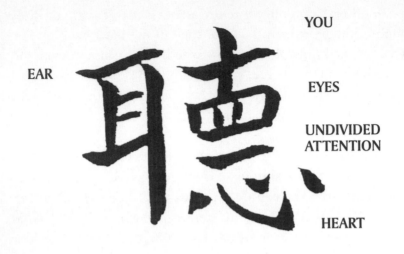

Look at this carefully. Study it. It's everything you need to know about listening to your wife.

THE MOVE

When my daughter, Greta, was in elementary school, it was my job to pick her up at school in the afternoon and bring her back home. We lived in rural Massachusetts then, and the ride back took about twenty-five minutes. I'd be in the driver's seat, Greta would be in the passenger's seat, and I'd ask her to tell me everything that had happened in her day—from the moment she left the house in the morning to the moment I picked her up—that she wanted to tell me about. She'd begin with Douglas Shea pulled her hair *again*! and continue on from there, while I listened and asked pertinent, interested questions along the way. When we got home, she'd grab her backpack and run up the stairs into the house and make herself a sandwich, then go into the living room and watch *Little House on the Prairie* and then go into her bedroom and call Douglas Shea.

You can do that with your children, and you can do it with your wife. Pick your spot this week, ask your wife a question that shows that kind of interest in her life—"When you walk from the train to your office in the morning, what are some of the things you usually see along the way? I'm just curious"— and then when she answers and tells you about her life, listen up.

CHAPTER 14

Be Prepared to Process

We had a silly quarrel over nothin'
Both got mad and it soon turned into somethin'
But we made up like we always do
Because you love me and I love you
We're supposed to do that now and then

George Strait

I have some bad news and some good news for you.

The bad news is, if you want to be a good husband in a good marriage, you're going to have to "process" the relationship. In other words, you're going to have to sit down with your wife and talk about the relationship from time to time. About the *state* of the relationship. And how you loused it up last week. And that knucklehead thing you said a minute ago in the kitchen. And the completely outrageous way you've been for twenty years in this marriage that's got her spittin' mad.

That sort of thing.

Did I say "from time to time"?

I meant many, many, many times.

That's the bad news—you've got to be willing to *process* the relationship with her.

An additional piece of bad news is that women actually seem to like this, and as far as I can tell, could be doing it all the time.

The good news is that if you're willing to process the relationship on a semiregular basis, you can keep the relationship in a pretty good state, which means you don't have to process it so much.

Yesss!

Here's how it works:

You're going along in the relationship, getting along pretty well with each other, and then something happens. Something *you* said or did, something *she* said or did, something you *both* said or did—action, reaction, etc., etc.—that got so tangled up in itself that the two of you ended up in a fight. Now you're both in a funk. One or both of you has hurt feelings . . . feels offended . . . mistreated . . . misunderstood . . . distrustful of the other, withdrawn and distant.

Happens all the time. Even in great marriages. It's the nature of marriage. The more work you do on yourself and the marriage, the less frequently it happens, but it still happens.

Connection . . . and then disconnection.

Marital disconnection feels like crap to both of you and darkens every other aspect of your life—work, leisure, the way you relate to your kids, the atmosphere in the house—so you've got to deal with it.

Here's how:

Connection . . . disconnection . . . and then *reconnection*!

That's the way to go.

Women know how to go there—back to connection.

That's when they say, *"We need to talk."*

No man alive likes to hear those words.

"We need to talk. We need to process what just happened."

Really?

"Really."

Shit.

Because for women, the whole thing is about connection, and when there's been an incident of disconnection between you, women aren't like us, they can't pretend it didn't happen, they can't go blithely on and be all sugar and spice and have sizzling sex with us later that night.

They're weird like that.

They need to process it. They need to talk it over.

What happened? At what point did the disconnection happen, did the train start to jump the track? Who said what when? Who blew it? (Chances are it was you, so get ready.) *Let's talk about it. Let's sit down for five minutes* (forget it), *ten minutes* (never happen), *twenty minutes* (don't count on it), *and talk it through.*

Like Jan and Francesco were trying to talk through something that happened while they were driving over to therapy.

"When I said I wanted you not to try to beat that yellow light," Jan said, "and you said, 'We're gonna be late!' and went right through it, I didn't like that. I felt my words meant nothing to you in that moment, that you just took over, as usual, and what I wanted didn't matter because you wanted what you wanted and did what you wanted."

"You know I hate being late," Francesco said.

"And I hate being in danger in the car," Jan said.

"There was no danger," Francesco said.

"*I* felt in danger, Francesco. I want you to hear me on that one: *I* felt in danger. I often feel in danger when you drive. We're in therapy now, and it's time you started to hear me when I talk to you. What you did in the car coming over here was an example of something you do a lot in our marriage, and I don't like it."

Francesco was about to protest, but I stopped him.

"Francesco," I said, "a word of advice. Try to *get* what she's saying to you about this. Clearly that was a moment when Jan wanted one thing and you wanted another thing, and the thing that Jan wanted *lost* to the thing you wanted—you ran the yellow light—and that's no longer acceptable to Jan. Just cop to the fact that that's what that was, and that's something you do—acknowledge it, then maybe apologize for it, and then the whole incident will be processed, grist for the mill of your marriage getting better, and we can move on."

He thought for a moment, head down, his hand smoothing a crease in his pant leg. Then, raising his head to look at Jan, he said, "I do get it, Jan. I do do that. Even when I do it for what I think is a good reason, I still do it. I should have stopped. Though I still think we weren't in danger."

"*I* felt in danger, Francesco," Jan said again. "That's what I want you to hear. Me. Your wife. The one sitting in the passenger seat. I felt in danger."

"I hear you," he said.

"What do you hear?" Jan said.

"I hear you telling me you were scared, and I hear you telling me I don't hear you."

"Thank you."

If you're trying to be a good husband trying to have a good marriage, be prepared to process with your wife. If you're like me, you won't like it, and you'll never look forward to it, but be prepared to do it. It's the gyroscopic thing that you have to keep doing to keep the relationship upright and on course.

Don't worry if you're not good at it: Your wife will teach you how to do it.

Three last points:

1. The fewer knucklehead things you do and say in the relationship, the less you'll need to process.
2. If there have been many disconnections for a very long time in your marriage and none of them have ever really been processed—primarily because *you* haven't been willing to—don't think for a second that bygones will be bygones. Those kinds of bygones do not bygone well with women, so be prepared to process them.
3. In many marriages—perhaps yours—the conflict and the estrangement have been so chronic and long and the communication so bad that hardly anything has been processed, so you might need some help. Which is why your wife has been asking you for years to do some therapy with her—to learn how to talk to each other so you can process stuff.

With regards to therapy or no therapy, here's the rule of thumb: *If your wife thinks you need therapy, you need therapy, so go.* If it's good therapy, stay, and stay till you're done. That might take a little longer than you want—which is the bad news—but don't worry about it. If you do the therapy right and stay to the end—till the past is processed and the two of you have learned how to communicate with each other so you can process for all the future—*you won't ever have to do therapy again.*

THE MOVE

The next time there's a disconnection between you and your wife, you be the one to say, "We need to talk about this."

There's a 79 percent chance your wife will pass out at that point, so have some smelling salts ready.

When she recovers, sit down with her and process the disconnection.

What happened? When did the train leave the track? What was going on inside for each of you? What went wrong?

You say what you have to say, and listen to what she has to say.

Stay there awhile and do the processing. Figure it out. Figure it out to the point where both of you understand it so well that it doesn't have to happen again. It probably will happen again—these things tend to repeat themselves in marriages—but figure it out anyway, because each time you process something, there's a little less of it for the next time.

If there's anything you need to apologize for, apologize, and say you just don't understand how you can keep being *such* a knucklehead.

Break out the smelling salts again.

A WORD TO THE WIVES

Never underestimate a man's dislike of processing the relationship.

Our aversion to talking about relational matters runs deep. We don't like the vulnerability of it, or the accountability, or the time involved, and we certainly don't look forward to being told again about something else we did that was bad.

So not too many men will make this Move on any regular basis, which means that most of the time you'll still be the one who comes to him, as Jane comes to me, and says, "We have to talk" or "We need to process what happened this morning on the phone."

Accept that.

And don't get hooked by our show of resistance to that—the rolling of our eyes, the smirk, the scowl, the sigh of grudging capitulation, the little burst of anger: "Not again! I don't have *time,* Laura! What'd I do *now*?!"

Even in the face of all this, press forward, insist, persist, and don't let our resistance harden into refusal. Just get us to sit down on the couch with you, or while standing in the kitchen, and start the discussion.

If we seem bored, we seem bored. If we're petulant, we're petulant. Don't worry about that. Just stay there, processing, and for now take our staying there as a victory.

CHAPTER 15

Get in Touch with Your Feelings

*You men should get in touch with your feelings and
learn how to talk about them with us. They're just
feelings, for heaven's sakes, and everybody's got them.
There must be workshops or courses or trainings or
something you guys can go to on feelings.*

A former client to her husband and me

Yeah, right. Where do we sign up?

THE MOVE

Admit it. The very last thing in the world you want to do
is to get in touch with your feelings or to talk about them
with your wife or anybody. You're a *man*—why the hell
would you want to do that?

So turn the page.

CHAPTER 16

Really *Get in Touch with Your Feelings*

There's no crying in baseball!
There's no crying in baseball! No crying!

Tom Hanks, playing Jimmy Dugan in
the movie A *League of Their Own*

Tell her about it
Tell her everything you feel . . .

Billy Joel

Sorry to have to tell you this, guys, but to be good husbands, we really do have to get in touch with our feelings.

What feelings are you talking about? I don't have any feelings.

Yes, you do.

I like this passage from Robert Bly's book *Iron John:*

In high school a girl might ask, "Do you love me?" I couldn't answer. If I asked her the same question, she might reply, "Well, I respect you, and I admire you, and I'm fond of you, and I'm even interested in you, but I don't love you." Apparently when she looked into her chest, she saw a spectrum of affections, a whole procession of feelings, and she could easily tell them all apart. If I looked down into my chest, I saw nothing at all. I had then either to remain silent or fake it. Some women feel hurt when a man will not "express his feelings," and they conclude that he is holding back, or "telling them something" by such withholding; but it's more likely that when such a man asks a question of his chest, he gets no answer at all.

It's not that we men don't have any feelings, we just don't *know* we have them.

We've got plenty of feelings, thank you—in fact, all the feelings a human being can have. Just like everyone else.

Really.

Just like everyone else, we've got all the so-called positive feelings like happiness, joy, enthusiasm, self-confidence, wonder, peace, tenderness, love, and faith. And just like everyone else, we've got all the so-called negative feelings, the ones that cause us inner pain, like disappointment, discouragement, sadness, grief, guilt, shame, inadequacy and insecurity, self-doubt, self-hatred, hurt, fear, anxiety, anger, rage, and despair.

They're all in there. Every single one of them. All the emotions.

Here's the way I think of emotions.

The "e" in the word "emotion" stands for energy—emotions are inner energies—and energy, by definition, always wants to *move*, have *motion*,—so an "e-motion" is a piece of energy in us that wants to have motion, that wants to move.

Where does it want to move?

It wants to move *out* of us. It wants to come out. To be *expressed*.

What do other things that are in us want to do? Like, say, urine. It wants to come out of us—we have to take a leak, we go to the bathroom, and then we feel better.

Same with feelings. They're designed to come out, and they want to come out, and when we let them out, we feel better.

Only one problem, though.

We men have been taught from day one not to let feelings out. Especially the so-called negative ones, the ones that show our pain and our vulnerability.

Take crying, for instance.

For most of us men, our crying machinery is pretty well shot by the time we're twelve. Our society apotheosizes strength, performance, endurance, stoicism, and heroism in males, and anathematizes all feelings it deems contrary to those, especially fear, sadness, helplessness, and hurt. It especially prohibits any vulnerable expression of those feelings by men, in particular crying ("Big boys don't cry!"), and it enforces its prohibition against men crying by ridiculing and shaming males who do cry ("Crybaby! . . . Sissy! . . . Mama's boy! . . . Fag!"), and/or being violent toward them ("You're *crying*? What are you *crying* for? I'll give you something to cry about!").

There really is no crying in baseball. Or football. Or business. Or the military. Or *anywhere* men are.

On the playgrounds and hockey rinks I grew up on, there was no crying. When Marc Pomeroy went out for that pass and was backpedaling and tripped and tried to break his fall by flinging his arm out behind him, he lay there on his side screaming, "Ow! Ow! Ow!" while the rest of us boys stopped the game and stood over him.

"Get up, Marc! Walk it off! Just walk it off. You're not hurt, just walk it off!"

He did get up, and he did walk it off, but he couldn't stop crying for the next couple of plays, and then without saying a word he walked whimpering off the field and went home, and we learned later he had broken his arm in two places.

Watch any male professional athlete get hurt and you won't see tears. You'll see his face grimacing with pain, you might even see him writhing in pain on the ground, but you won't see tears, and you won't hear sounds. He's holding it all in . . . because there's no crying for men, and there's no whimpering or whining or griping or complaining or bellyaching either. There's no way for us to let those feelings out, no way to even say that they're in there.

Believe me, though, they're in there. Some of us guys are able to get in touch with feelings in movies, crying silent tears in the dark when Kevin Costner plays catch with his dad at the end of *Field of Dreams*, and many of us can cry at times of great personal tragedy, like a death in the family, but some of us can't even do that, and most of us are embarrassed by it.

So now many of us are walking around with sixteen tons of feelings inside us, some of them from so far back in our childhood we have no idea what to do with them, and no way to move them out, so we spend our lives living in the emotional effluvium rising off them, which we call anxiety and depression and a hot temper and another-one-of-Dad's-bad-moods.

No wonder we're spending long, vegetative hours sitting in front of television sets flipping channels. It beats feeling feelings.

The same conditioning didn't happen to women. They're allowed to have feelings and to feel them and to let them out. For them, there *is* crying in baseball, and everywhere else they go. One of my wife's favorite places is crowded restaurants.

Women are great at knowing, expressing, and feeling their feelings. For many women, it's like they're sitting at a piano playing the whole keyboard of their emotions like impresarios, striking every note in sight with masterly skill and baroque abandon, while we men are sitting there at our pianos looking bleak, mostly hitting clunkers, and basically waiting to get up and mow something.

Kind of a drag for the women. Lonely. Playing solos.

So I hate to be the one to have to tell you this, guys, but to be good husbands we *do* have to get in touch with our feelings, and feel some of them, and share some of them with our wives.

Here's a scene from a recent therapy session of a man, George, getting in touch with his feelings and sharing them with his wife, Kathleen:

They were arguing about a time last week when, arriving home from work, George walked into the kitchen and Kathleen did not greet him or seem at all glad to see him.

"I was very busy," Kathleen said. "The kids were—"

"You're *always* busy when I come home," George said. "You don't even acknowledge when I come in. You're rushing around the kitchen like a banshee—"

"I'm cooking dinner!" she yelled. "I'm getting dinner on the table for you and the kids! What do you want from me?!"

"Nothing! And that's what I get! Nothing!"

"George," I said, "how do you *feel* when you come home from work and Kathleen doesn't stop to greet you?"

"I feel that she's an anal personality who cares more about her clean counters than she does about me."

"Uh, George, that's not quite a feeling," I said.

"Whaddaya mean?"

"You're not talking about your feelings, you're talking about something Kathleen does, and you're blaming and accusing her of it."

He thought about that for a moment. Kathleen was watching him hopefully.

"The feelings we're trying to get to as men," I said, "are ones like hurt and sadness and fear—those kinds of feelings. So, George, when Kathleen didn't greet you when you came into the kitchen that night, what did you feel?"

"I felt bad." He paused. "Is that a feeling?"

"Almost," I said. "What kind of bad? Hurt? Sad? Lonely? Rejected? Insecure?"

"Rejected. I felt rejected."

"Do you often feel rejected by Kathleen?"

"Yes. A lot. Most of the time. Sexually, big-time."

"Turn to Kathleen and say that: 'I feel rejected by you.'"

"She knows that."

"Tell her anyway, right now, and use her name: 'I feel rejected by you, Kathleen.'"

"It'll sound phony."

"That's okay. Just say the words."

He turned toward her, and they looked at each other for a moment. "I feel rejected by you, Kathleen," he said.

"And how do you *feel*, George," I said, "how would a little boy feel, how do you think any human being would feel, when they feel rejected?"

He thought about that for a moment. "I don't know . . . hurt, I guess."

"Say that to Kathleen: 'I feel hurt when you don't seem happy to see me when I come home from work.'"

"Kathleen, I feel hurt when you're not happy to see me when I come home."

They sat there looking at each other. George looked tired. Kathleen's face was soft.

"It's good when you tell me you're hurt, George," she said. "I don't want to hurt you. I'm sorry."

Men, really try to get in touch with your feelings and tell your wife about them. *Tell her about it, tell her everything you feel.*

We men should do this not because we want to, not because anything in our training as men prepares us for it, and not because our society encourages or rewards us to do it, but because somewhere inside us we *do* want to know and experience everything that we are—human beings with feelings—and everything that our wives are—human beings with feelings—and we want to be able to talk to them about being a human being with feelings.

THE MOVE

Think of a time in your life when you felt disappointed, afraid, insecure, sad, lonesome, or embarrassed. If you have to go all the way back to boyhood to find a time like that, go ahead, go back to that boy and remember a time when he felt bad.

How about the time you were nine and pitching in a Little League game and they scored *eighteen* runs off you in the fourth inning and Mr. Conlon came to the mound and took you out and you couldn't help crying in front of everybody as you walked to the bench.

Or the time when your dog Corky ran away for three days and you lay in your bed those nights crying, unable to be comforted.

Try to name the feeling you felt then. Were you sad? Were you scared? As you sat on the bench with Mr. Conlon's arm around you, with everybody looking, unable to stop the tears running down your face, were you ashamed? Eighteen runs in one inning? Everybody was looking. Were you mortified? And as you lay alone in bed those nights, unable to sleep, convinced that Corky had been hit by a car and you'd never see him again, was that fear? Grief?

And now go find your wife where she is in the house and tell her that story. Tell her both stories. And how they made you feel.

Tell her about it, tell her everything you feel.

CHAPTER 17

Her Anger: Take the Hit

*I don't know if fury can compete with necessity
as the mother of invention, but I recommend it.*

Gloria Steinem

*Out of the ash
I rise with my red hair
And I eat men like air.*

Sylvia Plath

When his wife is angry at him, a good husband understands where her anger is coming from and is man enough to take the hit.

Her anger is coming from two places.

It's coming from about ten thousand years of women getting pushed around and mistreated by men, and all the women are *furious.*

The other place her anger is coming from is the fact that you have somehow recently managed to be a jackass yet once again in your marriage, and she's really pissed at you. She has a right to be. Given the way you just acted, her anger is the appropriate emotion.

In an article called "Revisioning Women's Anger: The Personal and the Global," the psychiatrist Jean Baker Miller has an interesting definition of anger: "Anger is an emotion which arises when something is wrong or something hurts and needs changing . . . [and] prompts us to act against wrong treatment or violation of us, against injustice. Anger notifies the people in the relationship that something is wrong and needs attention, and moves people to find a way to make something different come about."

That's pretty much all you need to know about your wife's anger at you.

In other words, your wife is not an "angry bitch," and her anger at you is (mostly) your fault—it's a notice she's delivering to you to stop doing what you're doing. To *change*. I don't know what it was you just did, but you did *something*, and you should figure it out and not do it or anything remotely like it ever again.

Then she won't be angry at you for that.

This is simple stuff.

In Hinduism there's a goddess named Kali. She's the warrior goddess—in fact, the fiercest warrior of all the deities—with blood dripping from the corners of her mouth, eyes fiery red, carrying a sword and noose, the Righteous One, Slayer of Demons.

When your wife is angry at you, her face right up in your face, see her face as the face of Kali fiercely determined to slay *your* demons.

It was Kali who in the form of my wife, Jane, in 1970 over-

turned a dining room table toward me for my vehemently arguing that it was okay for me to have lunch with an old girlfriend
who had gotten in touch with me, even though Jane was saying,
repeatedly and loudly, "It is completely *not* okay with me for you
to do that." (I'm not recommending throwing the dining room
table in the direction of her husband as a model of good marital
behavior for a woman, but given the lunkhead I was in those
days, what was a girl to do?) That was Kali in the form of Jane in
1970, and it's been Kali in the form of Jane who, for the last
thirty-five years, has been waging unremitting holy war against
whatever is still unholy and unhusbandly in me.

So when your wife's angry at you, take the hit, man.

In hockey, when you go into the corner to dig out a puck, you
go in knowing you're going to take a hit, that somebody's going
to take aim at you and take a run at you and check you into the
boards, *hard*. You can feel it coming before you hear it coming,
and you never do see it coming, but it comes, slamming into your
back and you into the boards, and you take the hit and sometimes land on your ass. And if you're honest with yourself, there's
something in you that actually *likes* taking the hit, is proud of it,
and welcomes it, especially when you're able to get up right away
and skate back into the game.

Same thing here.

You willingly take the hit of your wife's anger. Her irritation
with you. Her indignation. Her frustration. Her fury.

She's angry at you because you've been doing stuff—sometimes for years—that has *made* her angry at you, and she needs to
get angry at you, and you need to listen to her anger and change
according to what she's angry about.

Justine came into therapy one day seething. Her husband,

Andrew, took his seat, crossed his arms over his chest, and sat staring at the floor.

"What's going on?" I asked.

"You tell him, Justine," Andrew said. "Tell him you haven't talked to me in two days."

Justine was silent for a moment and then erupted. "I'm so fucking mad at him I could scream. He doesn't get it. He'll never get it. And if he thinks I'm ever going back there again, he's out of his mind."

"Where?" I asked.

"To his fucking mother's! I try to be nice to that woman, I really do, I've tried to be nice to her for eighteen years, but she's such a bitch to me, she treats me with complete disdain, like I'm not even part of the family, like I'm the whore of Babylon that somehow captured her precious son . . . and *he* . . . *he* . . . takes her side! Every time! There's a fucking war going on between his mother and me—over *him!*—and he takes *her* side! He's more married to her than to me! This is what I've been living with for eighteen years!"

She sat there with her eyes closed. There was a faint hum, like a ringing, in the sudden silence of the room.

"Andrew," I said, "is there any part of you that sees what Justine is talking about here? This issue of your mother's treatment of Justine and your relationship with your mother keeps coming up in the therapy, and it doesn't seem to be going away, and I want to know if there's any part of you that sees Justine's side of it."

"I do see it," he said. "I didn't when therapy began, I thought Justine was just crazy, but now I see it differently, I see what I'm supposed to do here, to choose my wife over my mother, but it's hard, it's *hard* to oppose my mother, and then Justine gets so *angry* at me, like *raging*, I don't know what the hell to do."

"Do two things," I said. "Actually, three things. First, understand that Justine's anger at you is what she's *supposed* to be feeling—because she's been wronged. Like if I came over there right now and punched you in the face, you'd get angry at me, and you *should* get angry at me—I did something wrong to you. Right?"

He nodded.

"Then the second thing is to say something like that to her. *Validate* her anger."

He looked at Justine. "I see how my mother treats you when we go over there, and I know I don't take your side the way I should, and I know you're pissed."

"Okay, Andrew, good," I said. "You understand the reason for Justine's anger at you, and you've validated it, so now see if you can let her *get* angry at you. For the next few minutes see if you can just listen to her without getting angry back at her, or getting defensive, or shutting down. Just sit there and take the hit and see it as a good thing, a healing thing that needs to happen on the road of the two of you clearing all this stuff up. Think you can do that?"

"I can do that," he said.

And he did. He sat there while she got angry at him for a few moments. She yelled at him. At one point she shouted at the top of her lungs, "I HATE YOUR MOTHER! AND I HATE WHAT SHE DID TO YOU!" At the end of it Andrew was fine, his head held high, looking at Justine, who was holding back tears.

Is your wife angry at you? Probably.

Should she be angry at you? Probably.

Can she *get* angry at you? Why not?

It's okay. You're a man. You can take it. You can take the hit.

Believe me, for what you just did a short time ago, for what you've been doing for a long time in this marriage, for what we men have done to women since the beginning of time, we deserve it.

So be a man and take it.

THE MOVE

The next time your wife gets angry at you, don't try to stop her, don't walk away from her, don't get angry back at her, don't get combative, and don't get defensive.

Just stay there listening to her until she's done—take the hit; you can take the hit—and then apologize to her for what she's angry at you for, and say you're going to do your level best not to do it again. And mean it.

While you're at it, tell her, for future reference, that you *want* her to express her anger at you—you can take it and you know you sometimes need it.

Tell her this even if you think it's not true.

It is true.

CHAPTER 18

Your Anger: Cut the Shit

*Basically, anger is a trick you play on yourself
and others, to get your own way.*

A sage

*There's a woman on my block
Sittin' there in a cold chill,
She say, "Who gonna take away
his license to kill?"*

Bob Dylan

Your anger is a completely different thing than her anger, so if you like double standards, here's a doozie:

Her anger at you is mostly okay; your anger at her mostly isn't.
Sorry.

And don't go getting angry at *me* now. It'll just slow us down, and I can explain.

The only situation I can think of where your anger at her is okay is when she's completely off the wall—as only *you* know *how* off the wall she can sometimes get—and she's either taking it out on the kids or she's accusing, blaming, and attacking you for something that you totally didn't do, and you need to stop her. Then, looking her in the face and making eye contact, you can raise your voice to a firm, emphatic volume, using your voice and your face and your eyes for the single purpose of letting her know that this attack isn't fair and it isn't right and it must stop.

There are three things you must remember about that use of your anger:

1. It must be controlled, something you're using temporarily for a discrete purpose, like a tool, and then when the purpose is accomplished, you put your anger down, like a tool.
2. There must be an underlying gentleness (see the next chapter), an intention to maintain connection with her, a respect for the connection with her, underneath your anger.
3. There can be no violence, nothing physical, no threat in your anger, no menace in your body or your voice, nothing intimidating.

You can say it like this: "Margaret, this isn't okay. I'm being blamed for something here that is not my fault. I did nothing bad, and your apparent compulsion to always *make* me bad is something I wish the hell you'd get over. You always tell me I need to grow up. Well, so do you. I love you, and I know you love me, but there is no need to speak to me like this, and I won't stay here and listen to it."

As for the rest of your anger at her, forget about it. All that impatience and annoyance and irritation and wrath—the stewing and the fuming and your explosions of temper—all that yelling and criticizing and blaming and bellowing that you do—all that sound and fury—cut it out.

Just cut it out!

Because it scares the hell out of her.

You see, we're bigger than women. We can hurt them. We *have* hurt them. Based on their history with us, a history that they all share deep down in their collective experience, they have no idea, when our anger starts to come at them, how *much* of our anger is going to come at them. With us a raised voice could easily turn into a raised hand, and a raised hand could clench into a fist, and a fist could be thrown at them and hit them, hit them bad and hurt them bad.

How do they know, when our anger starts, how much of it's coming? How do they know if it'll turn into violence?

They don't.

If you don't believe me, ask Nicole Brown Simpson. Or Laci Peterson. Go ahead. Ask them.

Women have already had plenty of experience of male anger and male violence with their fathers, brothers, boyfriends, ex-husbands, God knows who else, and maybe you. They read stories about it in newspapers every day, see examples of it on TV every night, and are flooded with it in videos and movies. They see it all over the world—because it *is* all over the world—and all over human history.

Male anger.

It scares your wife.

Do you understand that?

You're a man; your anger scares your wife.

If anger at your wife comes up inside you, that's fine, that happens, we're human, and once a decade or so we're even right, but your job is to keep it inside you until it isn't scary and ugly anymore. To do that, you use something called self-restraint. It's a discipline. The discipline is to stop getting angry at your wife in the ways you've gotten angry at her in the past.

Just cut it out. It's very unmanly. It's cowardly.

For those of you who are saying, "But anger's a *feeling,* and you just told me to get in touch with my feelings," please realize that most of your anger at your wife and the way you've expressed it in your marriage is not a feeling; it's you thinking you're completely entitled to whatever you want from her at a particular moment and then freaking out when she won't give it to you.

I hope that clears that one up.

And for those of you who have a problem with the double-standard thing—the one that says it's not okay for you to get angry at her, mostly, but it is okay, mostly, for her to get angry at you—yes, you're right, that is definitely a double standard, and if you've got a problem with it, tough.

THE MOVE

Go ask your wife what it's like for her when you get angry at her. Annoyed. Irritated. Raising your voice at her. Glowering at her. Yelling at her. Fuming. Exploding.

Tell her you really want to know and then listen carefully when she tells you.

Believe every word of what she's saying.

When she's done, sit quietly for a few minutes pondering what you've heard, and then, taking her hand and looking her solemnly in the face, say that you now know it's wrong—*not* okay—to direct that kind of anger at her, and there's no reason, no excuse, no justification, no rationalization, no provocation, that makes it okay, and from this moment forth you renounce and repudiate it.

CHAPTER 19

Gentleness

Hey, that's no way to treat a lady,
no way to treat your baby,
your woman, your friend.

Helen Reddy

I want to see you game, boys. I want to see you brave and
manly. And I also want to see you gentle and tender.

Theodore Roosevelt

A good husband is a gentleman to his wife.

A good husband is a gentle man.

When he is called upon to protect or defend himself or his family against aggression or threat, he's not gentle at all, he's a warrior, using firmness and force and ferocity as necessary to repel danger, but at all other times, and *always* with his wife, he is gentle.

I didn't start out gentle with Jane. I would sometimes be harsh, angry, mean, and insulting to her. I would glare and fume.

Sometimes, to my shame, I'd shout and yell at her, and once, many, many years ago, in a rage I pushed her.

I was like that for four reasons: because I was immature, because there is lots of ungentleness swimming around in the Alter family gene pool, because I'm a man, and because for some strange reason I thought it was okay to act like that with a woman.

Now I know it's not okay. Jane taught me that. She taught me how to speak and behave gently to her. My whole marriage has been a training in gentleness. It has had to be. Because Jane as a child was abused and terrorized by a great-uncle and -aunt for many years, she has very high requirements for and standards of safety in our marriage. That means she doesn't let me get away with any of my ungentle, intimidating, scary stuff around her. My male stuff. My Alter stuff. My angry, peremptory tones. The edge in my voice when I'm impatient with her. She'll call me on it every time, and I mean *every* time.

Living with my wife, I have learned that I must not in any way or for any reason or to any degree be rough or scary with her, and I must never yell or otherwise raise my voice to her.

That's what I tried to explain to my client Gary the other day in my office. He was recounting a story from the weekend when he had come into the living room where his wife was going through the mail and said, "This time, *please*, sort the bills *right*."

"Stop yelling at me," she said.

"I'm not yelling at you," he said.

"Yes, you are."

"I'm just telling you—"

"You're yelling at me! And I want you to stop it!"

At which point he stomped out of the room.

"But I wasn't yelling at her, Robert. I was just telling her something."

"Nah, you were yelling at her, Gary. You don't hear it inside yourself as yelling, but that's the way women hear it. I can remember back when my daughter, Greta, was a teenager and I'd be in the kitchen going off on one of my famous rants about 'Nobody is doing enough around this damn house!' and Greta and Jane would be standing there staring at me like I was a lunatic, until one of them said, 'Stop yelling at us!'

"I didn't get it then, but I get it now: Women and children hear yelling in our voices that we don't hear. When there is impatience, annoyance, irritation, frustration, exasperation, or any kind of anger in our voice, they hear it *all* as anger—and they're right: It *is* all anger—which is when they get scared of us and get angry back at us and they say to us, 'Stop yelling at us!'

"So that whole scene in the living room with your wife, Gary, was a great teaching to you: Be gentle with her, be ever more gentle with her, always practice gentleness with her."

There's something about women, I think, that is all about gentleness.

And don't get me wrong: When I say gentleness, I don't mean weakness.

Women aren't weak!

Spend more than two hours studying women's history—what women have done in this world, their service to the world, what they've suffered and endured, the social changes they've fought for and won, the odds they've gone up against. Spend more than two minutes watching a woman give birth to a child and then taking care of that child and all her children pretty much nonstop for the next two decades. Spend more than two *seconds* having to live with *you* on a daily basis . . . Believe me, *women are not weak!* They are, in fact, tough as nails—when they have to be.

And gentle as doves—that's in their nature to be.

And that's the way they want us men to be. They want us to find the gentleness in our own nature and to practice that gentleness with them. They want us to be *nice*.

When they've asked us to wake them up from a nap, they don't want us to barge into the bedroom and shout, "Hey! Get up!" but to come in softly and sit down on the edge of the bed and touch their hair and whisper, "Time to get up, honey," and then when they don't, you tiptoe out and let them sleep another half hour. (Jane taught me that one.)

My whole marriage has been a teaching in gentleness, and yours is too. It has to be—you're married to a woman.

Gentleness, gentlemen.

Let's stop all our yelling at women. When we speak to them, when we look at them, when we touch them, whenever we're around them, let's be gentle men.

THE MOVE

Go to your wife and ask her if she's ever been treated ungently in her life, including by you.

Listen to what she tells you. Listen as she tells you about her father, his belt in his hand screaming at her to stay out of the way as he chased her little brother through the house.

She might cry. That's okay. Stay there right next to her.

When she's done, take her gently in your arms and whisper in her ear, "I will always be gentle with you . . . I promise to always be gentle with you."

CHAPTER 20

Discipline

For the very true beginning of wisdom is the desire of discipline, and the care of discipline is love.

King Solomon

Discipline, 007, discipline!

James Bond in his Aston Martin in *Goldfinger*, reminding himself to focus on his spy work rather than chase after the gorgeous blonde who just drove by in a Mustang

A good husband is disciplined. Like everyone else in the world, he's got all kinds of impulses that come up inside him, but he practices self-control and doesn't let those impulses come *out* of him as actions or words that might upset his wife. He knows how to contain those impulses within himself, head them off at the pass, and not let them turn into bad behavior.

This takes effort. Willpower. Sometimes a lot of willpower because the inner forces you're trying to restrain—to *keep* inner—have a lot of their own power.

Feelings, like impatience and anger. Propensities and tendencies, like to make others feel bad when you're in a bad mood, or to sulk when you don't get your way. Desires and cravings—to have that third beer. The temptations of the senses—to stare at that billboard with the half-naked girl on it. Male idiocy. Addictions.

That's why discipline takes strength. You've got to keep that stuff inside. Draw a line and hold it. It takes resolve. And muscle. Discipline is a manly kind of thing.

Every great athlete practices discipline. Every great coach demands it. Every soldier, every successful businessman, every common hardworking man who's spending his life just doing his job, practices discipline. Every man who really is a man practices discipline, because discipline is the very essence of manhood.

Discipline is the power—the *choice*—to do something that's hard because it produces, in the short or long run, something that's good.

Like a happy wife who feels loved by her husband.

To choose to do something that's hard is what we're doing at the health club when we're sitting at the shoulder press machine doing our twelve reps at a new weight. The first eight are pretty easy, feels good. It's the last four where it gets hard, where the *work* is, where the muscles are burning, where there's effort needed. And—no pain, no gain!—it turns out that those are the four reps, the hard ones, where the muscles are being toned and built, where the benefit is.

The benefit, it turns out, is almost always in the hard.

It's like Jimmy Dugan, played by Tom Hanks, says to Dottie

Hinson, played by Geena Davis, in the movie _A League of Their Own_. Dottie, the star catcher for the 1940s women's baseball team the Rockford Peaches, is telling Jimmy, the team's manager, that she's quitting the team in the middle of the season to go back home with her husband. "It just got too hard," she says, and Jimmy Dugan, old-school, says, "It's _supposed_ to be hard. If it weren't hard, everybody would do it. The hard is what makes it great."

The hard is what makes it discipline. Baseball is a discipline, and marriage is a discipline. Not out of onerous obligation to her, or fear or guilt or fawning servility, but out of your respect and love for her, you are a disciplined man in all your relations with your wife.

Discipline really _is_ love. It's doing what you have to do to take care of what you love.

The discipline of a husband is to do what he has to do to take care of his wife, whom he loves.

To not hurt her. Not upset her. Not cause her pain. Not be (mostly) at fault anymore for the difficulties in the relationship, because now he's so disciplined the relationship hardly has any difficulties.

Here's what I'm talking about. Here are eight examples of a husband practicing discipline and not causing difficulties in his marriage:

- You're paying credit card bills, and you see a rather hefty charge at a woman's boutique. You want to call your wife into the room and ask her ominously what this charge is for. But you know your wife. If you do that, you know she'll feel bad, and her pleasure in wearing whatever she bought will be gone. You look at the charge again: $295! For a dress! Gadzooks!

Ah, it's only $295. She doesn't do this often, and once in a while you can afford it, and she's going to look so pretty in it. Why make her feel bad? So you pay the bill without saying a word, and when you see your wife later, you ask her to put on the new dress she bought and show it off to you.

• You're sitting at the computer in a really bad mood. Grouchy. Crabby. Your wife comes into the room to tell you something. You feel like being short with her, snapping at her. That'll startle her, hurt her. There'll be a scene. It'll be a bad scene. So you make an inner adjustment. It takes half a second. You turn to your wife welcomingly and ask her sweetly what she wants.

• You're sitting at a restaurant with your wife. The waitress comes over to take your order. She's young and pretty. As she walks away, a strong impulse arises in you to follow her with your eyes, to check her out, to do The Scan. But you know your wife, and you know she'll see that, and you know she'll be upset by that, whether or not she says anything about it. *Discipline, 007, discipline!* The waitress walks off. You keep your eyes on your wife. (See Chapters 30–32 for more about sexual discipline in marriage.)

• You're sitting in the living room and hear a glass break in the kitchen, where your wife is preparing dinner. You feel annoyance, and there's criticism arising in you. You feel like going into the kitchen, surveying the damage with a frown, and saying something like, "Jesus! Again?! Would you *please* be more *careful?*" That's your impulse, but you know she'll feel hurt if you do that, and defensive and angry. So you don't do that. You get up and go into the kitchen and say, "Be careful of the broken glass, honey. Here, let me clean it up."

• Your wife's best friend from college is coming from out of town to visit tomorrow. You don't like the woman—never have—and as usual feel like saying something negative about her. This, you know, puts your wife in a difficult position between two people she loves, so with great effort you suppress your negative comment about her friend and offer to pick her up at the airport.

• You're about to make some really juvenile sexual comment having to do with your wife's breasts, *again*, the twelve-year-old junior-high-school kind of comment, where she just said, "We have to get two new doorknobs for the closet," and you say, "The only knobs I want to get are the ones under your sweater," or something equally moronic, and then you giggle like an idiot and reach for a feel and think it's really funny. It's almost irresistible . . . but you know from past experience she won't like it and feels annoyed and violated by it. So you don't do it. Summoning all your inner strength, you squelch it and somehow manage to pass for an adult in that moment.

• Your wife is feeling blue for some reason this morning and needs attention. You know that what she really needs is to be held (by you), to talk about it (to you), and maybe have a good cry (with you), and then she'll probably feel better. The problem is you don't have any attention. You're busy. You're about to go buy a new leaf blower. The very last thing you want to do in the whole world is sit with a crying woman. But there she is, picking up after the kids, looking so sad. You put down your car keys and go to your wife and take her hand and say, "Come, sit on the couch with me and we'll talk."

• You're having sex with your wife. Your penis is being pleasured and you're excited. Ready to orgasm. Like, *really* ready. But you know yourself: If you orgasm, your sexual interest in your wife will plummet along with everything else, and you'll just want to turn over, read for a while, and fall asleep. With Herculean self-control you pull your body back and your penis to safety and you turn your attention to your *wife's* sexual pleasure. For the next half hour or so you give her the time of her life till *she* orgasms . . . and then it'll be her pleasure to help you out with *your* pleasure.

Get the point about discipline?

It's a pretty simple point: Draw a line between what you might think and feel inside and what you say and do outside. And then, like they say in football, you *hold that line.*

That's the discipline.

It's the key to changing yourself.

And there's a reward! From all your discipline you receive something.

Her respect and her love and her lifelong devotion to you.

One woman client, whose husband had stopped drinking six months before and was maintaining his sobriety, said, "There is so much more there now for me to love."

"Everyone wants to be loved," says Scott Peck, "but first we must make ourselves lovable. We must prepare ourselves to be loved. We do this by becoming ourselves loving, disciplined human beings."

By practicing the disciplines of love with your wife, you receive everything.

THE MOVE

Start practicing disciplines like the examples above with your wife. Of course add your own.

It's not necessary to tell her that you're doing them. Just do them.

Realize that these little moments of effortful self-control make you feel strong and manly and proud and are actually *fun*.

So keep doing them and have fun doing them.

CHAPTER 21

Sober Up!

*Alcoholism isn't a spectator sport.
Eventually the whole family gets to play.*

Joyce Rebeta-Burditt

Every form of addiction is bad.

Carl Jung

If you're an alcoholic, sober up.

If you're a workaholic, sober up.

If you're addicted to *any* substance or behavior, sober up.

That means drugs, cigarettes, food, sex, TV, sports, ogling women, pornography, masturbation, money, gambling, and work.

You can't be a good husband and an addict at the same time. You may think you can, but you can't.

Here's why:

An addiction is a particular kind of *relationship*, a very strong and consuming and *exclusive* relationship you're having with a substance or behavior. An addiction is a relationship that binds you so tightly to itself that it takes you away from all the other relationships in your life—like with your wife and children. You're tied up, man. Your dance card is filled. You are not *there*.

Even when you're there, you're not there.

Ever try to relate to someone who's drunk? There they are, in the same room with you, sitting right next to you, looking at you and talking to you . . . but look into their eyes—they are not *there*.

An addiction is another isolation booth you've gone and built for yourself. The sign on the outside of the door, facing your wife, says, "No Entrance!" The sign on the inside of the door, facing you, says, "No Exit!"

Get honest with yourself. This addiction of yours—whatever it is—is taking up your time, affecting your health, probably shortening your life, and creating distance between you and your wife.

Take my lifelong TV addiction, for example. It's (mostly) under control now, but I wonder what it was like for my wife all those years when she'd come into the living room to be with me and talk with me, and I could literally not take my eyes off the rapid-fire flow of channels I was flipping through like someone in a permanent state of brain mania. That was probably not her favorite experience in our marriage, and it was *totally* my fault.

You can't be a good husband if you're not really there with your wife when you're physically there with her.

A good husband faces his addictions and is using whatever means are available to him—therapy, therapy groups, twelve-step programs, books, spiritual counseling—to find his way out of them, to find his way back to his wife.

THE MOVE

All addictions, at bottom, are attempts to go somewhere else than where you are—to go into a pleasant or exciting or numbing sensation or stimulation in order to get out of the *un*pleasant emotion you're usually feeling at the moment, like stress, nervousness, boredom, frustration, self-judgment, loneliness, depression, that sort of thing. All addictions, in other words, are attempts at *distraction*.

Since these pleasant and exciting and numbing sensations and stimulations work pretty well as distractions, *but only temporarily,* we have to repeat them ad infinitum . . . hence, the addiction.

So when you want to go somewhere, remember this:

There's nowhere to go.

There's nowhere to go!

Drink as much as you want, little fishcake, watch all the football games there are on TV, surf the Web, eye the women, have a snack, have a smoke, have sex with everything in sight, go up, go down, get high, get off, search out every imaginable kind of stimulation and sensation, and yes, it'll all feel so good!

It really will. It'll feel like a rush, a flush, a quiver and a shiver, a thrilling little trip outside yourself . . .

And then the little trip will be over.

You'll come right back to yourself.

Really. That's what's going to happen. Every single time. You'll come right back to yourself.

So just forget it.

It's hopeless. You can't get away from yourself.

Using whatever means are available to you, learn to stay right where you are—it's the only place to be—and become free of all your addictions. Break all your consuming relationships with substances and behaviors.

It's possible.

And then you're free to have a relationship with your wife.

A WORD TO THE WIVES

He has his addictions. Do you have yours? To food? Sweets? Television? Those two glasses of wine you so enjoy in the evening? Shopping and spending?

While he's working on his addictions, you work on yours.

Think of your addictions as the substances and behaviors you chose to form a close relationship with because you weren't able to form a close relationship with your husband—he's been incapable of it.

What could you do? You had to go *some* where with that need. Good choice—for the time. Not your fault.

But now it's a different time. Now your husband is starting to be capable of close relationship with you. Now he's coming back from his addictions, and from everywhere else he's been hiding out all these years, and coming back to you, to form a real relationship with you.

So now it's time for you to come back too.

Using sound diet programs, twelve-step programs, books, friends, therapy, and plain old willpower, start to break your relationships with the things you've been addicted to. They've served you well, but they're no longer necessary. Say a sweet and grateful good-bye to them, turn away from them, and turn to your husband now.

Chapter 22

Cheer Up!

If I were asked to diagnose the spiritual disease of modern men, I would not concentrate on symptoms such as our lust for power, our insatiable hunger for gadgets, or our habit of repressing women and the poor. I would, rather, focus on our lack of joy.

Sam Keen

Snap out of it!

Cher, slapping a morose Nicolas Cage
in the movie *Moonstruck*

Here's a scene I see often:

I'm in a restaurant, airport, store, or a park, some public place, and there's a family there—husband, wife, and two or three young kids—and the kids are running around, fooling around, with lots of energy, lots of smiles and laughter and noise and activity, and the wife is smiling too, watching them, enjoying them . . . and I look at the husband and he's sitting there looking *bad*. Grim. Glum. Fretful. Grumpy. Every once in a while he'll erupt and tell everyone to Shut up! Calm down! Knock it off! Cut it out! and everybody'll get startled and look at him for a second, then get quiet for a minute, but the energy really is irrepressible in them—it is, after all, the energy of play, of *joy*—so they'll start back up again in a few seconds, the woman and children smiling and laughing again and having a good old time, while the man sits there like a sourpuss.

Frankly, he looks *depressed*, like a lot of guys look depressed, and I suppose I should feel bad for him, which I do, but I also feel like going over there and slugging him.

"Hey! Cheer up, fella! C'mon! Pull yourself together, man! Your wife and kids are having fun, and you're sitting over here looking like the grim reaper. Perk up! It's not that bad! Snap out of it!"

That's what I feel like saying to him. It would be a very brief therapy.

If you can't *snap* out of it, start dealing with your moodiness and irascibility and general unhappiness—do some therapy maybe?—and *come* out of it.

Call it moodiness, call it grumpiness, call it clinical depression or whatever you want—a lot of us men can be pretty dismal characters sometimes, real *bummers*, and we're bumming out the whole family.

A good husband doesn't do that.

He does what he has to do to revive the spirit of play and fun and lightheartedness and silliness and joy in himself, and he brings that spirit into his family, and he hears the laughter of his wife and children ringing like bells all around him.

THE MOVE

This week, every time you catch yourself wearing your habitual mask of seriousness and grumpiness, take it off. Lighten up, put a smile on, and play with your family.

Choose to do this all week. Even if you don't feel like it, do it. Do it for them.

Get up and start running around with them . . . and dancing with her.

Yes, you have a lot of responsibilities, but your first responsibility is to make them happy. So don't be an old stick-in-the-mud.

Play with them this week.

You remember play? You spent your whole boyhood playing!

So play with your family.

You've got a *great* family. Play with them!

Lighten up, man!

Come on!

Have a good time!

CHAPTER 23

Lookin' Good!

*A true lover considers nothing good except
what he thinks will please his beloved.*

Andreas Cappellanus

*He's so fine!
Gonna make him mine!*

The Chiffons

A good husband tries to stay young and healthy and look as good as he can for as long as he can for his wife because he knows that she has to spend the greater part of her life being with him and looking at him. And going out with him in public!

Bearing this in mind, a good husband tries to eat well, exercise regularly, stay groomed and fit, and stay clear of things like alcohol and drugs that make him feel and look wasted. He's into health and hygiene—for himself, yes, but also for his wife, whom he dearly loves and whose tender senses he doesn't want to subject day after day to a *zhlub*.

Speaking of *zhlubs*, one of my male clients in individual therapy was complaining one day that his wife never wanted to have sex with him.

"You want to know why, Wayne?" I said.

"*You* know why? You've never even met her."

"I don't know all her whys, but I can tell you one of them, because I've met *you*."

"Go ahead," he said.

I sat there just looking at him for a moment. "You don't look well, Wayne. Actually you look like shit. There's no way you can be attractive to her. You drink beer and eat bad food, and too much of both, so you're kind of soft and shapeless, you look like you dress out of the hamper, and you always smell like something is fermenting in you.

"What woman in her right mind would want to have sex with you? I don't think even a woman water buffalo would want to have sex with you. If you ever want to have sex with your wife again, Wayne, you've got to get yourself in shape. Spiff up, man! Look good—for her! Be the good-lookin' guy to that pretty gal you married. Pull your whole physical trip together."

"That 'pretty girl' I married is *fat* now," he said. "You think *I'm* out of shape? You should see *her*. You should see her *eat*."

"To whatever degree your wife is overeating herself into fatness, Wayne, take that on—as you take *everything* about her on—as something not to judge her for, never to make her feel bad about, but help her with. The best way to help her is to realize that part of the reason she's feeding herself with food is that she feels so *unfed* in the marriage with you—'*My marriage isn't fulfilling, but I bet that bagel will be!*'—and then get to work on changing yourself, learning how to truly connect with her, and making your marriage a veritable feast of love instead of the empty plate it now is for her. That's the best diet plan of all for her! In the meantime you get your act together and change your lifestyle by eating better and exercising regularly—*on your own*—and become a model of fitness and health that your wife can use for inspiration. Our culture has so messed up women's minds about food and fat and physical appearance that, when it comes to eating, they need all the inspiration and support they can get from their husbands. Also remember that there is a natural and healthy weight increase in women that comes with maturity— that, with some ectomorphic exceptions, most women are *supposed* to get heavier as they get older. Rounder, fuller, curvier, earthier—more voluptuous is the best way to think about it, and fat is the wrong way to think about it, so be careful with that word."

When it comes to his wife's physical appearance, a good husband is supportive and encouraging. When it comes to his own physical appearance, he basically just wants to give pleasure to her, so he wants to *be* a pleasure to her senses. He wants to be pleasant for her to look at, and lie next to, and touch and hug and kiss and breathe in—so throughout his life, out of love for her, he makes the daily effort to practice his personal disciplines of health, hygiene, and physical fitness.

THE MOVE

Tell your wife that you're starting a new regimen: You want to get healthy and fit and make yourself attractive and pleasing to her eye.

Start by turning off the TV (just how important *is* the Northwest Regional Two-Man Chain Saw Challenge from Koyuk, Alaska?), getting up off your keister, and inviting her to go for a nice long walk with you right now.

CHAPTER 24

Still Crazy After All These Years

> *When I'm broken down and cannot stand*
> *Will you be strong enough to be my man?*

> Sheryl Crow

> *But true love is a durable fire . . .*

> Sir Walter Raleigh

Yup. Sometimes she's crazy.

As a loon.

Unreasonable. Off-the-wall. Psycho. A *wreck*.

Stubborn. Mean. Moody. *Weird*.

Sometimes she's so needy you can't stand it. Full of anxiety. Insecure. Immature.

And sometimes she's so *angry*. Pissed off. Accusing. There's no pleasing her. No matter what you do, it's never enough, never good enough, she's *never* satisfied.

Okay, I get it: Sometimes she's crazy.

I know.

Believe me, I know.

Here are four things to understand about your wife when she's crazy like that:

One. It's not (mostly) your fault (finally! a first!), it's not at *all* your fault (hallelujah!), it's not her fault either, it's just *her*.

Two. We're all crazy somewhere inside us, and we all *go* crazy at fairly regular intervals. You do too.

Three. Most of us come from pretty crazy families, with a wide variety of mental disturbances floating around the family gene pool, so no wonder we're crazy. Take a moment and think of your wife's family. Her mother and father. Her sisters and brothers. Her aunts and uncles and the cousins on Long Island. Think about those people . . .

Cousin Bernice?

Oy.

Uncle Murray?

Oy vay.

Coming from *that* family, whatever loose grip on sanity your wife has gained over the years is a miracle of mental health.

Four. Most important, understand that her craziness is like a fire for you. The very way she's crazy and immature is burning out all the ways that you're crazy and immature.

I'll explain that.

Some years ago I was seeing a couple who was at an impasse. The wife, Rachel, was a wonderful person in every way. She was also the most defensive person I'd ever met. She was a *phenomenon* of defensiveness. I would match her against anybody, anywhere, anytime. Her defensiveness took the form of her getting instantly explosively angry and argumentative whenever anybody, particularly her husband, Joel, tried to give her information about herself that fell half a millimeter short of, "You're totally perfect, honey." Anything he said less than that, like, "Did you remember to pick up the sponges at the supermarket today, Rachel?" elicited from her something like, "Yes, I did. And you don't have to remind me, Joel. I know you asked me yesterday, but I just couldn't get to it! I was too busy. Stop making me feel bad! I just didn't get to it! And tell me, Joel, do *you* always get stuff right when I ask you to?!"

When Rachel's defensiveness kicked in like this, there was no getting through to her. All she knew how to do was retaliate. This drove Joel nuts. She was so defensive she couldn't be called on it—she couldn't admit she was being defensive when it was clear as day she was. She'd just retaliate again. This drove Joel completely nuts.

From the point of view of what Joel knew about Rachel's relationship with her parents in her childhood, her extreme defensiveness made perfect sense, and Joel fully understood it. From the point of view of trying to get through to her as her husband, however, Rachel, in Joel's opinion, was "out of her cotton-pickin' mind . . . crazy!"—and made him crazy.

"I don't know what to do," he said to me. "If I have *any*, even the slightest, critique of her, or a suggestion of how to do something better, or even an innocent request, like the sponges, she freaks out. Then I get freaked out, and at that point we're toast."

"Here's what to do," I said. "Take the fact that your wife is crazy in this way as a golden opportunity to work on the way you get *driven* crazy *by* it. Take your focus off her 'action'—in this case, her getting defensive—and put it on *your reaction*.

"What *is* your reaction to not being able to get through to her? How *do* you get when nothing you're saying is getting through to someone? . . . Hmmm . . . Joel goes crazy inside. You feel all alone, and angry, and helpless inside. You feel frustrated and furious . . . Hmmm . . . I wonder if it's the same way you went crazy in *your* childhood when nothing you said ever got through to *anybody* . . . I bet it is . . . Hmmm . . . A little window into your past perhaps? . . . A chance to know your past better, bring more of it into your consciousness, free yourself a little more from it?

"By seeing that in you, by focusing on your reaction rather than her action, you now get a chance, in the present, to *change* your reaction from the past, to try your hand at having an approximately *adult* reaction to not getting through to someone, which would be a novelty for you.

"Do you understand?

"It's called not getting *hooked* by what your wife does or doesn't do, or how sane or insane she is on a given day. If she listens to you, fine. If she doesn't listen to you, not so fine, but fine enough so you don't have to go crazy like the little ignored boy you were. You're not a little ignored boy anymore, Joel. You're a grown man, and you can have a grown man's reaction to your wife's *meshugas*. Calmly you can point it out to her, and say that it's sometimes very hard to talk to her, and say that you wish she'd continue her work on dismantling it. When she's coming from *her* childhood wound, in other words, you don't *have* to be coming from yours; you can be using hers to get beyond yours."

Their next session he brought in a note he had written and left on Rachel's pillow the day after the previous week's session. He asked her if he could read it to me, and she smiled and nodded.

Dear Rachel,
In the same way that there have been several things in our relationship that I have had to work on alone, that were

completely mine and had nothing to do with you, your defensiveness—i.e., what happens to you when you think you're being criticized—is yours, and yours alone, to work on. I still love you if you don't, but I want you to know that your defensiveness is very hard for me and makes me very reluctant to tell you I need something different from you than what I'm getting in a particular moment. Please keep working on it, and I'll keep loving you.

Love, Joel

Have this understanding: When your wife is still crazy after all these years, lost in her stuff, off-the-wall, her total psycho self, whatever form her craziness takes is helping you get free from your own craziness and grow up. She—as she is, *exactly* as she is, as crazy as she is—is the purifying fire that burns out of you everything that's holding you back from being the adult man and good husband you want to be.

Sit down in the fire.

You already have. You married her.

Didn't anybody tell you that marriage is a fire?

Marriage is a fire.

A good husband kind of *likes* the fire. It's challenging, kind of exhilarating actually, kind of awesome when you understand what's really going on in it.

THE MOVE

The next time your wife is being crazy and driving you crazy, completely take your focus off how she's being crazy and put it on how you're *going* crazy.

Now say to yourself, "This isn't about her, this is about me and what I'm feeling right now."

Identify how you're feeling right now. Anger, maybe?

Feel it. It's okay to feel it. It's *good* to feel it.

Just don't act on it. In other words, don't *get* angry, just *be* angry, inside, and contain it. Like fire is contained in a furnace.

You're the furnace.

Meanwhile, outside, let her be however crazy she's being—she's probably having a rough day—and you just be supportive and loving.

CHAPTER 25

Is There Good Sex After Marriage?

> *Take me in your arms and never let me go*
> *Whisper to me softly while the moon is low*
> *Hold me close and tell me what I want to know*
> *Say it to me gently, let the sweet talk flow*
> *Come a little closer*
> *Make love to me.*
>
> Jo Stafford

When you get married, is there any good sex after the honeymoon?

You bet.

After the first year?

Yup.

Great sex?

Yes.

Frequent?

Yes.

After five, ten, twenty, and thirty years?

Absolutely.

Forty, fifty, and sixty?

I'll let you know.

Just don't believe all the comments out there in our culture that say that marriage makes the sex go bad. Those comments are said by people in bad marriages having bad sex, and they're not true.

The opposite is true.

Marriage improves and enhances sex. Marriage *perfects* sex.

If you get the marriage right.

After an evening of good marital sex, you and your wife are lying next to each other in bed holding hands, silent in the dim light, sweetly tired and slightly dazed, and one of you gently interrupts the silence and says, "I can't believe we're *married* and actually get to *legally* do this."

THE MOVE

Try to believe what I'm saying here about good sex in marriage.

I'll make that easier for you:

It's totally true!

Now go to your wife and ask her what she thinks needs to happen in the marriage for the two of you to have better and more frequent sex. She might say:

- "Talk to me more."

- "Share your feelings with me more."
- "Be nicer to me."
- "Learn how to be affectionate with me without being sexual."
- "Don't be so busy all the time."
- "Lose some weight."
- "Cancel your subscription to *Playboy*."

Try to believe everything that she's saying, and start to do those things.

CHAPTER 26

Her Sexuality

> *Our love is kind of stalled, baby*
> *But it ain't about the sex*
> *I'd trade the roses and the negligees*
> *If we could just connect.*
>
> Bonnie Raitt

> *You can get it if you really want*
> *You can get it if you really want*
> *You can get it if you really want*
> *But you must try . . .*
>
> Jimmy Cliff

Your wife's sexuality is one of the greatest gifts that will ever be given to you on this earth. You already know that. She's given it. And it blew your mind.

To make sure her sexuality is a gift that keeps on giving, make sure you *understand* her sexuality.

It's *female* sexuality.

In case you hadn't noticed, it's not exactly the same as male sexuality.

Male sexuality, as I see it, is basically a man somewhat clumsily fiddling and diddling with the sexual parts of a woman until she gets fired up enough to pay attention to *his* sexual part, which has been hard and throbbing and actually *steaming* for hours, so he can finally have his orgasm and relax. There are more sophisticated versions of this that can involve restaurants and wine and candles and the Mantovani strings, but it's basically the same thing.

Up to this point in history, female sexuality has been when a woman believes that that's the best sex she can get from a man, and then uses all her willpower to keep from yawning, laughing, crying, or leafing through the J. Jill catalog during it.

Now let's talk about how female sexuality actually works.

First off, to get it, you can't just show up at her body with a blazing hard-on at some random moment of the week and say, "Here I am!"

Most of the time it doesn't quite work like that for her.

The way her sexuality works is that it starts much earlier than you think it does. It's a long ramp that starts way back with how you've actually been *relating* to her, *treating* her, all the rest of the week.

Imagine that.

Are you attentive to her? Are you nice to her? Do you talk with her about her life? Are you interested in her feelings? For her, your hug in the morning, your phone call in the afternoon, and your pleasant conversation at dinner, your thoughtfulness and kindness and gentleness and sweetness, all that warmth you send her during the day is what gets her hot at night.

The trick is to *stay connected* to her, because female sexuality is completely connected to how connected she feels to you.

Got that?

Just in case you don't, I'll repeat it:

Female sexuality is completely connected to how connected she feels to you.

Imagine *that*.

All that time you spend out of bed with her, the thousand and one little connections you create with her, are *erotic* to her! All the ways that you show love to your wife are—in that slow, softening, melting, liquefying way of a woman—turning her on!

The ancient Greek poetess Sappho said it long ago:

> *How love*
> *the limb-loosener*
> *sweeps me away!*

That's it! For a woman, the limb-loosener is *love*.

A good husband is a great lover.

He is making love to his wife basically all the time.

THE MOVE

Be nice as pie to your wife from now on in your marriage.

Sweet as honey. Considerate. Attentive. Supportive. Helpful. Gentle. Kind.

In the way you talk with her, in the way you are with her, always show your love and respect for her.

It's all foreplay, man.

CHAPTER 27

All Women Have Curves

The nakedness of woman is the work of God.

William Blake

She'll let you in her house
If you come knockin' late at night . . .
If the words you say are right
If you pay the price
She'll let you deep inside
There's a secret garden she hides.

Bruce Springsteen

The other thing you want to remember about your wife's sexuality is that it's like her body, with lovely contours curling and curving all over the place.

This part of her body curves into this part which slopes down to this other part which is now miraculously sweeping back up to this other part over here, where it does a complete loop-de-loop and swirls around to oh my god *this!*

She's all curves!

There's not a straight line on her!

She's got spheres and coils!

She's even got spirals!

And folds within folds!

Hallelujah!

It's so multidimensional and curving and moving through so many planes at once, it's kind of dizzying, and you can spend a whole lifetime learning how to make love to it all.

And you do.

A good husband spends a lifetime learning all the planes and dimensions of his wife's sexual body and also the planes and dimensions of her sexuality. She's a piece of work, this girl, and he *likes* the work, *loves* it, because the reward—a wife who feels completely sexually known by her husband and therefore completely sexually open to him—is heaven on earth for a man.

So you want to have sex with her? Great idea!

Now get to work.

The work is to know her.

For example, if you want to have sex with her, you might try asking yourself—or, better, her—does she want to have sex with you? How's she feeling physically? Is she tired? What kind of day has she had? What part of her menstrual cycle is she in? Is she premenopausal? Postmenopausal? How does that affect her sexuality? How's she feeling emotionally? Is she in a good or bad mood? How's she feeling in the relationship with you? What's the latest meathead thing you've done that you haven't apologized for yet? Is she stressed and busy? Is she feeling shy today? Did you already have sex today, or yesterday, and maybe she's done with you, bozo? When was the last time you touched her *non*sexually, like just hugging, or a foot rub, or snuggling with her on the couch without heading for a breast? Have you *ever* touched her nonsexually? Are you keeping yourself healthy and fit and looking physically attractive to her these days? How's she feeling these days about her *own* body? Attractive? Insecure? Sexy? Old?

In other words, is she up for it right now?

Go ahead. Figure it out. You can do it.

A word of caution: If the answers to the above questions add up to she doesn't want to have sex with you right now, don't even *think* about *blaming* her for that! And if she doesn't want to have sex with you right now and that old word "frigid" comes up in your mind and you actually think that she's frigid, as opposed to the truth, which is that you're an insensitive oaf, I don't know if I can help you.

If the answers to the above questions add up to she never wants to have sex with you, if her sexual interest in you has completely disappeared, here's what to do:

Find out why.

By asking her. By talking to her about it.

Don't get angry at her, don't turn away from her, don't reject her even though she's sexually rejecting you (that takes strength for a man!), but be her friend and stay her friend and keep gently inviting her to talk about herself. And don't always try to steer the conversation into sex; women hate that ("All he's interested in is sex!"), and it'll get you nowhere. Let her take the conversation where she wants it to go. Remember that it's your interest in *her,* not in sex, that feels intimate to a woman. So whatever you do, stay in relationship with her, and keep talking with her, and be her friend. Speaking as her friend, you could suggest that the two of you read some marital self-help books together and talk about them, or go to a marriage or sex therapist and talk there.

Remember that the sexuality of a woman is a high and holy temple that you may enter only through the labyrinth of her feelings about you, her feelings about men, her feelings about herself, her feelings about her body, her feelings about sex, the doctrines of her religion, the phases of her life, the phases of the moon, and her entire sexual trauma history with men, including you—all of it swimming around in a rather choppy sea of hormones that we men never even heard the names of.

You have to walk through the labyrinth with her. You really do. Don't worry about how long it may take. Just stay by her side and on her side. There's no other way into the temple.

Female sexuality.

You have to learn it.

Your wife is your teacher of it.

Whatever the state of your wife's libido, whatever her feelings, age, history, or mood, the best thing to do is to know that woman so well and respect her so deeply that your relationship with her is a work of genius, and then your wooing of her and your lovemaking to her, both in and out of the bedroom, will be a work of genius.

This is doable.

When you're making love to your wife in the bedroom, you pay attention to every curve and contour and dimension and plane of her beautiful female sexual body.

All you have to do now, in and out of the bedroom, is pay attention to every curve and contour and dimension and plane of how her beautiful female sexual body actually works—that's a lot of attention, but she's a *woman*, she's your *wife*, she's worth every second of it.

THE MOVE

Tell your wife you want to learn about all the different factors that go into her feeling sexual toward you or not.

Go for a walk with her, hold her hand, and ask her questions about it.

Use the questions listed above and any others you can think of.

When she starts to tell you about it all, listen with great interest, and ask more questions, and keep holding her hand.

Treat the information she gives you as sacred and always use it sensitively. Don't ever pressure her for sex. Basically just keep asking her questions in a kind way and listen.

A WORD TO THE WIVES

If you have little or no interest in sex with your husband, do everything you can to revive your interest. Even if you don't feel like it. I'm asking him to do things in this relationship for the sake of the relationship that he doesn't feel like doing, like talking to you, and I'm asking you to do the same, and for the same reason—for the sake of the relationship.

Think of it this way:

You're in a marriage. Sex is very important to a marriage. It strengthens the marital bond. It is connection, closeness and intimacy, benevolence and blessing, bestowal of affection, and pleasure and play and joy and fun with someone you love.

You're in a marriage to a *man*. Sex is very important to a man. It's an acceptably manly way of feeling open and vulnerable and strong and proud and *intimate* with a woman, and it feels better to a man than anything you can imagine.

So don't give up on sex. It's important to him, so make every effort to make it important to you. Read the articles about marital sex in magazines. Read the good books out there on marital sex.* If your husband makes the Move I've asked him to

*There are a number of good books on marital sexuality: Barry and Emily McCarthy, *Rekindling Desire: A Step-by-Step Program to Help Low-Sex and No-Sex Marriages* (Brunner-Routledge, 2003); Wendy Maltz, *The Sexual Healing Journey* (Harper Perennial, 2001); Sallie Foley, et al., *Sex Matters for Women* (Guilford, 2002); Robert Butler and Myrna Lewis, *The New Love and Sex After Sixty* (Ballantine, 2002); Patricia Love and Jo Robinson, *Hot Monogamy: Essential* make in this chapter, if he takes your hand, take his hand and open up and start to talk to him about you and your sexuality. Teach him your sexuality, how it *really* works. Teach him that your sexuality spans the whole spectrum of sensuousness and sensuality—from sitting next to each other on the couch to intercourse in bed—and take him up and down the spectrum. Get him to go to marital therapy with you, or sex therapy, or get yourself into individual or women's group therapy and talk about your sexuality there. When it feels right, you might want to try having sex with your husband by bringing him into the bedroom and getting the lights and the music just the way you want them, and then, by prior agreement, teaching him what feels good to you by stopping when it's not feeling good and trying to get the poor guy back on track.

Don't give up on sex. In the past, sex with your husband may have been anything from traumatizing to irritating to disappointing to boring, and once it goes dormant in a marriage, it can be tough to get it going again—and it may take a while—but do your best. Sex is worth it. Sex is *good*. It is a great gift given to women and men by God, who gives us marriage as the perfect place to enjoy it.

Steps to More Passionate, Intimate Lovemaking (Plume, 1994); David Schnarch, *Passionate Marriage: Love, Sex, and Intimacy in Emotionally Committed Relationships* (Owl Books, 1998); and Michele Weiner-Davis, *The Sex-Starved Marriage: A Couples Guide to Boosting Their Marital Libido* (Simon & Schuster, 2003).

There are also sex therapists. They can be found through the American Association of Sex Educators, Counselors, and Therapists, P.O. Box 5488, Richmond, VA 23220, http://www.aasect.org, 804-644-3288.

CHAPTER 28

A Man's Sexuality

See, the problem is that God has given men a brain and a penis, and only enough blood to run one at a time.

Robin Williams

Who touches this touches a man.

Walt Whitman

I have often thought that an honest book written by an honest man about his sexuality, and the role his penis plays in his sexuality, would be a very easy book to write.

It would be titled *Please Touch It*, and all the chapters would be titled "Please Touch It," and all the words in all the chapters would be "Please touch it."

A man with rudimentary grammatical skills, very little time, and almost no vocabulary could write this book.

THE MOVE

Find a good time and tell your wife about the role that your penis plays in your sexuality. Read this chapter to her, look up bashfully . . . and burst out laughing together!

CHAPTER 29

The Gauntlet

*Girls and women who are sexually violated experience the most
extreme form of a process that occurs for all women.*

Jean Baker Miller

In their third month of therapy Corrine, a twenty-nine-year-old
sales representative for a pharmaceutical company, and her husband, Ned, a restaurant manager, were describing their sexual
difficulties.

"She seems grossed out by it," Ned said. "We'll start it, and it
seems to be going well for a time, but then there'll come a moment when she, like, *shudders*, and kind of gets disgusted, and she
has to stop right away—can't go on. I know she loves me, and I
love her, and we're attracted to each other, but this always happens."

"Is this the way it is?" I asked Corrine.

"Yeah, that's pretty much the way it happens."

"Are you aware of any sexual abuse in your background?" I asked.

She thought about it for a moment. "Not unless you count being stared at by men most of my life," she said, laughing.

"I count that," I said.

A good husband understands what his wife has been through sexually in her life and treats her accordingly.

What she's been through sexually is various forms of sexual abuse.

Our entire culture is a long gauntlet of sexual abuse that every girl and woman runs from birth to death. Sexual abuse is just what *happens* to women in this culture, including to your wife, and men are completely at fault for it.

Here's the way I see it:

Any woman who has ever been stared at, leered at, eyed, ogled, or looked up and down for the purpose of sexual appraisal by a man has been sexually abused. Any woman who has ever had her blouse stared down or her skirt stared up has been sexually abused. Any woman who has ever seen a movie, television show, commercial, billboard, or magazine in which a sexually suggestive woman was displayed has been sexually abused. Any woman who has ever been sexually spoken to, joked about, or propositioned by a man who feels he has the right to do that simply because she's a woman has been sexually abused. Any woman who's been obscenely spoken to has been sexually abused. Any woman who has ever been invited into or exposed to male pornography has been sexually abused. Any woman who has ever been forced to see any gesture of disrespectful and aggressive male sexuality has been sexually abused. Any woman who has ever been touched, pinched, patted, petted, rubbed, stroked, hugged, or kissed without her invitation or against her will has been sexually abused. Any woman who has ever said no to a man who didn't immediately stop his sexual advances has been sexually abused. Any woman who's ever been stalked has been sexually abused. Any woman who has ever been made to feel that her job, her financial security, her physical safety, her marriage, her womanhood, or her human worth was a function of the way she looked or dressed or sexually performed has been sexually abused. Any woman who has ever been misled, deceived, or emotionally manipulated by a male for sexual purposes has been sexually abused. Any woman who has ever given in to a man's command or demand or ultimatum or threat to have sex with him has been sexually abused. Any woman who has ever been physically forced to have sex with a man has been sexually abused.

All of these are violations of a woman's psychological, physical, and sexual boundaries. They all put the woman on notice that she is being seen, talked about, thought of, and treated as a sexual body that could be approached, possessed, and used for the sexual pleasure of a male.

It happens to all women in our culture.

And worse.

What's happened to your wife?

Do you know?

You should want to know.

Ask her about it.

What's the gauntlet been like for her? What's her story?

She's got a story. If you show real interest, perhaps she'll tell it to you.

And when she does, when she tells you about the stranger in the elevator, or her cousin in the attic that time, or her uncle all those years, or her counselor, or neighbor, or her high school boyfriend in the car that night at the golf course, or her first husband when he'd be drunk, when she tells you about the looks, the comments, the lies, all the *hands*, and the tremendous pressure that's been brought to bear on her, when she tells you, listen.

And if she cries, hold her and listen.

And if she gets angry and screams, let her scream, and hold her and listen.

And when she's done and sitting there silent and distant, just sit there with her and love her.

Your wife has run the gauntlet and made it to you, thank God, the man she's completely safe with, the strong and loving arms she finally falls into.

THE MOVE

Ask your wife to read this chapter, and sit with her while she does.

After she's done, ask her if she'd be willing to tell you her story.

If she says yes, listen with rapt interest from beginning to end.

When she's done, thank her, tell her you're beginning to get what she's been through and that you want someday to get it totally.

Assure her that she'll never have to go through any of it with you.

CHAPTER 30

Fidelity!

When he is late for dinner and I know he must be either having an affair or lying dead on the street, I always hope he's dead.

Judith Viorst

"Dan, you seem to have the perfect marriage.
How do you do it?"
"You just pick the right one to be in the foxhole with,
and when you're outside of the foxhole,
you keep your dick in your pants."

Topher Grace and Dennis Quaid in
the movie *In Good Company*

A good husband is so completely sexually faithful to his wife that he doesn't think of it as sexually faithful. He doesn't think of faithful or unfaithful. He doesn't have those categories in his head. When he thinks of sex, he thinks of his wife, and that's the end of that.

Many men have to take a journey through various forms of unfaithful to get to faithful. "Fidelity seems to come harder to us," says Sam Keen.

Yup.

Actually, many of us men are sexual *addicts*, if you define addiction as an energy inside you that operates outside your control, and if you define *sexual* addiction as the uncontrolled sending of sexual energy—*in any form and to whatever degree*—to any woman other than your wife.

In our culture this sending of sexual energy to women other than our wives hides under such quasi-benign, laundered terms as "hanky-panky," "fooling around," "playing around," "messing around," "womanizer," "woman chaser," "skirt chaser," "philanderer," "ladies' man," "libertine," "rake," "wolf," and "boys-will-be-boys-ha-ha-ha," but it's anything but benign.

It's addiction, and it's infidelity.

Your fault.

The sending of sexual energy to women other than our wives could be anything from having sexual intercourse with another woman (as in an extramarital affair) to sexual touching that stops short of sexual intercourse but is still sex (as in, "I did *not* have sex with that woman!") to flirting, which is a sexual transaction with words, to making eyes at that woman at the party across the living room over the guacamole . . . and all the other times you can't keep your eyes off women, including all the pornography you look at in all the places it is, which is pretty much everywhere.

All of it's addiction, and all of it's infidelity.

Your fault.

All the little seduction games you play with other women? All your sexual shenanigans?

Addiction. Infidelity. Your fault.

Anything you might say in defense of these behaviors is, at best, delusion and, at worst, dishonesty—in either case, bullshit—so save your breath.

Just listen.

Be completely sexually faithful to your wife, which means that every form, aspect, and degree of your sexual energy gets directed *exclusively* to her.

There is no exception to this.

To whatever degree and in whatever form your sexual energy is directed to another woman—whether it's the neighbor lady "who's always so friendly" to you, or your secretary, or colleague, or your friend's wife, or that bar girl leaning over that table with the cleavage, or that actress on the movie screen, or just a cute little thing that you spot on the street—*that's* the addiction, right *there*, *that's* infidelity, and hurts your wife deeply (believe me, she sees it *all*) and pisses her off royally, so cut it out.

Lose the concept of "another woman." In any form she appears. There is no other woman. For all your sexuality the only woman is your wife.

It's really important that you understand this. Once and for all, *get* this fidelity thing.

Recently I heard a story about a woman in New Hampshire. She was forty-five, married for twenty-three years to the same man, with three college-age, well-adjusted children, a good wife and mother and neighbor and citizen, a good woman living a comfortable and happy life.

Then she found out her husband had been having an affair for the past three years.

She hung herself in the garage.

This is not a story about a woman's problem with codependence or depression. And it's not a story about a weak woman. It's a story about the enormous effect that a husband's infidelity has on a wife, the rotten betrayal that it is, the ethical *wrong* that it is, and the devastation that it causes.

She hung herself!

Get it now? Get what infidelity does to women inside?

Fidelity!

THE MOVE

Being really honest with yourself, identify all the behaviors you're involved in where your sexual energy—*in any form and to whatever degree*—is directed toward a woman other than your wife.

This other woman might be an actual person in your life—a coworker in your office or that teenage girl who lives across the street—or she might be an image on your computer or in some commercial or movie or magazine.

What women and what parts of women are your eyes looking at?

What women are you talking to, and what's going on in all that talking? What other women besides your wife are you touching, and why are you touching other women besides your wife?

What do you do, by the way, when the Victoria's Secret commercial comes on the TV? How long do you stand in the drugstore leafing through the swimsuit issue?

Being really honest with yourself, check it all out.

And then cut it all out.

Right now.

Here's how:

Right now remember a time recently when your thoughts or eyes began to stray to a woman other than your wife—the one in the short skirt sitting with her legs crossed at the airport last week. Feel the familiar urge: to look at her, to go over to her and talk to her, to get something going with her, to touch her, to look more at her, to *really* get something going with her . . . feel that urge . . . you know that urge . . .

And hold it right there—at the level of urge—and don't take one single action that it's urging you to do. Don't do the things you've done in the past. Don't look at her anymore. Look away. Look down.

I *said,* Look down!

You're a man: You can bear the pain of not acting on your urges. You're strong. You do what's right. It's not right for a husband to direct any of his sexuality to a woman other than his wife.

Now go back to what you were doing.

This is manhood.

It's a magnificent energy, your sexuality—the crest jewel of your manhood—but only when it's with your wife.

CHAPTER 31

Aging Wife, Younger Woman

*I'm going to see you through getting tired, getting sick,
getting old. And there's nobody else in my mind. Just you.*

Beau Bridges, playing Sonny Webster,
to Sally Field in the movie *Norma Rae*

Until you're a hundred
Until I'm ninety-nine
Together
Until white hair grows . . .

Japanese folk song

One last point about fidelity, especially for us older guys with aging wives.

The fact that your wife is aging (or is someday going to age) does not constitute a loophole in your promise to be faithful to her. Get it? The fact of her aging is not your license to leave her, cheat on her, or otherwise betray her for a pretty young thing. Stop all that shit.

Eliot, a fifty-five-year-old college professor in individual therapy, came in one morning looking troubled.

"I'm a mess," he said. "Me and Angie are doing a lot better these days, and she's still the finest woman on the face of the earth, but you know what, Robert? She's getting *old*. She has one of those age spots on her forehead now, and when I look at her hands, they look old—wrinkled and lined like an old lady's hands. Meanwhile I have a graduate student in one of my classes this year who's incredible—beautiful!—she actually looks a little like Angie at that age. We had coffee the other day, and I swear—"

"Don't do what you're thinking of doing, Eliot."

"What am I thinking of doing?"

"Something so incredibly dumb and morally wrong I'm going to fight you every step of your stupid way on it."

Your wife may be a youthful twenty-one, or thirty one, forty-one, or fifty-one, and physically she may be cute as a button, pretty as a picture, drop-dead gorgeous, or beautiful beyond compare.

Whatever.

It's not gonna last.

This woman is going to age. Everything physical about her will change. Her skin, hair, hands, breasts, her face and figure, it's all going to age right before your very eyes.

It's like Gypsy Rose Lee once said, "I've got everything I've always had. Only it's all six inches lower."

It's going to happen. You ready, Freddie?

Well, *get* ready.

Get ready because if you use the fact of your wife's aging to leave her for a younger woman, you're a jerk.

Let me reword that:

Get ready because if you use the fact of your wife's aging to leave her for a younger woman, you're a complete asshole.

Take your pick.

It's (mostly) your fault?

This one's all your fault.

Grow up. In this world there are certain things you do and certain things you don't do, and one of the things you don't do is discard the woman who has given you *everything*—her hand in marriage, her trust, her body, her youth, babies, her *life*, man—and you don't dump her, you don't just discard her, you don't throw her away because she's getting older and some nubile young thing is jogging with jiggling breasts down your street.

That's *betrayal*, pal, and you just don't do it.

Don't you get it? There's *always* a woman younger than your wife jiggling down your street. Plenty of them. A whole new crop of pretty young things jiggles up every year. Whatcha gonna do? Go jogging with them *all*? Don't be an idiot. Forget about it. Stay home.

All you have to do to stay home is to love that wife of yours so deeply, madly, truly, that when you look at her and see the aging in her, the creases in her neck and the gray in her hair, *it simply doesn't matter to you*. It's not that you don't see that stuff—you see it—but it doesn't matter to you. You see way past it. You see *her*. You see your *wife*.

"There is no old age. There is, as there always was, just you."

They say beauty is only skin-deep. I say that for a good husband there's a beauty that's deeper than skin-deep, and that's the beauty you see when you look at your wife. It's the beauty of the woman you married, your wife whom you love, the life that you've shared, the heart she entrusted to you forever. It's the fact that she knows you better than anyone on this earth will ever know you, and befriends you and loves you in a way that no young thing ever could, no matter how perky her nipples.

When you look at your wife, your heart overflows with such love of her that there are no younger women because there are no *other* women, there is only one woman, there, standing, with lines now in her face, figure changing, eyes tired perhaps but bright and filled with love of you, smiling at you, sunlight all around her, the most beautiful woman you have ever seen or will ever see.

THE MOVE

- **If you and your wife are young . . .**

Go get a recent photograph of her and sit down somewhere and look at it.

See her youthfulness. Love her youthfulness. That's partly why you married her. That's fine. Sit there looking at her in all her youthful beauty.

Now close your eyes.

In your mind's eye see her get older—no longer twenty-one, but thirty-one . . . forty-one . . . fifty-one . . . eighty-one! Like time-lapse photography. Imagine that happening. Look at that happening. In your mind's eye see the inevitable, that she will age, and love her at every age she will be.

- **If you and your wife are older . . .**

Go get a recent photograph of her and sit down somewhere and look at it.

See her as her not-so-youthful self. That's her now. Sit there looking at her. And let your heart melt for sheer love of her.

If you're having any difficulty doing this, if you're still entertaining any fantasies of a younger woman in your life, put the photograph of your wife down, go to a full-length mirror, take off all your clothes, and look at yourself.

Go ahead. Take a good look.

Hello?

Are you kidding?

Are you *crazy*?

Chapter 32

Lust for Wife

The king went with lifted head to the holy loins
He went with lifted head to the loins of Inanna
He went to the queen with lifted head
He opened wide his arms . . .

Sumerian wedding poem

You're the cutest thing I ever did see
I really love your peaches
want to shake your tree . . .

Steve Miller Band

A good husband feels sexual desire for his wife. Lust. Lots of it.
And only for her, exclusively, for all your years together.
Till the two of you are too old for lust.
But until then . . . lust.
The kind of lust that when you see her—her face, her lips, her

hair, her curves—you want to move to her and touch her, to kiss her, to move forward to her and reach for her, rising up to her.

And when you do reach her and touch her and rise up to her, when she rises up to you, somewhere inside you you're still sixteen and going, "*Oh, thank you! Oh, thank you! Thank you! Thank you!*"

That kind of lust.

You feel that for your wife.

And she for you.

Dancing in the darkened living room to Marvin Gaye's "Let's Get It On."

All evening getting it on.

Lucky man.

Married man.

THE MOVE

Tell your wife she's the cutest thing you ever did see. And the prettiest. And the sexiest. And the most gorgeous and the most voluptuous and the most delicious and the most sumptuous and scrumptious. And you can't wait to get into bed with her and do all kinds of wonderful things with her body for hours.

That's your lust for her. It's a wonderful form of your love for her.

CHAPTER 33

The World-Class Apology

When you make a mistake, there are three things you should do about it: admit it, learn from it, and don't repeat it.

Paul "Bear" Bryant

Woman, please let me explain
I never meant to cause you sorrow or pain . . .

John Lennon

A good husband is trying to be good all the time, but sometimes he's not. Sometimes he blows it.

We all blow it.

We're not perfect yet, and even if we're close (ha ha), most of us have been *far* from perfect in the past. It really *has* been (mostly) our fault.

What to do?

Apologize!

If you've made mistakes in your marriage, committed violations, even committed sins, apologize to your wife.

The neat thing about apologies is that when they're coming
from new understanding and true remorse, and include a complete cessation of the hurtful behavior, they *work*. They work
with God, I've heard, and they work with your wife because they
validate her sense of injustice and injury, and open the door to
her forgiveness.

So you've got to learn to apologize.

Easier said than done. Almost impossible for some of us guys.

Because an apology is an admission of having done something
wrong or bad, and most of us guys can't *stand* being wrong, or
thinking we're bad, or our wife or anybody thinking we're bad, or
that we've ever done, said, felt, or thought anything bad.

Deep, deep in our hearts we're good as gold, and we know it,
but it's really shaky in there because we're also stuffed to the gills
with guilt, a kind of chronic, constitutional guilt that we feel
most sharply with our wives, so the slightest suggestion from her
that we've been anything less than perfect—anything remotely
resembling critique or correction from her—triggers us into an
angry, defensive reaction of sometimes nuclear proportions.

Ask your wife if you do this.

Then duck.

In the old black-and-white TV westerns I used to watch as a
kid, the bad guys were always hiding out in the badlands. I never
quite knew where the badlands were, but it seemed they were so
bad that nobody ever wanted to go into them and look for the
bad guys. This is the way it is with men. Once we go into the badlands, the I-AM-BAD-lands, once we start shouting, *"Oh, you're
just saying I'm bad! Everything I do is bad with you! You're right! I'm
a shit! I suck! I'm bad! Guilty as charged!"* the moment we go into

that one, we're gone, ungettable, and our poor wives can just forget about trying to critique, correct, or confront us on anything.

Do you have any idea what it's like to live with somebody whose behavior is often bad, sometimes outrageous, but who cannot be corrected or confronted on it? Do you begin to understand what it's like to be your wife?

What to do?

Here's what to do:

Grow up. You need to *get*, once and for all, that you're not bad, you're not a bad person, you're a good person who has committed errors, done some bad things, wrong things. Some of us have done some *very* wrong things. Some of us have caused grievous pain and harm to our wives. Come on. Own up to that.

And here's what to do next:

First, remember that an error is an error, and we've all committed them in the past, and even the best infielders commit flagrant errors. I've seen ground balls go right through the legs of Brooks Robinson and Ozzie Smith. The errors were in the past. The past is past. Now move on. It's like Maya Angelou says: "You did what you knew. When you knew better, you did better."

So do better. Start by going to her and saying you're sorry.

Here's how. Here's what I call The World-Class Apology. There are ten steps. They take four or five minutes.

Step 1. Name quite specifically the thing you did that was wrong, like making light of that fight she had with her sister that she tried to talk to you about yesterday, or getting pissy and mean when she was too tired to have sex with you the other night, or forgetting to thank her for the dinner she put on for your boss.

Step 2. Say that you now know it was wrong and you shouldn't have done it.

Step 3. Say you're sorry. Say it from your heart, with true remorse for not having behaved in the best way toward her.

Step 4. Tell her you're aware that the thing you did is part of a larger pattern of your behavior toward her that you don't want to do anymore: "I know I have a tendency to not pay attention to you when you need me, but I really want to change that" . . . "I always have a bad, immature reaction when you won't do something I want, and I think I need to make a stab at maturity sometimes" . . . "I don't voice my appreciation of you nearly enough, and I'm going to start doing it more."

Step 5. Say you're sorry for each and every instance of that behavior, from the day you met to today. Say *that* with remorse too.

Step 6. Remember that *true* remorse is to be sorry enough to completely stop the behavior that causes you to have remorse.

Step 7. Stop the behavior. Just don't do it anymore. *Promise* her you won't do it anymore, and keep your promise.

Step 8. Ask for her forgiveness for having wronged her. Depending on the severity of your offense, you will get this either immediately or in time. Tell her to do it in her own good time—that this apology isn't about her forgiving you, but about you saying you're sorry to her.

Step 9. Look at her contritely. If you find yourself getting teary at the very thought of having neglected or disrespected or frightened or hurt or betrayed this wonderful person, good. Let her see that. It's part of the contrition.

Step 10. Stay for her response.

A couple I'd been seeing for over a year was in crisis. The husband had a history of yelling at his wife through all the eleven years of their marriage, and she had had enough. "It's *abuse*, Brad, and I won't take it anymore." Like many abusive men, Brad tried to excuse his behavior by saying that she provoked him—"Sometimes you do such unbelievably stupid, incompetent things, like losing the checkbook or backing the car up over our bikes, that I can't help myself"—and they left their therapy session the week before at an impasse, looking wretched. This week, though, they came in looking a lot better; their faces were relaxed, and the wife, Jackie, was actually smiling.

"What happened?" I asked them.

"After our therapy session last week, we spent the whole day fighting," Brad said. "Twelve hours of it. But then in the evening something changed, and I asked Jackie to write down a list of all the times in our marriage that I had been abusive to her. She did—there were nine major times when I yelled at her or broke something in a fit of anger in her presence. So I looked at the list and realized that I did do all those things. So I stood there in the kitchen holding the list and went down it and apologized for each one. I meant it too. Basically what I was saying was that 'I'm sorry I have yelled at you, Jackie, or been violent to you in any way, and I don't want to do that anymore, no matter how many bikes you run over.'"

"And that's all I needed to hear," said Jackie. "All I need to know is that Brad has woken up and owns his behavior, and knows it's wrong, and is sorry. My heart changed to him as soon as he did that. We even had sex later!"

Those are the big apologies. They're great. Then there are the smaller day-to-day ones, for minor infractions, misdemeanors, and lapses of consciousness.

The other day, a drizzly day, Jane and I were driving to a restaurant for lunch, and she asked me to park the car as close to the restaurant as I could get, and she pointed out an open space right in front of it. The parking space was small, and it was going to be hard to get the car into it, so with an immediate "That won't work!" I drove right past it and ended up parking in a lot two blocks away. On our walk back to the restaurant, arm in arm, Jane said she didn't like the way I had handled that; it had felt dismissive; she hadn't wanted to walk in the rain. At first I felt my usual indignation that she would even *think* to impugn my always impeccable behavior toward her, and tried that tack for a while, but it didn't work at all, and I then went into one of my famous sullen silences for a few moments. The whole scene felt bad, and the lunch was going to be bad—and then it struck me that I was the one *causing* it with my ridiculous reaction to her correction. In order for me not to have that reaction, I would have to remember that I don't *always* do everything right in our relationship, that sometimes I'm off, sometimes *way* off, that I'm not perfect, I make mistakes—and that that's all okay.

So I remembered that. I *do* make mistakes. I'm *not* perfect. I'm a work in progress. I'm still learning and growing. There's always room for improvement.

When we got to the restaurant, I apologized to her for not handling the situation better. She accepted my apology, and we had a nice lunch.

Two weeks ago Jane told me about an interaction she had on the phone with her friend Ella where she felt she hadn't really been there for her. She was feeling bad about it, and we talked about it for a few moments. Then it completely slipped my mind, as these things do. Last week I remembered it, so I went to her and said, "I want to apologize for not asking you how you were doing with that thing that happened with Ella on the phone. Totally forgot about it. Sorry. How're you doing? Did you call her back?"

She liked that. Out of the blue. She really liked it.

So . . . do those kinds of apologies too. The minis. They work too. They're like hydraulic stabilizers that keep autocorrecting the balance in the relationship when something you did has thrown it off balance.

Except they're not quite auto.

You have to *do* them.

And remember: There is no expiration date on apologies. You can apologize one second, five hours, two weeks, or ten years after the fact. However long the time, your apology, if sincere, tends to have the same effect on your wife: It touches her heart, makes her feel better, and gets both of you back to feeling close to each other.

THE MOVE

Find in your memory something you've done in your marriage—years ago or recently—that has caused significant hurt and pain to your wife, and she still carries the wound in her heart.

Following the steps of the World-Class Apology, go to your wife and say you're sorry.

If you feel like getting on a roll, try to remember everything you've done that has *ever* caused her hurt or pain, and apologize for those too—World-Class.

And do your best to never do any of it again.

A WORD TO THE WIVES

If you're trying to get us husbands to see that we've done something wrong or bad in the relationship, do everything you can think of to keep us from going into the badlands.

Good luck.

Preface your correction of us with something kind and exculpatory, like, "Terrell, I am *not* saying this to make you feel bad or because in any way I think you're bad. Please don't go there. You're *not* bad, you're *good*. I just wish, for future reference, you'd ask me before inviting your mother over to spend the whole day with us on Mother's Day."

Or you can sandwich your correction of us between two ringing praises of us, like, "Vernon, you are one of the best automobile mechanics the world has ever known, and I'd appreciate it if you'd not reassemble any more fuel pumps on the dining room table from now on, and thank you for being your big old lovable galoot self."

Or you can do it while you're watching football with us, or the World Series.

Or do what my wife does when she's "bringing something up" with me and I start going into my badlands: When I start going into "Do I ever do anything *good* in your eyes, Jane?! I can never win," Jane just says, "Don't you dare go there, Robert, or I'll kill you."

That works pretty good. Anything. Just keep us out of the badlands.

Good luck.

CHAPTER 34

Getting All A's

For years I've been taking for granted the most wonderful thing that's ever happened to me. You! I've never shown you the appreciation you deserve, Alice. Baby, you're the greatest!

Ralph Kramden

A good husband takes complete responsibility for helping his wife feel good about herself.

He realizes that most human beings, as a general psychological condition, feel not so good about themselves, that women in our culture have been particularly conditioned to feel bad about themselves, and that his wife has her own personal life story that did a number on her self-esteem.

Her low self-esteem may take the form of insecurity about her looks, competitiveness with other women, a general sense of inferiority, timidity, self-judgment, self-denigration, or outright self-hatred. To whatever degree she feels bad about herself, a good husband assumes the responsibility to help her feel good.

It's pretty easy to do, actually.

Just do a lot of nice things for her and say a lot of nice things to her.

I want that to stick in your mind, so I'm going to repeat it:

Just do a lot of nice things for her and say a lot of nice things to her.

Every time you do something nice for her, every time you treat her with love and respect, you're helping her believe that she's worthy of that, that she's likable and lovable, that she's attractive, that she's *good*. And every time you say something nice to her, something positive and appreciative and admiring and loving, those words go all the way down to her heart and help make her feel better about herself.

It's really true.

You have a huge role to play here.

Words count, and *your* words count the most to her. So if you're in the habit of saying negative, critical, demeaning, unkind words to your wife—*words that make her feel bad about herself*—cut it out immediately and start saying words that make her feel good about herself.

Compliment her. Commend her. Praise her. Acknowledge her.

And thank her—for everything you can think of.

If she's discouraged, say words that encourage her.

If she's feeling down or putting herself down, say words that'll lift her up.

Never get tired of this. Do it when you're feeling good and do it when you're feeling bad. You can even be depressed and feeling lousy about yourself and your life, and still do it. Just do it.

It's *the* way to use words with your wife. It's the language to speak to her in. Learn it.

Here's your first lesson: It's called Getting All A's.

At any given moment, if you're wondering what words to say to your wife, say words that carry the message of one of these A's:

Awareness of her: "You seem kind of stressed today, honey. Want any help with anything?"

Attention: "I'd be happy to sit with you and talk about your career. Sure, I have time."

Affection: "When I was watering the lawn, I was looking at you through the kitchen window and realizing how much I love you."

Acknowledgment: "I noticed you got new skates for the kids this week. That must have been quite an outing! Thanks!"

Appreciation: "I really appreciate all the help you gave me in the garage last weekend. I've been avoiding it for months, and your doing it with me made it actually fun."

Affirmation: "I'm really proud of the way you behaved with Jody and how you feel about it all. You're right, she's full of shit."

Admiration: "I admire the daughter you are to your parents. They're very lucky."

Apology: "I'm sorry I get so wrapped up in myself sometimes that I forget about you. I should have taken better care of you last week when you had that cold."

Assurance: "Of course I'll still love you when we're sixty-four! Are you kidding? I'll love you more!"

Amusement: "I love seeing you sort through all your mail-order catalogs each week and arrange them alphabetically. It's so *you* and so nuts it always gives me a laugh."

Amazement: "How you manage to do all the things you do for this family blows my mind! You're awesome!"

Amorousness: "God, you're pretty! Got any plans tonight?"

Adoration: "I adore you, my darling . . . Je t'adore, ma chérie . . . Te adoro, querida mia . . . Ti adoro, mia cara . . . Ya tebya obozhayu, moya dorogaya . . . Habibati, azizati."

See what I mean?
All A's.
Simple.
Speak like this to her in little loving notes that you leave on the kitchen counter in the morning, and in e-mails during the day, and in phone calls you make to her at odd moments, and in voice mails when you don't reach her. If you're really wealthy, you can hire a blimp to float over the town with "I LOVE YOU, EVELYN!!!" blinking in large red letters on the side of it. But for most of us a simple voice mail message from you would do the trick: "Hi, honey. Just called to say hello and see how you're doin'. Call me back if you get a chance. I love you, and look forward to our little date tonight."

Say words like these frequently. To whatever degree your wife doesn't feel good about herself, make her feel good with your words.

When I say "frequently," by the way, I don't mean four or five times a year on birthdays, anniversaries, and major holidays; I mean four or five times a day over all the days of your marriage.

It takes a long time to wear down a person's negative self-judgment and help her feel good about herself.

Marriage is a long time.

If speaking like this to your wife feels unfamiliar and awkward to you, don't worry about it. When you were first learning to drive a stick shift, hit a golf ball, or do anything worth doing, how unfamiliar and awkward was that?

Because it was new.

Then you practiced it and got used to it and got good at it, and now it's second nature.

By practicing speaking like this to your wife, it, too, will become second nature. It'll just be the way you speak to her.

The point is to take complete responsibility for how that woman feels about herself. Not the kind of responsibility that says you caused her to feel that way (for the most part, you didn't) or the kind that says you can totally fix her (you can't), but the responsibility that says you can do a lot to help—which you can: *Just do a lot of nice things for her and say a lot of nice things to her.*

Help her feel as she deserves to feel: great about herself.

She's a great lady. Help her come to know her greatness.

THE MOVE

When you're about to say words to your wife, before speaking them run them through this inner filter: *Will these words make my wife feel worse or better about herself?*

If they'll make her feel worse, don't say them.

If they'll make her feel better, if they're one of the A's, say them.

CHAPTER 35

A Good Father

For Greta and Matt

Whenever I try to recall that long-ago first day at school,
only one memory shines through: My father held my hand.

Marcelene Cox

I'm gonna watch you shine
Gonna watch you grow
Gonna paint a sign
So you'll always know
As long as one and one is two
There could never be a father loved his daughter
More than I love you.

Paul Simon

You can't be a good husband and a bad father at the same time, because bad fathering causes so much pain and distress to your wife that it ends up being bad husbanding.

So be a good father.

Be a *great* father.

It's not hard.

Protect and support your children.

Guide and instruct them.

Feed them lunch.

Fix their toys.

Do the laundry sometimes.

Hang out with your kids—a lot. Read to them, talk to them, listen to them, smile at them.

Play with them—a lot—and get down on the floor and play *their* games. Even Candyland. And when the game's over and they say, "Again, Daddy!" play it again.

Yup, even Candyland.

Always be gentle with them. Your gentleness with them means your wife doesn't have to be always looking in to see how you're doing with them. She can go take a nap or a walk or a weekend off because she *knows* how you're doing with them: You're always doing gently with them. "The father's role," says the philosopher Joseph Chilton Pearce, "is to support the mother right down the line and provide her with a safe space that is free of fear, so that the child's safe space, first within the mother and later with her, is never in question."

Ask them lots of questions about their lives and their feelings about their lives, and do not make them ashamed of any of their feelings. Whatever age they are, remember what it was like when you were that age, and the feelings normal to that age, and make them feel okay about it all. "It's a wise father who knows his own child—hood," goes an old saying.

As they get older, keep asking them questions about their lives, but expect fewer answers. When they're teenagers, forget it.

You'll hardly get a hello, never mind answers, but keep asking the questions anyway—teenagers won't say so, but they appreciate your interest—and whatever you do, make sure they're not down in the basement making bombs. Or drinking or drugging. Or doing weird stuff on the computer.

Clean up your own life so you can be a living model of everything you want them to be. "Dear God," prays the Jewish sage Rebbe Nachman of Breslov, "teach me to embody those ideals I would want my children to learn from me. Let them find in me the values and the behavior I hope to see in them." "Example is not the main thing in influencing others," says Albert Schweitzer. "It is the only thing."

Remember you're the father. The parent. The adult. Along with your wife, the voice of authority for your children. Set clear limits and boundaries for them. Teach them that there are rules and regulations, moral precepts and principles of right behavior on this earth. Teach them that actions have consequences on this earth, that *their* actions have consequences in this family, and impose the consequences consistently, fairly, and authoritatively. Permit what is permissible and don't permit what is impermissible.

Always exercise your authority with respect.

Love them and serve them.

Help them and hold them.

In every possible way give them a sense of safety, security, and inner well-being.

Spend tons of time with them. Pay great attention to them. Not bullshit attention, like the father I saw at the pool one day.

I was sitting on a chaise lounge at a hotel swimming pool last summer. Across from me was a man on a chair reading a newspaper. His son—maybe ten years old—was in the pool.

"Look, Daddy!" said the boy. "I can swim the whole way across *underwater!*"

The father unenthusiastically lowered the newspaper and looked at his son.

"Watch, Daddy!"

The boy took a deep breath, checked one last time to see if his father was looking, and dove in. Immediately the father raised the newspaper again and started reading. Frog-kicking like crazy, the boy swam underwater to the far side of the pool and came up gasping for breath along the wall just below his father. Blinking water out of his eyes, he looked up at his dad, who was completely hidden behind the newspaper.

The boy's head fell. He hung there on the wall, silent, for a minute or two, and then slowly swam off.

That father should have made that moment about his child, not about the news. The only news this man needed to hear is that when you're a father, on some deep level of your being you make *every* moment about your child, running everything you do and everything you say and everything you are through the inner filter of, "How is this going to influence my son? How is this going to affect my daughter?"

Remember that your children are affected by everything you do, say, and are, and they're always watching you, and they're always watching for *love.* They are particularly watching for love and respect between their father and mother because when they look up from their games and their books and see that all's right in the adult world, they don't get hijacked into that world but can go back to their world with a great feeling of peace and security inside, and be free to grow and develop in their world as nature intended. That's why, as Leonard Cohen says about the children in his song "Suzanne," "They are leaning out for love, and they will lean that way forever." And that's why, as one author puts it, "The most important thing a father can do for his children is to love their mother."

A team of child psychologists once posed the question *What does love mean?* to a group of four- to six-year-olds. Here are a few of their answers:

- "When my grandma got arthritis, she couldn't bend over and paint her toenails anymore. So my grandpa does it for her now all the time, even when his hands got arthritis too." (Maureen, aged six)
- "Love is when my daddy makes coffee for my mommy and he takes a sip before giving it to her, to make sure the taste is okay." (Darnell, aged five)
- "Love is when you kiss all the time. Then when you get tired of kissing, you still want to be together and you talk more. My mommy and daddy are like that." (Heather, aged five)
- "When you love somebody, your eyelashes go up and down and little stars come out of you." (Kassia, aged four)

Realizing that his children are watching *this* closely, and they're watching for *love*, and they're *always* watching for love, and they're always watching *him*, a good husband finds it rather easy to be a good father.

THE MOVE

Ask your wife to tell you the ways in which you are already a good father.

Bask in her acknowledgment and keep being those ways.

Now ask her to tell you all the ways in which you could stand some improvement as a father.

Listen up.

Get to work.

CHAPTER 36

My Father's Teaching

The great man does not think beforehand of his words that they may be sincere, nor of his actions that they may be resolute—he simply speaks and does what is right.

Mencius

I leave this rule for others when I'm dead:
Be always sure you're right—then go ahead.

Davy Crockett

When I think of the greatness of men, I don't immediately think of famous men like Abraham Lincoln or Albert Einstein or Martin Luther King Jr. I think of my father.

My father, Jack Alter, owned a small furniture store in Boston. He worked six days a week to support his wife and two children and somehow managed to come to most of my Little League games. He was tall and well built and handsome. He was funny.

And tough. At the age of fifty-nine he started having a hard time with his health, suffering two heart attacks, a number of different cancers, and finally, for the last four years of his life, his kidneys gone, dialysis. He died in 2000 at the age of eighty-seven. He was really tired.

By the world's standards he wasn't a great man. He never got rich or famous or powerful, he didn't compose symphonies or discover vaccines or hit five hundred home runs. But he embodied an aspect of manliness that to me is the *essence* of manliness. My father's teaching was, *Always do right.*

"Do it right, Bobby," he would say—about everything. About washing the car, shoveling snow, my stance in the batter's box, my jump shot, my homework, the way I spoke to my mother and sister, the way I lived my life. "Do it right, Bobby. Don't ever do anything wrong."

On hearing about some wrongdoer in the news, like an embezzler or a wife beater or a corrupt politician, he would say, "That isn't *right*," his voice coming down like a hammer on the word "right"—and that was *it* for him. A man's behavior was either right or wrong for Jack Alter. If a person did right, if a man was a mensch, my father liked that man. If a person did wrong, that person was *off his list forever*.

My father was a great man in my eyes because he taught me that the greatness of a man is the degree to which he does what's right.

A true man, a real man, a great man, wants to do *only* what's right. He wants to get his actions, his thoughts and words—*himself*—right. By getting himself right, he ends up creating rightness all around him.

A right man, in other words, creates a right world.

You are that right man.

Really, you *are*.

You have an innate sense of rightness in you, and you aspire to live it.

That's manhood, that aspiration. That's greatness. The always aiming for, the reaching high for the right and the good. That reaching is what the erect phallus is *really* about. It is greatness in a husband to want to become a greater husband.

When I am trying to get a man to do this good-husband work, to keep going, to keep changing, I tell him, simply, it's the right thing to do.

Always do the right thing, I tell him.

When I am telling him that, I am simply passing on what my father told me. That was my father's teaching. That's Jack Alter's message to the world.

THE MOVE

Measure everything you do this week (and forever after) according to this criterion: "Is it right or wrong?"

That action, that thing I just did . . . the way I just spoke to my wife . . . spending so little time with my kids this weekend because of golf . . . declaring the trip to New York as a business expense . . . this thing I'm thinking of doing to get a leg up on my competitors . . . that stunt I pulled last week to get out of jury duty . . . what I do in my private time when nobody's looking . . . Is it right or wrong? Is it the right thing to do?

Be like my father. Measure it *all* by *Is it right?*

If you're confused about what's right and what's wrong, seek guidance from someone who might be less confused.

Like your wife.

Go to her and say to her, "Could you help me out here? I don't know if the way I just spoke to you was right or wrong."

She'll like that, and she'll know.

CHAPTER 37

Respect

> *R-E-S-P-E-C-T!*
> *Find out what it means to me!*
>
> Aretha Franklin

> *Anything you want, you got it*
> *Anything you need, you got it*
> *Anything at all, you got it . . .*
>
> Roy Orbison

Whatever you want, honey . . . It's up to you . . . Whatever you want to do is fine with me . . . Whatever . . .

I find myself saying words like these to Jane a lot. More and more.

Whatever you want, hon . . . Fine with me . . . Let's do what you want to do . . .

What's going on here? This isn't the way a man's supposed to be with a woman! A man's supposed to be *decisive, in charge.* A man rules the roost. Holy mackerel, have I turned into a complete nerd? A pansy? A wuss? Am I . . . am I . . . am I . . . *whipped*?!

No, that's not what this is at all.

It's the opposite of that.

It's a man finally being a man—a man who's in love with a woman. It's Barry White singing, "Whatever you want, girl, you got it, and what you need I don't want to see you without it," and Al Green, "I'm so in love with you, whatever you want to do is all right with me."

It's me finally learning what mature manhood is. It's me growing up and finally getting it that as a man I'm here on this earth to serve and I'm in this marriage to serve Jane. It's me finally learning to *respect* my wife.

Respect means "high regard, considerate attention, deferential esteem." Etymologically it means to "re-spect"—literally to "look back at," to "see again." It means looking at your wife, and looking at her again, and seeing again and again the particular person that she is, and what she might be feeling or wanting or needing from you in that moment.

There she is, standing by the mirror brushing her hair before bed. Looking pensive. You know that look. Sad? Maybe. Tired? Probably. It's been a long day for her. You know that about her day today. That's *seeing* her. That's respect. Most days are long for her. You know that too. That's respect. She puts the brush down and turns toward the bed. Yes, she does look tired. You see that. That's respect. As she comes into bed, you hold the covers open for her because you know she likes that. You know what she likes and what she doesn't like. That's respect. She lies down, and you don't do or say anything sexual to her, even though you might

want to, because that's not where she's at. That's plain as day, and
that's respect. She lets out a long breath, and you stroke her hair.
That's respect.

When she wakes up in the morning, it'll all be different. To
respect her then is to see that she's got about two million things
to do before she can get out of the house to go to work, and you
serve her by doing some of those things for her. You pull the car
out of the garage for her. You put up the coffee. You handle the
kids' breakfast. You do all this out of respect for her, because you
can actually *see* her—what she's thinking, feeling, wanting, and
needing.

This respect I'm talking about, though it's always changing
and it never stops, is really quite simple: You just pay attention to
her. You attune to her. You attend to her.

Here are five things that happened this week that in the past
Jane and I would have had conflict over, but we didn't this week
because I'm growing up and learning to respect my wife:

• We're driving in the car to visit our daughter, son-in-law,
and grandchildren, who live in the next town over. I'm driving.
I want to go the usual way on the main road. Jane wants to go the
back way, to avoid possible traffic. I know for sure there won't be
traffic this time of day, and for a moment I want to argue the
point, but I don't. I let it go. *Whatever*. She wants to go the back
way? We go the back way.

• I'm watching a rerun of *NYPD Blue* on TV. I love *NYPD
Blue*, and I'm into it. Jane comes into the living room, looks
through the *TV Guide*, and asks if she can watch a show about
French impressionism on PBS. I'm about to put up a pretty big
fight (as in, "What?! This is *NYPD Blue*!"), but . . . on second
thought . . . *whatever* . . . and I give her the remote, say a sad,

silent good-bye to Simone and Sipowicz, and settle in for some good ol' Toulouse-Lautrec.

• Jane calls down to me, "I'm going for a walk. Want to join me?"

I call back up from where I'm writing. "Now?"

"Yeah," she calls down. "I have to go right now so I can get to work on time."

The writing is going well, and I really don't want to go for a walk, at least not right now, but I know she wants me to, she likes the company, so . . . *whatever* . . . I tell her I'll be up in a minute, and I am.

• Jane's in a really bad mood today and answers irritably when I ask her a question. I feel stung, upset, a little pissed off. I'm going to bring it up to her. I'm going to *object*! Goddammit, I'm going to make her feel bad for treating me like that!

Nah.

She has a right to be in a bad mood sometimes. She hardly ever is. I don't need to say anything. *Whatever*. I go over and rub her neck for a few seconds and then leave her alone.

• Jane says the house is too hot.

I say it's not, it's fine.

She wants the air-conditioning on.

I don't. I'll be too cold.

We talk about it for a few minutes. Battle lines start to get drawn. Argument coming! Uh-oh.

Suddenly I get it. I remember. I'm a *man*, I'm supposed to take care of her. This moment isn't about me, it's about her. If I get cold, I'll put on a flannel shirt . . . I'll put on a wool sweater . . .

hell, I'll put on my arcticwear! *Whatever*. I'm a man; I want my wife to be comfortable; I can be cold; I can deal.

The hidden cause of marital conflict is *your* attachment to what *you* want—so the way to achieve marital harmony is for you to let go of your attachment.

"But she's attached to what she wants too, y'know!" you're saying.

Right. You're absolutely right. She is.

So *you* let go, dingaling.

The moment you do, you're doing what you're supposed to do as a grown-up man in your relationship with your wife: You're respecting her.

A real man really *sees* his wife, and sees every moment as another opportunity to show respect for her.

THE MOVE

This week, whenever the potential for disagreement and discord arises between you and your wife, whatever your side of it is, let it go.

Just let it go.

A good way to practice letting go—to see how easy it really is—is to pick up something right now, like this book or a paper clip, and hold it in front of you.

Go ahead. Pick something up and hold it.

Now let it go.

Drop it. Just drop it.

It drops.

It's that easy.

So this week, whenever the potential for disagreement and discord arises between you and your wife, whatever your side of it is, let it go, just drop it.

Whatever you want, honey . . . Fine with me . . . I'm so in love with you, girl, whatever you want to do is all right with me.

Maturity.

Manhood.

Respect for your wife.

CHAPTER 38

Connection and Love

Connect *vt to join or be joined; fasten together;
link; couple; be closely or intimately associated;
be in relationship; tie; bind; unite*

Are you ready for the thing called love?

Bonnie Raitt

Has your wife ever said to you, "I just don't feel connected to you" or "We're not connected"? Have you ever thought about that—what she means?

Think about this:

Your wife is physically, psychologically, and spiritually built for connection. She thrives on connection. Her sense of self and her sense of well-being grow out of connection. I don't know what you thought you were promising to do when you said, "I do," on your wedding day, but let me break it to you: What you were promising to do was to connect with her.

Connection is love. The first time you said, "I love you," to her, and every time since, you are promising to be connected with her.

So keep your promise.

Connection is not something that just automatically happened when you got married to her; it's something you have to do—*you* have to do—on a regular basis. You have to do certain things and say certain things and be certain ways. It's a constant effort, a practice, your lifelong daily labor of love.

Here are some ways to connect with your wife, to love her. Some of them I've already written about in this book, but we're nearing the end of the book now, so I thought I'd put them all together here, organized for your easy reference.

You can connect with your wife:

- **With your face.** You smile at her. You smile back at her when she's smiling at you, you smile at her because you like her, and you smile at her for no particular reason, just to be smiling at her, just because that's her. Your eyes light up when she walks into the room. When she's talking to you, there's attention and interest in your face. When she's not feeling well or just having a hard time of it in life, there's kindness and caring on your face. When she's all dolled up looking snazzy, there's that glint in your eye. Wherever she's at, whatever she's going through, your face is there for her, expressive and empathic, like a mirror that always reflects back to her the kind of love she needs in that moment.

- **With spoken words.** You talk to her. You talk to her *a lot*. You always use a gentle tone with her. You leave her loving voice mails every day. You say loving, supportive, understanding, kind words to her—every day. You ask her lots of questions about herself, her life, her needs, her feelings, and you say, "Tell me more about that" a lot. You say words to show her your high regard for her, words of acknowledgment and appreciation and gratitude and praise. You say, "I love you" a lot, and "You're my girl," and "I'm your boy," and "You're so pretty I can't take my eyes off you," and "How do I love thee? Let me count the ways," and then you start counting.

• **With written words.** You write little thank-you notes every day to her for everything you can think to thank her for. On birthday cards and anniversary cards and Valentine cards and other holiday cards, you write more than "Love, Dwight"; you write, "Dear Lucia, You are a wonderful wife to me," and go on from there, celebrating her existence. You leave little scrap-paper notes on the kitchen counter when you go to work, or to the store, or to nap, or to the shed to organize the tools: "Hi, hon. I'm in the shed organizing the tools. Come in and say hello. Love ya, Donny." You e-mail her humorous little loving messages during the day. Every once in a while, when the impulse strikes, you write her long, loving letters on nice stationery, extolling all her wonderful qualities and expressing your deep love and devotion for her. If you really like to write, and if you fancy yourself a writer, you can even write a book about becoming a good husband to her.

• **With your body.** When the two of you are walking together, you give her your arm or take hers or hold hands. When the two of you are walking together and you're both feeling young and frisky, you swing hands. When you're driving in the car or you're at the movies or sitting on the couch watching TV, you hold her hand or put your hand on her knee or put your arm around her. Sometimes you take her in your arms and you hug her, hold her, enwrap her in your strength and love. You come up behind her in the kitchen and hold her around. You hold her when she's feeling down and sit with her and hold her when she's crying. You offer foot massages, neck massages, shoulder massages, head massages, back massages—and you don't try to turn any of them into sex. (If *she* tries to turn them into sex, that's a different story.) When it's time for sex, you serve her sexually by making long, heavenly love to her. On impulse and for no particular reason, you get up from where you are and go to wherever she is in the house and just touch her—her cheek, her hair, her waist, her arm—not to get sex from her, not to get anything from her, but just to connect with her, just to let her know that even when you're not with her, you're with her, you feel connected to her, you're in love with her.

• **With your actions.** Everything you do, every behavior, every act you perform, whether it's in her presence or not, you do it with her in mind. What effect will this action have on her life or feelings? Is this thing I'm doing a service or a disservice to her? Is it loyalty or disloyalty? Will it please or displease her? In this way, you stay connected to her in all that you do on this planet. You do lots of nice things for her—gentlemanly things, helping hands, acts of kindness, civilities, chivalries. Big things like sitting down with her for an hour or two and helping her map out a strategy to get the promotion she wants at work, or helping her reorganize her filing cabinet, and little things like helping her put away the groceries she just brought in, or going to the cellar to get the batteries she needs for her alarm clock, or making sure the paper tray on her printer always has paper in it, or taking the kids to the park Saturday morning so she can have some alone time. You take her to nice places, give her nice gifts, treat her like a lady. You encourage her to tell you what she needs from you, and when she does, you fall all over yourself trying to provide it. When you're in doubt about what to do or not to do in your life, you remember that you have dedicated and devoted your life to her, and then you act accordingly.

In all these ways you connect with your wife. In all these ways you're telling her, *I'm thinking about you. You are always in my consciousness. I feel connected to you. I'm in love with you.*

And remember: When it comes to connection with your wife, what you give, you will get. What you sow, you reap. That's the way it is with women. They're givers-back. A woman said it perfectly in my therapy office the other day. She was talking to her husband, who was asking for more attention and connection from her.

"The way to ask me for it," she said, "is not to ask me for it, but to give it to me, because when you give it to me, I feel like giving it to you."

THE MOVE

Are you ready for the thing called love?

Using this chapter as a resource, come up with a written list of some of the connecting, loving things you could say or do with your wife. Customize the list to her—to what you know feels like connection to her. For example, if your wife likes you to get up from the couch (where you're watching *Celebrity Poker Showdown* on Bravo—with celebrities you never heard of) and come to the back door and greet her when she comes home from work and take her tote bag or briefcase or whatever she's carrying, you put that on your list.

And then you *do* the things on the list.

You can immediately start doing them all, or do them gradually, a few at a time, adding new ones over time, until you're doing them all, all the time.

CHAPTER 39

Change!

Women . . . want more than to be understood
by their men; they want men to change.

Terrence Real

After marriage, all things change.
And one of them better be you.

Elizabeth Hawes

Bottom line: We're men who have married women who want us to stop being (mostly) at fault for the problems in our relationships, who want us to learn how to connect with them and have truly intimate relationships without any problems. So we have to *change*. Our ideas and attitudes about women and marriage and manhood have to change, and our behavior toward our wives has to change.

It's like all those makeover shows on TV these days. We men

need a makeover. Some of us need an extreme makeover. This book is about the supreme makeover of husbands that women are totally fed up with into good husbands they love and admire.

There are two ways that change happens in a human being: instantly or gradually. If you're the kind of guy who can finish this book and it makes enough sense to you that you immediately become the good husband it's telling you to become—boom! you're a changed man! If you're quick like that, a regular Mercury Morris, great, do it—your wife'll be delighted with you, and your marriage will feel great to you. If you're like most of us and you change gradually, that's fine too, because you end up at the exact same place as the guy who changed instantly—with a wife who's delighted with you and a marriage that feels great to you. It just takes a little longer.

For us gradual changers, it's important to understand how change really works, so right now go back and read about the three Cs in "Her Introduction" (pages 44–45). That's how gradual change happens. First, our *consciousness* changes as we learn and accept new ideas about how we're supposed to be in our marriages; then the change moves into our *conduct* as these new ideas settle in and become new behaviors; and then if we practice the new behaviors long enough and consistently enough, the change finally enters our *character* as the new man we have become.

Voilà, a good husband!

Here are two stories from my therapy practice of men who sailed the three Cs of change and made it to good husband.

Cal

Because of his father's physical and emotional absence from his family, Cal had been enlisted throughout his childhood as the primary emotional support for his depressed mother, often having to sit with her for long periods and listen to her woes. As a result, he found it close to impossible to be emotionally attentive to his wife, Carole, for anything but the briefest moment, and he would always find ways to go off by himself—to his office, to television, to his neighborhood coffee shop—when she needed him. This, of course, drove Carole crazy, and she spent long periods of time— and twelve years of marriage—lonely and dissatisfied in her marriage, and furious at Cal.

So they came into therapy, and Carole and I started making it very clear to Cal that it was his responsibility as her husband to give her the attention she needed when she needed it. Carole told him that every time he saw that she was sad or upset, his face changed, got dark and distant—like inside he'd *gone*—and within a few minutes he'd be really gone, in his office working or in the den watching the news. I told him that what he's supposed to do in such moments is to stay with Carole even though it was uncomfortable for him. I told him that when as a boy he had to pay attention to his mother instead of the mother being a mother and paying attention to him, his ability to pay attention to his wife in his adult life got damaged. In his case, I told him, it was big-time damage, which is why he couldn't sit for more than a minute with Carole when she had emotional needs. Cal listened to all this with interest. It made sense to him—he saw the cause and effect of it. For the next few weeks in therapy he told us stories about his mother, what it was like having to sit on the couch with her for an hour after dinner while his father was on the porch reading the newspaper and chain-smoking cigarillos.

At the end of one session I gave Cal an assignment. "For this next week," I said, "whenever you feel the urge to leave Carole's presence, don't succumb to it, *don't* leave, but do the opposite: Stay with her and do everything in your power to let your atten-

tion flow out to her. Just sit there and give her attention. Don't
tell her how hard this is for you, or what it's bringing up in you,
or *anything* about you—that'd be just another form of the attention flowing to you, and we want it flowing to Carole. This week
the entire flow of attention should be from you to your wife.
Think you can do that?"

"Yeah, I can try."

He spent the week doing that and reported in his next therapy session that it was hard, and it did bring up a lot of stuff inside, particularly anxiety and inadequacy, but he did it. It didn't
feel good to him, it didn't feel like anything he knew how to do,
and most of the time he was faking it—but he stayed.

I asked him if he'd be willing to "reenlist," to practice the
same new behavior of staying with Carole and giving her his attention for the next *two* weeks. He agreed.

He practiced staying with Carole for the next two weeks and
started to get a little more comfortable with it and better at it.

Then one session he reported this:

"I was sitting with her in our bedroom, and she was upset
about a phone call she had just had with her stepbrother, and I
could tell she wanted me to stay with her and talk to her about
it. Seeing her need, I kind of regressed at that moment—everything in me wanted to get the hell out of there and get back to
the remodeling project I'm doing in the bathroom. Then it was
like I heard a voice in my brain talking to me, saying, *Cal, nothing new or good happens here if you do that, if you go away from Carole. Let me do something different this time. Let me stay with her and
try to get my attention to come out of myself and pay attention to her.*

"Then I realized that in order to do that I would have to first
acknowledge the little boy inside me, the one we've been talking
about who used to sit with his mother for all those hours, and tell

him I would see him later, but it's time for him to go to bed now, that this moment was not for children. A grown-up was needed here. A man was required. It didn't feel fake or driven by guilt. It felt like a very deliberate decision on where to put my attention—on my wife. And so I did that, and stayed with Carole and felt good about it. It felt *adult*. It was great."

That was the moment that the change in Cal started to move from conduct to character. Carole reported that ever since that day the quality of Cal's attention to her changed dramatically: Now it felt real, now it felt like she had a husband who cared about her and knew how to care for her.

"For the first time in our marriage I feel like I'm married to a *man*," she said.

Tomás

Tomás, a fifty-one-year-old executive at a biotech company, had been married for seventeen years to Rita. She had brought him into therapy because he could be so controlling and critical around the house, especially when he'd come home from a business trip, that she and the kids just tried to stay out of his way. During a recent dinner he had gotten angry at his oldest son because he was chewing too loudly, "masticating like a goddamn cow!"

"This behavior has to stop," said Rita. "I can't live like this anymore. And he's blowing it with the kids. He's losing authority with them. I can see it. They don't listen to him anymore, except out of fear."

"Tomás," I said, "the behavior that Rita is describing is not okay, and I know that on some level of your being you know that. So let's figure out what part of you thinks it *is* okay for a husband

and father to act like this in his family, and then you can cut it out. Are you game?"

He thought about it for a moment. "I'm here," he said.

So we did that. We spent the next few weeks talking mainly about Tomás's father, and the horrible scenes at the dining room table when Tomás was growing up, including the time his father suddenly smacked Tomás off his chair because his fork was scraping the plate too loudly. In the meantime Tomás was disciplining himself at home, restraining his impulses to criticize the kids' behavior all the time, letting go of his need to control every moment and dictate how everybody was supposed to be.

"I'm getting it," he said at the end of one session. "I understand now that I'm just doing my version of what was done to me, and thinking that's the way I'm *supposed* to be in my family. I've been really wrong about all this."

There was a long pause as he sat there thinking.

"I have to stay close to this," he said. "I know I could lose this. I have to remember this."

"In order to stay close to it," I said, "it'd be good if you could name it. What's the thing you're trying to stay close to? What's the thing you want to remember?"

He sat there thinking. I expected him to say, "Being different than my dad was with us," or "Being a good husband and father," or "Remembering the past," or something like that.

He didn't.

"*Honor,*" he said. "I need to remember *honor.*"

The room got very still for a moment. Rita was looking at him intently.

"What do you mean, Tomás?" I asked.

"It's a question of honor. I have to remember that for me to be a man of honor, I have to realize all this, I have to become a different man than my father was. This is about the fundamental principles and values by which I live my life. Listening to what Rita and you are telling me about all this, and changing the way I've been with her and the kids, is a question of my honor as a man."

Tears welled up in Rita's eyes. She got up from her chair and went over to Tomás and hugged him.

"You're really changing, Tomás," she said. "Thank you!"

Change happens. Big-time change, permanent change—*transformation*—happens. It happens because you're a good man and a smart man and you come to the understanding that it needs to happen, so you make it happen. The big change. The makeover. The supreme makeover into a good husband.

THE MOVE

Go to your wife and say this:

"At this point in our marriage, if you could give me a makeover as a husband, the way I talk to you, the way I behave to you, the way I behave in the family, the way I look, the way I dress, our sex life, everything, if you could give me a complete makeover, what would you do to me? How would you change me? How would you change me so that when I became the new man, you'd be amazed and stand up and applaud wildly and think that I was now the man of your dreams?"

Tell her to take a couple of days and make a list of all the changes she wants to see in you and to put "ASAP" next to the ones she wants you to make right away, and to give it to you when she's done. Her list might look something like this:

1. Show interest in me. Ask me what I'm doing and where I'm going that day. ASAP.
2. Remember things I say. ASAP.
3. Take my advice.
4. Hang up your clothes. ASAP.
5. Empty the dishwasher sometimes.
6. Take the kids with you on your errands more often so I can have some time to myself. ASAP.
7. When you come home from basketball Tuesday nights, don't always be in a bad mood if you lost.
8. When you ask me to do something for you and I say I can't, accept that, and don't get angry at me or try to pressure me into it. ASAP.
9. Don't always be commenting on how I *look*. Say things about me—*inside*.
10. Don't lecture me.
11. Be nicer to me. ASAP.

When she hands it to you, thank her, and think of it as your "honey-do" list for the rest of your life, and start doing all the things on the list.

CHAPTER 40

Consistency

Like a rock, I was strong as I could be
Like a rock, nothin' ever got to me
Like a rock, I was somethin' to see
Like a rock . . .

Bob Seger

All this great changing you're doing?

Being gentle and kind and respectful to her? Listening to her? Actually sitting down and *talking* with her? Really learning to *connect* with her?

Good going!

Keep going!

They're great changes. Sea changes.

And whatever you do, don't change back!

Don't go back and forth, the good husband one day, *in rela-*

tionship, and then suddenly out of relationship, clueless and closed up, back to jerk, the next.

Women hate that.

Remember: The whole goal here is to make them feel *safe* with us so they can relax with us.

One of the reasons women *don't* feel safe with us is that we can be so inconsistent. One moment we're sweet as honey, attentive and loving, connected with them, and the next moment we're totally disconnected—silent and withdrawn . . . or angry . . . surly . . . in a *mood*. We turn on them.

And there's no predicting. No warning. No explaining. Out of *nowhere* we're disconnected again.

There, and then not there.

Nice, and then not nice.

Dr. Jekyll and Mr. Hyde.

Do you have your own version of that? Does your wife not know from one moment to the next which husband she's going to get?

She should know.

She should always get the good husband.

One woman client, Marie, referred to her husband as "Al One and Al Two." Al One was a nice, attentive man, soft-spoken, funny, interesting to talk to. When he was stressed, though, Al Two showed up. Al Two was, in her words, "a dictatorial little shit."

"And then," said Marie, "if you *oppose* him when he's like that? If you don't want to do what he wants to do? If you say any kind of 'no' to him? Watch out! He becomes *furious*. All bets are off at that point. I swear there's two of him."

Another woman referred to her husband as "good Gus and no Gus," depending on his mood. Good Gus liked to do things with the family, play with the kids, talk to her, have some fun, but sometimes he got dark, quiet, head down, eyes down, mouth set, barely speaking to anybody, and if she or one of the kids had to speak to him, they'd get a sharp, gruff reply.

"When he's in one of those moods," she said, "he's one big 'Leave me alone!' I can never *rely* on him. I don't know who's going to show up. I don't know who I'm going to get."

Be a man your wife can rely on.

A good husband is reliable, and a reliable man stays staunch and steady at his post. Dependable. Consistent. Constant. Solid. Like a rock.

A woman wants this kind of man. She wants her man to finally *get* it—to get it so deeply and completely that there's no *ungetting* it. Then she will know, from one moment to the next, that the husband she's going to get is the husband who has gotten it, the good husband, a man she can rely on to always be there for her, a man she feels safe with.

THE MOVE

There will be times—many times—when you're stressed or busy or out of sorts, *really* in a mood, or something will happen between you and your wife that'll throw you off your game—a disagreement, a rejection, one too many corrections of your behavior—and you'll find yourself feeling some of the old feelings you thought you had gotten beyond—mainly anger at her—and starting to go into some of the old behaviors you thought you had changed. You'll lose patience, raise your voice, turn away, disappear, and sulk and stew and generally make life miserable for her again. Just like in the old days. That will all happen. All that's still in you.

What to do?

• **Before it happens**. If any of these old feelings are rising up inside you, the trick is to catch them before they come *out* of you as behaviors. Head 'em off at the pass. Pause. Count to ten. Take a few deep breaths. Pray. As the feelings arise, ask yourself, *What will be the result if I let these feelings come out as words I say to her or those old ways I used to behave? What effect will that have on her and on our relationship? Is it worth it? Do I want to go back there?* Use any technique you can think of to practice self-restraint. The discipline you'll need in order to do this will be considerable, but it's way easier than the mess you're going to cause—and will have to process later with her!—if you let those feelings come out as behaviors (review Chapter 14).

• **While it's happening**. If bad words and bad tones are already coming out your mouth to her, if you've already lost it, the instant you become aware of that, stop! *In miten drinnen* just stop. Take a deep breath . . . another . . . another . . . get control of yourself, man . . . don't go on. You're stronger now. You don't have to go on. It's stupid to go on. The harmony you've been enjoying in the relationship is much more important than spewing this momentary feeling at her . . . Now relax, let your face soften, and say to your wife, "That was a lapse. I'm sorry. Let's try this discussion again. Let's start over. I'm sorry."

• **After it's happened**. If you've already blown it and there's been an argument, maybe a fight, and a disconnection, and you're off by yourself being pissed and punishing, surprise everybody on the planet, including yourself, by suddenly coming to your senses, going to her wherever she is in the house, and apologizing (review Chapter 33). Don't let yourself think, *This one's her fault.* Remember that it's (mostly) your fault . . . and then go to her . . . go to her . . . go to her.

In the meantime try and try and try to be consistent in the great changes you've made in your behavior to her. Try and try and try to not lapse or relapse into the old stuff.

This might help:

Close your eyes.

In your mind's eye see yourself standing upright, strong and steady and stable, like a post, like a pillar.

Stand there unwavering, unmoving, sound and firm.

Like a mountain.

Like a rock.

Like a *man.*

Steadfast. Unchangeable. Immovable.

That's *you.* You are that man. That's the essence of your manhood. That's a beautiful part of you.

That's what she wants from you.

Consistency. Constancy. Total reliability. Strength. Manhood.

Give her that.

Chapter 41

Who's the Boss?

Wisdom is the principal thing; therefore get wisdom.

Proverbs 4:7

If I could only learn to always turn to you
Instead of thinking I always know what to do
Why does it take the darkness for my eyes to see
There's never been a time when you weren't there for me?

Paul Overstreet

A marriage between a husband and wife is not just between the two of them. There's a third party involved. It's a triangle, a ménage à trois.

The third party is the truth.

When I say "the truth," I mean right perception of one's moral obligations on this earth, right understanding of the meaning and purpose of life, and right behavior in your marriage and everywhere.

Wisdom.

A marriage is a covenant between a husband and wife that they will always strive to obey the truth, to perform the constant practice of trying to do right by each other and by all others, to follow the dictates of wisdom.

So it doesn't matter to a good husband who's the boss, who commands and who obeys in his marriage, who leads and who follows. He doesn't care. He's happy to lead when he's nearer to the truth than his wife is, and happy to follow when she's closer. Makes no difference to him. He's mature now, so he has no need to be the king of the castle, the lord of the manor, the head of the household, or the boss of his wife.

Giving instruction or taking instruction. Obeying or commanding. Following or leading.

Irrelevant.

Who's the boss?

The truth is the boss.

Did you know that the words "audio" and "obey" have the same root? The implication is that when we hear the truth being spoken to us—by *any*one: our inner selves, our wives, our children, any person in our lives—we're supposed to obey it.

With respect to how to behave on this earth, it doesn't get any simpler than that.

If you've got a problem with obedience as a general principle of human behavior, get over it.

Obedience is a beautiful thing.

The beauty of obedience, when you're obeying the truth, is that by virtue of the power of your obedience, you acquire the power of the truth and can then speak with the authority of the truth. This gives you the authority to instruct and guide and even command others when it's necessary. This, by the way, is the true authority that children respect.

"Only he who obeys can command," say the sages of the Vedas.

The Christian sage Thomas à Kempis echoes it: "No one can firmly command save he who has learned gladly to obey."

And the two things are really the same anyway, obeying and commanding, for in the realm of the truth, there's really no obeying and commanding, and no one who is bossing anybody else; there's just the truth and two people trying to live by it in their marriage.

My clients Sophia and Bob were talking about her parents' upcoming visit for Thanksgiving. Bob was sullen because Sophia had been angry at him for a few days.

"Ask her why she's angry at you, Bob," I said.

"I *know* why she's angry at me," he said.

"No, you don't," Sophia said. "You've never asked me."

"Go ahead, ask her, Bob," I said. "Say, 'Why are you angry at me?' and put her name at the end of it."

"Why are you angry at me, Sophia?" he said.

"Before you answer, Sophia," I said, "appreciate him for asking that question."

She nodded. "Yes, I do like it when you ask me questions like that, Bob. I do appreciate it."

"And now answer his question," I said.

"I'm angry at you because of the way you always get whenever my parents come to visit. For twenty-two years. I can't stand it anymore. I can't stand the sniping comments at my mom. I can't stand the hostility coming out of you. I can't stand that you're reading—*reading!*—at the dining room table when people are sitting around talking. I can't stand your wandering off without saying a word to any of us and the next thing I know you've gone to bed!"

"Sophia, tell him how you want it to be this Thanksgiving," I said. "And, Bob, I want you to listen to Sophia like you're listening to the official set of instructions on how to have a happy wife who's pleased with you this Thanksgiving."

"I want you to be nice to my parents for the whole time," she said. "I want you to engage them in conversation and stay at the table with us talking, and if you do get tired before we do, politely excuse yourself to go upstairs. That's for starters."

"On what authority are you asking this, Sophia?" I said. "What gives you the right to ask this of Bob?"

She thought about that for a moment. "Well, I'm telling him what I want, but I'm really just telling him what the right thing to do is," she said. "That's the way my husband is *supposed* to be with my parents."

I turned to Bob. "See how easy this is, Bob? You don't even need to think about what to do; all you need to do is believe that your wife often knows what to do, what's the *right* thing to do, and then follow her instructions. Then you'll have a wife who's often pleased with you and a marriage and a life that work a lot better because you're doing the right thing."

If you've got a problem with obedience to your wife (*Me? Obey a woman? Obey my wife? I don't think so. I wear the pants in this family!*), get over that. Grow up. Get a different pair of pants.

Get over it because your wife and my wife and a lot of women in this world know the truth about how life is supposed to be lived in this world, and from their mouths are dropping pearls of wisdom about life, and we men should be sitting at their feet listening to them like our lives depended on it.

Trust me on this one.

Our lives do depend on it.

So let your life be guided by your wife. Listen to the wisdom flowing from her mouth. When you're trying to live your life guided by truth, you listen for it from every mouth, and when you hear it, you do what it's telling you to do—which means that sometimes you'll be doing what your wife's telling you to do, and you're totally fine with that, thankful that you have such a great, wise being in your life.

THE MOVE

To get the hang of this obedience thing, try following your wife's lead all week. In small and big things, just do what she says. Don't even think about it. Literally just do what she says.

Make the internal adjustment to get into a state of obedience to her. If you don't like the word "obedience," call it followership or willingness.

For a week.

If you feel any resistance to this Move coming up inside you—anything from a mild scrunch of discomfort to a full-blown aneurysm of rage at the very idea of it—think of your resistance as a bubble of really foul gas your digestive system is trying to expel from something really bad you ate a long, long time ago . . . and let it pass.

Make sure no one else is in the room when this happens, except maybe the dog, who probably won't care.

After your resistance passes, try again: Make the internal

adjustment to get into a state of obedience to your wife. All week, in matters great and small, just do what she says.

Keep doing this until it feels comfortable and then *keep* doing it until it feels *good,* like a great new way to do your whole life . . . and then sit back and relax and watch how much easier and smoother the rest of your life becomes.

CHAPTER 42

Look at You!

*You gotta look inside yourself. You gotta look
inside your inner self and find out who you are.*

Robert De Niro, playing mob boss
Paul Vitti in the movie *Analyze This*

To enter one's own self, it is necessary to go armed to the teeth.

Paul Valéry

I watch the History Channel a lot, especially the documentary
films they always have on about war—World War II, Korea, Viet-
nam. When I see footage of men going into battle, like those GIs
crouched in the landing craft heading for the beaches of Normandy on D-Day, or the soldiers at Chosin reservoir, or the
marines at the siege of Khe Sanh, it's hard for me to imagine
what that's like—the *fear* a man must have going into battle. The
courage it takes to do that. I am in awe of guys who have that
kind of physical, warrior courage.

There's another kind of warrior courage. It's psychological courage. It's the courage to look inside yourself and see what's there within you. *Whatever's* there. Whether it's good or bad, strong or weak, noble, deplorable, or pathetic, you're not afraid to look at it—because it's *there*.

It's an important courage for men to have these days because things really need to change in our marriages and in this world, and the main thing that needs to change is us men, and it's going to take psychological courage for us to do that.

Because here's the thing: *You can't change what you can't see.*

Psychological courage is when you're not afraid to go into yourself and take a long, hard look at yourself and really see yourself and come to really know yourself. By doing that, by looking at all that stuff inside you and really *seeing* it, seeing the way you're wired, you come to know why you behave the way you do, and then you can change the way you behave.

It's like a car engine that needs repair, or a window, or a faucet, or anything that's broken. I can probably fix it, but first I have to be able to *see* it.

So you have to learn to see yourself.

Here's how to do that:

First, be willing to do it. That's not easy for us men. Looking inside ourselves is not our strong suit. Most of us don't even have that pitch. That's something that the girls do. They go in—must be a vagina thing. I go out, like a penis. While they're at their therapists and yoga classes and discussion groups, I'm busy out here repointing the chimney. They're watching *Oprah* and *Dr. Phil*, and I'm watching reruns of *Gunsmoke*. They're reading self-help books, and I'm doing *important* stuff like going to the boat show. Look inside myself? Forget it. I'm a guy. Not going there.

So let me make it easier for you:

You have no choice.

Because for real and deep and permanent change in the way you are and the way you act, for *transformation* of yourself and therefore of your marriage and your family, for a good marriage and a happy family in a peaceful world, *for everything you yourself want in your life*, there's no other way. You *can* get to there from here—a marriage and a family and a world that *work*—but it's going to take you through *yourself*.

So here's what to do:

With whatever help you need—from your wife, a therapist, a marriage counselor, a clergy member, a friend, meditation, or (ahem!) a book—you learn how to look inside yourself and you start to see what's there. You get the lay of the land. Like Lewis and Clark going up the Missouri, you get to know the new territory, the stuff you're made of, the inner realm of yourself with all its interesting terrain.

And you make a map.

It'll look something like this. Here's a map of a representative man:

Childhood Stuff

My childhood stuff is pretty much everything that happened to me in my childhood:

- **In my family of origin.** *What was it like growing up in my family? Does what happened to me back then have anything to do with who I am now? Like the fact that my father was always on my case, always busting my chops. I wonder if that has anything to do with the fact that I can't hear any criticism from my wife and whenever she tries to say, even nicely, that I did something she didn't like, I have a total conniption fit. The fact that my oldest* *brother seemed to actually* hate *me, I wonder if that might have anything to do with how hard I am on myself. I wonder if any of that family stuff actually* affected *me.*

- **In school.** *"My seventh-grade teacher Mr. Lavier told me in front of the whole class that I was a pimple on the ass of life, and no matter how hard I tried all through school, I could never seem to pull an A. I wonder if any of that could have anything to do with the fact that I feel so insecure about myself all the time at work.*

- **With my friends.** *I wonder if the time Teddy Saviano showed me those pictures of those two couples beating off a little boy, I wonder if that has anything to do with my premature-ejaculation problem. The time when Billy Parker shot the hockey puck at Rebecca LeBeau and hit her in the shin and she fell down on the ice and cried and all us boys laughed our heads off, but inside I felt really sad for Rebecca LeBeau—I wonder what that was all about. Maybe I should think about all this stuff.*

Gender Stuff

My gender stuff is my male conditioning. When you go into this stuff, you will almost certainly find your sexism, also called male chauvinism, a.k.a. *patriarchy*—the social, economic, and political world order in which men hold power and wield authority over everybody else on the planet. In my opinion it's impossible to understand how your marital problems are (mostly) your fault and to really *get* this good-husband thing unless you get the patriarchy thing, so it's important to see its major features inside you. Here, in my opinion, are the major features of patriarchy inside you:

- **Dominance.** *I wear the pants in this family . . . If I say our son should sit up at the table, he'll sit up at the table . . . I don't care* *what you say, we are not spending the whole long weekend at your mother's . . . We are not buying a new dishwasher, the old one is fine. Do you hear me? It's fine!*

- **Centrality.** *Whaddaya mean you're busy? I need you right now . . . No, we're not stopping at this service area so you can pee. I don't need to pee. Just hold it in till we get there . . . Where's my laptop? Where's my blue shirt? Where's dinner? Where did you say you were going tomorrow? The doctor? For what?*

- **Autonomy.** *Yeah, yeah, yeah, I'll get to it when I get to it . . . I'm watching the game . . . Whaddaya mean you want me to change? This is who I am. Take it or leave it.*

- **Entitlement.** *Give me sex . . . And handle the house . . . and the kids . . . and your job . . . I'll be playing golf tomorrow when my parents come over. Deal with them, will ya?*

- **Superiority and condescension.** *That's a girlie idea . . . Yeah, yeah, yeah, I'm hearing you, boy am I hearing you, all I ever do is hear you 'cause all you ever do is talk! . . . Of course, dear, if that little meeting of yours is so important, run along, I'll clean up . . . If I get behind one more woman driver, I'm going to freak out.*

- **Misogyny.** *If I get behind one more goddamn woman driver, I'm going to run this car right up her ass . . . Henry's wife is a manipulative bitch . . . You're all a bunch of bitches . . . That woman deserved whatever he did to her.*

- **Enforcement.** *I will physically and emotionally withdraw from you when I don't get my way with you . . . I will raise my voice when I'm annoyed with you, I will yell at you when I'm mad at you, and I will hit you if you provoke me . . . Oh, and by the way, if I don't get sex from you, there are a lot of other women out there, you know.*

Social Conditioning

Social conditioning is all my ethnic, religious, racial, national, regional, and class background stuff:

- *I wonder if the fact that I'm Jewish* (or Christian or Muslim or whatever) *has anything to do with the way I feel about women and treat my wife . . . I wonder if the fact that I'm Latin* (or Italian or African American or whatever) *has anything to do with the way I treat my wife . . . I wonder if the fact that I grew up rich* (or poor or middle-class) *or come from South Carolina* (or South Boston or wherever) *has anything to do with anything.*

Sexual Stuff

- Oy.

Spiritual Stuff

- *What are my beliefs about religion and God? How did I come by these beliefs? Are they true? What is true? . . . What are the teachings of my religion about women? Are they true? . . . What is the purpose of my life? What exactly am I doing here?*

Human Nature Stuff

- *I wonder if everybody struggles with the same things I struggle with. I wonder if everybody has a lot of negative thoughts about themselves, like I do. Is everybody as screwed-up as I am? Maybe I'm more normal than I think. Maybe everybody who's starting to look at this stuff is finding pretty much the same stuff!*

It's like Anne Lamott says: "Sometimes this human stuff is slimy and pathetic . . . but better to feel it and talk about it and walk through it than to spend a lifetime being silently poisoned" by it.

The Parts of You

LOOK AT YOU!

There's a whole world in there to look into, and like all worlds, there's a lot to see. There are ways you are, ways you speak and act, feelings you have about yourself, opinions, reactions, character traits, entire belief systems and political philosophies, a whole vast territory that is *you* and that you keep exploring while you keep drawing and redrawing your map as you keep seeing more and more of your stuff.

Now comes the tricky part: You have to get all the bad and false and childish and unhealthy stuff out of you without thinking that you yourself are bad for having any of it.

It's tricky, but not *that* tricky. All you have to do is divide it up, divvy it up. Like apples and oranges. You divide the mature you from the immature you, the good from the bad in you, the stuff you're proud of from the stuff you're ashamed of, your nobility from your imbecility, the old wine from the new bottle.

You discern, you distinguish, you discriminate, you separate it all out.

It's like separating the wheat from the chaff.

Or knowing your ass from a hole in the ground.

I'll give you an example. In me, in my gender stuff, in my attitude toward women, there's a part of me that totally honors and reveres women as the strong, wise, beautiful, beneficent beings that they are, and there's another part of me that totally dismisses them as inferior and insignificant beings. It's my form of disdain for women, like when Jane tells me—for the gazillionth time—to clean the hair out of the drain after I shower, or to not take swigs of grapefruit juice right out of the carton, I can hear a voice inside me that's going, *Yeah, right. Forget it, lady. Not a chance. I ain't doing it because it's just a woman who's telling me to do it.*

That's really the way it sounds in my head. After all these years. I guess there's more stuff in me than I thought. What to do?

Easy. Once you've seen it, once you know what the apples and the oranges are, what's your ass and what's a hole in the ground, once you've divvied it all up—the good, the bad, and the ugly in you—you decide to keep the good stuff and you chuck the rest.

In other words, you change.

With great psychological courage you have landed on your *own* Normandy and fought your own ignorance and denial and laziness and habit to go way inland into your stuff. You have laid siege to yourself. You have looked yourself squarely in the eye, seen what had to be seen, and now you change what has to be changed. And you keep doing that, for as long as there's stuff in you that needs to be changed.

It's a lifetime kind of thing. And *very* manly, because it's so challenging and takes so much courage and strength and stick-to-itiveness to get the job done.

And, believe me, it's a dream come true for your wife.

To her, your willingness to look at yourself and change yourself is *everything*.

THE MOVE

This week go to your wife and say, "Got a few minutes?" She'll probably say yes.

Then ask, "Is there anything that happened to me in my childhood that you think I should look at? Is there anything there, like in my family, that you think kind of messed me up and I bring it into *our* family?"

There'll be a pause. She might breathe a big sigh of relief that you're finally asking this question. Then she might answer the question. She might say, "I've been trying to get you to see for *years* the extent of your father's narcissism and how angry you are at him and how you transfer all that anger to me whenever I try to say what I want from you."

Or something like that.

Then say, "I don't really see that. Would you help me here?"

She'll smile and nod.

Thank her and then ask her to go on.

Your job is easier. You don't have to figure out how to get rid of your bullshit and become a good husband. It's figured out and laid out for you in this book.

All you have to do now is do it.

And it's doable.

I'll prove it:

I've done it.

Lots of men have done it.

"When you see somebody who has done it," Oprah Winfrey once said, "it speaks to the possibility that it can be done."

Absolutely. It's doable.

II. It Works

One of the worst feelings for us men is helplessness, ineffectualness, the feeling that we're in a situation over which we have no power or control. Many of you feel that way about your marriages: *She's always angry at me, she's always nagging me, she doesn't appreciate me, she doesn't want to have sex with me . . . and I can't do anything about it.*

Bullshit.

You *can* do something about it. You are *not* in a situation over which you have no power or control. You have the power to have a wife who is not angry at you, is totally pleased with you, appreciative of you, and lying naked in bed with you. You have the power to have the great marriage you want and the great family you want. There is something you can do. Something *works*.

Become a good husband.

It's the change that changes everything. Trust me on this. I base this on the unassailable authority of my own experience.

It's like my client Rudy said at the end of his therapy with his wife, Brooke: "All these years I thought it was *her*. I thought she was just an unhappy person. I thought she *liked* being angry. I thought she didn't love me anymore and she'd never have sex with me again. Then we came here, and I rethought everything, and I changed *myself*. Then *she* changed. And now we're leaving here, and I can honestly say we're a happily married couple."

He looked over at Brooke, who smiled and gave the thumbs-up sign.

I'm telling you, this *works*.

III. It's the Right Thing to Do

When a man loves a woman, and loves her so much that he asks her to marry him and she says yes and they get married and she becomes his wife, becoming a good husband to her is the man's duty, his *job*. A true man always does his duty, just does his job, because it's the right thing to do. And for a true man, the right thing to do is the only thing to do.

When a man loves a woman, he takes her on, and he takes on everything about her: all the good and bad experiences she's had in her life, her wounds and hurts from all of that, her wants and needs, her likes and dislikes, all her hopes and dreams. That's how big the taking on of her is—when a man loves a woman. When a man loves a woman, you enter into a state of service to her. You husband her. You do right by her. You take care of her . . . when a man loves a woman.

IV. It's Good for the Kids

Some of you have kids. Some of you are fathers.

Being a father is like always playing in the major leagues. Everything you do, every word you say, every look on your face,

every way you are with your wife, is being watched . . . moni-
tored . . . recorded . . . remembered . . . by your children. The
children are *always* watching. It is through their eyes, I believe,
that God watches us. They come to bear witness of us.

And because they're our children, they're always modeling
themselves on what they're seeing in us. Your boy children, your
sons, are modeling their whole character on you, and modeling
their behavior with women on your behavior toward your wife.
Your girl children, your daughters, are developing their self-
respect out of the respect they see you treat their mother with,
and they're building an image of men's behavior to them as
women on the image of your behavior to your wife.

Remember that inside them the kids are shaping themselves
on the shape we're in, so if you're a father, you better shape up as
a husband. Don't expect your kids to be in good shape if the relationship between you and your wife is in bad shape. Doesn't
work like that. The kids become what they see, and they see
everything.

One couple I was seeing told me that every time they started
to bicker or argue, their seven-year-old son, Sam, would start to
sing very loudly and beat the sides of his head with his fists, and
their four-year-old, Krissy, would say, "Please no fight . . . please
no fight . . . please no fight . . ." with tears running down her
cheeks.

When you have children, every way you are is being watched,
everything you do gets seen, every word you speak gets heard,
everything that happens in your family gets written in their soul.

If you're trying to psych yourself up to be a good husband, tell
me, what more do you need to know than this?

V. It's Important for the World

We live in a troubled world. It's kind of a mess on the planet. Everybody's confused, sad, angry, scared. There are terrorists running around this world who want to blow up our beautiful children while they're shopping for jeans in the local mall, and other beautiful children are being blown up in wars all over the world. I think we're at the end of the line here. Something needs to change.

It's us men. We're (mostly) at fault for all this. We need to change.

I believe that when we men make the changes in ourselves that enable us to be good husbands to our wives, when we learn to love and respect our wives in the ways I have described in this book, when we men go through *that* change, the whole world will change.

We've got the whole world in our hands, men.

We can change it.

We can make the world safe for our children and grandchildren and all children and grandchildren. Search inside that great male heart of yours, and you will find that's what you really want—a world that's peaceful and safe for our loved ones.

Remember: All the children and all the people all over the world, they're *all* our loved ones.

We really can have it. We really can change it.

When we change.

VI. For the Points!

When I was growing up, it was all sports for me. Baseball and basketball in the spring and summer, football and more basketball in the fall, hockey all winter. My friends. Great athletes. Cabot Park and Edmunds Pond. Great games. Competition.

Points! It was all about scoring points. Runs. Goals. Jump shots from the side of the key. Touchdowns.

Score a lot of points, and you win. Don't, and you lose. Very simple. And winning feels *so* much better than losing.

It's a guy thing, the point thing, the winning and losing thing. I myself am completely into it.

Jane and I have a kind of point system in our marriage. The way it works is I do some good-husband-type thing for her, and I get points. Very simple. Like I'll go out of my way to run an errand for her, or I'll make a salad for our dinner that evening, or I'll be the one to make a social arrangement with our friends (this has actually never happened, and isn't likely to anytime soon, but I thought I'd use it as an example anyway) . . . and I get points.

I'll go up to her and tell her the good-husband thing I did— "I was *really* quiet leaving the bedroom this morning so I wouldn't wake you up"—and ask her, "How many points is that?"

She'll say, "Three."

I'll say, "Three? Are you kidding? I was on my tiptoes! I didn't even breathe! It took me forever to turn the damn doorknob. It's gotta be worth more than three."

"Okay, four," she'll say.

Shooting my fist into the air, "Yes!" I'll say.

And so on.

It's very informal and mostly a joke and we don't keep score and I start out at zero each day anyway. It's just one of those silly, fun marital games couples play.

But it's not. There's truth in it.

The first truth is, for a good husband, taking care of his wife is an infinite requirement, a job that just keeps rolling over from one moment to the next, a game that has no end. Which is fine with a man who loves sports, because for a true lover of sports, the game never really ends. Like when I was a boy, the game never really ended, it just changed with the seasons and got interrupted by our mothers calling us into dinner, or by rain, or school, or when it got too dark to see the ball or puck anymore. The next day we'd be right back out there, back in a game.

Marriage is like that. It's an endless game that we keep playing and, if we get good, keep winning.

The second truth is that even though Jane and I don't keep score, I know that there is an official scorekeeper sitting inside her where my points are quietly accumulating, and my loveableness to her is increasing, and it all comes back to me eventually as her love for me—in all the wondrous ways a woman who feels loved by a man can love.

So the next time you make a good-husband Move and do something nice for your wife, and you bring it to her attention and ask how many points you get for it, if she smiles and says, "Are you doing it just for the points?" smile back and say, "You bet."

THE MOVE

You're down a point, half second to go in the game, you've got the ball.

You've only got one move. Take the shot. Take the shot!

Love her. Love your wife in all the ways she wants to be loved. Love that woman!

That's it! That's the game! You won!

Celebrate! Everybody's congratulating you, slapping you on the back, mussing your hair, hugging you. There's your wife running up to you with a big smile, throwing her arms around your neck, whispering in your ear under the roar of the crowd, so it's only her voice that you hear: "I'm so proud of you! I'm so proud of you!"

And the Move is to believe her. When you become her good husband, it'll be hard not to believe her, because she'll say it so often: "I'm so proud of you! . . . You've become such a wonderful husband to me! . . . I'm the luckiest girl in the world!"

And it's true. You *have* become a wonderful husband to her, and she *is* the luckiest girl in the world, and she's totally proud of you and totally in love with you.

So here's your next Move:

Don't blow it.

This good-husband thing? It's a constant effort, a daily practice, a lifelong offering of love. There'll be times when you don't feel like it, you're tired, you're cranky, it's not fair, I'm not doing this anymore, forget it! There'll be times when you're *sure* it's her, *she's* the one who started this fight, *she's* the one who's acting crazy, *she's* the one who needs to change—and being a good husband will be the last thing you feel like doing. What you'll really feel like doing is giving in to your old feelings that'll be coming up like gangbusters in your mind and settling back into the BarcaLounger of your old behaviors toward her, those old comfortable ways. Oh yes, guaranteed, there'll be times when it's going to be so damn *hard*.

That's when I want you to remember two things. First,

remember that those old feelings and those old behaviors of yours got you nothing. Well, not nothing, they got you something—they got you a wife who was angry with you and distant from you and turned away from you, reading, in bed. Night after night. Silence. Loneliness. Remember that.

And then when the good-husbanding thing gets hard, remember Tom Hanks's line to Geena Davis in *A League of Their Own:* "It's supposed to be hard. If it weren't hard, everybody would do it. The hard is what makes it great."

He's talking to a woman about playing baseball. I'm talking to us men about being a good husband.

Remember that being a good husband makes us great.

CHAPTER 44

Reverence

As I see through a mist, One with inexpressible
completeness, sanity, beauty,
See the bent head and
arms folded over the breast, the Female I see.

Walt Whitman

She moves a goddess, and she looks a queen.

Homer

When Jane and I got together in 1970, my mother, who knew me better than anyone and who was not given to superlatives, said to me, "She's the best thing that ever happened to you, Rob."

What she knew about Jane then, I, who have always been a little slow on the uptake, have come to know over the years: My wife is a wonderful woman, and the love of a wonderful woman is the best thing a man can have in this life. I think there are other men who know that about their wives. I am glad that I know it about mine.

When I think of Jane, I think that a goddess entered my life thirty-five years ago and I had the great good fortune to marry her and I'm supposed to spend my marriage learning to have reverence for her.

You're supposed to have reverence for your wife too, I think. She, too, is a goddess, if you have eyes to see.

I see the goddess in my wife every day. I see her in the glowing love in Jane's face when she's with our daughter, Greta, and her husband, Matt, and our grandchildren, Gracie and Harper, just gazing at them, laughing with them, delighting in them. I hear the goddess when Jane is talking on the phone to her mother, brother, cousins, friends—her low, soft voice a soothing murmur from the other room. I see the goddess in Jane when she's meditating in the early morning, sitting wrapped in her shawl, eyes closed, serene and still and regal. I see her in the garden tending the flowers and vegetables and herbs she grows. I see the goddess in Jane when she's preparing and presenting the beautiful and nourishing food that we eat. I see the goddess when Jane is all spruced up to go out, made up, hair done, new dress, jewels sparkling, she herself a jewel, exquisite! the beautiful woman! the goddess *adorned*! I see her walking toward me in our bedroom—toward *me*, lying there staring and stunned and silent. I see the goddess when Jane is angry—the goddess Kali—full of fury at my or anyone's unrighteousness or untruthfulness. I see the goddess in my wife as she ages, the mature feminine, ripe and full, ever softer, wiser.

In the thirty-five years of my marriage I have not always treated my wife with the reverence due her as goddess. I have been discourteous, ungentle, unkind. I have been reclusive and rejecting, ignorant, arrogant, and horrendously stupid. In many ways over the years I have not been in right relationship to her, I have not been a good husband to her. The problems we've had in our marriage have been (mostly) my fault.

But I am learning.

Here's one thing I've learned about the goddess:

She is full of grace, overflowing with grace, but we men have to earn it. We earn it with our reverence for her. Our loyalty and devotion. The little and big efforts we make every day to be good husbands. The changes we make in ourselves. Our transformation.

"It is incumbent upon us that we should please the goddess and women at this time," said one man.

Absolutely.

Something big is happening on this earth of ours. It's a spiritual thing. It's the return, the reappearance, of the goddess from her long exile. No less. She brings relationship with her, and togetherness, and connection and kindness, and love, and peace on earth. She's the biggest thing happening in our time and the best thing happening in our time. Very quietly but very strongly, she's the great thing happening behind all the not-so-great things that are happening.

The return of the goddess who has come in the nick of time to save us all.

We need to win her grace, guys—with our reverence for her.

You heard it here.

That woman you married . . . your wife . . . she's a divine being to whom you owe reverence.

THE MOVE

Sometime in the next few days, find your wife as she sits on a chair, the couch, or the edge of the bed.

Go to her and kneel before her.

Put your head on her knees for a moment.

Then look up at her and say whatever is in your heart.

Then get up, give her a little kiss, and go back to what you were doing.

A WORD TO THE WIVES

The ideal marriage is a mutual and reciprocal exchange of love between a wife and a husband.

All the forms of love your husband is supposed to give you in your marriage—attention, care, appreciation, support, empathy, respect, reverence—you are supposed to give him. Your husband devotes his life to the loving service of you, and you devote your life to the loving service of him. Till death do you part. That is marriage. Mutuality. In its ideal state, marriage is a mutual admiration society, a mutual *everything* society.

See the goddess in your wife, I am telling him. *See the absolute best and highest in her, and revere the great soul that she is.*

And I'm telling you: *See the god—the absolute best and highest—in your husband, and revere the great soul that he is.*

To see the greatness in him, you may have to look hard, you may have to look under the not-so-great parts of him, and you may have to look long because it's going to take him some time to realize that this greatness is who he really is and to act like it. That's all right. Just keep seeing it. *By seeing the best in him, you bring out the best in him.* By having reverence for him as he is right now—the good man who is making a big effort to become a good husband—you are helping him become what he already is in his soul: a great man worthy of your reverence.

Closing Message to
Women Readers

*It is the most momentous question a woman is ever called upon
to decide: Whether the faults of the man she loves are beyond
remedy and will drop her down, or whether she is competent to
be his earthly redeemer and lift him to her own level.*

Oliver Wendell Holmes

Sweet woman, rising so fine!

Chris Williamson

I. NOW WHAT?

I don't know what you're feeling now that you've read *It's
(Mostly) His Fault*. You could be feeling angry at the book for
pointing out the inadequacies of your husband and the unsatis-
factoriness of your marriage; or you could be feeling confused as
new ideas and old ideas about husbands and wives and marriages
grate against each other in your mind; or you could feel affirmed

and validated in what you've known for ages about your husband and have been trying to get into his head in every conceivable way short of total brain replacement; or you could feel a huge sense of relief, a happiness inside that you're not alone, that you're finally seeing all this in print—written by a man, no less— so now there's hope that your marriage might improve, that you might someday even have the marriage of your dreams, and now you just have to figure out what the hell to do next.

Here's what to do next:

Try to get your husband to read this book.

You can rush right over to him the moment you finish it, and say, "Pete! I just read this book on husbanding, and it's written by a guy to guys just like you, and I really think it's gonna help us, and I really want you to read it!" Or you can wait for just the right moment, maybe his birthday or your anniversary or Valentine's Day or before, after, or during sex, and ask him in just the right way: "Chuck, I know you don't go in for these books, and I know you're busy, but I want to ask you a favor. I read this book on husbanding recently, and I really think it has some good ideas in it that would help our marriage a lot. And it's short and easy and kind of fun, actually, to read. And it's written directly to men by a man. Would you be willing to read it—for me? For us?"

One of four things is then going to happen:

1. He reads *It's (Mostly) His Fault* and understands it and likes it and starts to use it, starts to make the Moves, and he begins to change, either rapidly or slowly, and eventually transforms into a good husband. Yay!
2. He doesn't want to read it (some men are just not readers of books like this), but agrees to listen to you read it to him,

probably in installments, and he understands it and likes it and starts to use it, and changes, and transforms. Yo!

3. He agrees to read it but doesn't understand it, doesn't like it, *really* doesn't like it, slams it shut one night, and gives it back to you with a "This is bullshit!" and turns over and goes to sleep.

4. He totally refuses to read it or let you read it to him and gets up abruptly from the couch and stomps by you on his way out of the living room to get new batteries for the remote.

The first two lead to major change in him, the marriage, and you. The latter two also lead to major change, but of a different kind, which I'll talk about later in this section.

II. IF YOUR HUSBAND CHANGES

If your husband reads this book or lets you read it to him, and the ideas get into his head, embed themselves in his consciousness, and become part of him, he'll change. He'll change either fast or slow—the fire of transformation burns at different rates for different husbands. Some men get it very fast—they're like dry tinder that bursts into flame the moment the match is applied. One woman whose husband got it very fast exclaimed, "It's amazing! What happened? Where did it come from? Was it in him all the time? What the hell was it *doing* in there for twenty-three years?!" And some men are more like wet logs, which when lit by the match catch fire and then smolder over a long period of time. More men burn slow than fast—which is harder on you, of course, because that means you have longer to wait for a good husband—but as long as he's burning . . . moving . . . changing . . . growing . . . getting it . . . *really* getting it . . . you're okay.

Really getting it, by the way, means he *becomes* it.

A good husband.

Transformation!

Worth the wait.

Here are nine important things for you to keep in mind along the way of your husband's transformation:

1. Do Your Part

By agreeing to read this book and be open to its ideas, your husband has stepped onto a path that starts with him owning his faults in the marriage and ends with him becoming a good husband to you. While he's walking this path, do everything I talked about in my opening words to you in "Her Introduction":

- Know that you're right in wanting what you want from him.
- Hold him to your highest standard of behavior toward you.
- Trust your dissatisfaction and anger with him and when necessary *get* angry at him.
- Stay on his case.
- Remember you're in a fight. Fight hard, and fight long, and don't worry about losing some battles, but win the fight.
- In everything you do or say, be strategic.
- Get the help and support you need from wherever you can find it.
- Know that you're the teacher of your husband and teach him well.
- Do your own inner work and address your own issues around relationship and intimacy.

- Be both impatient and patient with your husband as he takes his journey of change.
- Know that *you* are the goal of his journey, that all his efforts culminate in your being pleased with him.
- Keep a steady stream of appreciations flowing to him in the form of grateful words and whatever other ways you know he likes to be thanked. As your husband does his work and walks the path of his transformation, never underestimate the power of your acknowledgment, appreciation, and admiration of what he's doing.

2. Acknowledge Yourself

While you're giving him all that acknowledgment for what he's doing, make sure to acknowledge, appreciate, and admire yourself for what *you're* doing. What you're doing is no picnic. You are a woman trying to change a man in a deeply entrenched global culture of male autonomy and superiority and dominance that decrees that a man should not be subject to change by a woman. You are trying to assert a right—the right to have a husband who always treats you with utmost respect—that has never been asserted so strongly and on such a large scale on this earth before.

It's hard.

"Disciplining masculinity that takes its superiority for granted," says psychoanalyst Marion Woodman, "demands as much strength and vigilance as training a wild horse that's never known a harness."

Yes. Strength. Vigilance. Courage. Conviction. Stamina.

Remember that the expectation of superiority and control over a woman, the expectation of her submissiveness and obedience, is so deeply ingrained in a man that any form of her trying to assert herself—any form of disagreement, contradiction, oppo-sition, or refusal from her—any form of her "No, I don't want to, and I don't want you to, and I'm going to stand up to you on it" literally shocks him.

"Who *are* you?" he wonders. "Where did my wife go? When are you coming back to yourself, Sheila?"

"This *is* myself, Anthony. I finally *found* myself. If you're ask-ing when I'm coming back to my *old* self, try 'never.'"

"But you're being so difficult, Sheila."

"This isn't called *difficult*, Anthony. This is called 'Some of the ways you treat me are unacceptable, and you must change.'"

Even though your husband is open to change and walking the path of change, let's not kid ourselves: He's a *male*, so he's going to put up a lot of resistance along the way, and you're going to have to struggle with him, you're going to have to take him on.

It's *really* hard.

Stand in awe of yourself at what you're trying to do here.

3. Rising So Fine

In order to take your husband on, you must rise from the second-class citizen place, that swamp of inferiority, guilt, fear, dependence, and self-effacement that our culture conditions into a woman—the poor self-esteem place where you think that your wants are unreasonable and your need for connection is patho-logical and your loneliness is a weakness and your anger is unladylike and his mistreatment of you is deserved—*that* swamp—and you are going to have to rise to another place in your being, a strong, clear, self-respecting place where you know what kind of behavior you want from your husband and what you don't want. You know it and you say it and your voice has such authority when you say it—like, "This is not up for argument, Sean, this is the way it is"—that it surprises both of you.

In that kind of voice—low, slow, steady, sure—one woman in my office told her husband he had a year, one year, to change. "I will not go into the next year with this marriage like it is, Jim. I will not."

Jim stared at her for a moment. Her gaze was steady back on his.

"I don't like being given ultimatums," he said.

"Call it what you want," the woman said. "I just call it a fact. I will not go into the next year with this marriage like it is. Change, or you lose me, Jim. I mean it. Become the kind of husband I'm telling you I want, or I will leave you."

Another woman, Tara, in an individual session, described her rising this way: "For so long I allowed him to treat me in an abusive way. Over the twenty years of our marriage he had come to accept my complacency, my stupidity, my quickness to forgive him, my low self-esteem, my belief that I was always the one who was wrong. I'm no longer any of that. The other night I told him how I wanted him to be treating me, how he *should* be treating me, and I was so clear, *so* unbelievably sure of myself, that in the moment I was saying it, it didn't matter whether or not he got it—all that mattered was I was saying it to him."

4. Bring It Up!

In order to keep your husband on the path of change, you must come out of your long silence and find your voice with him. You must address things with him. You must bring it up with him and challenge him on all his disconnective, disrespectful, or neglectful behavior toward you.

One woman, talking about how she knows when she needs to

address something with her husband, to call him on something he's just done or said, explained, "It begins with a tiny little feeling, an inner sense that this doesn't feel right, the way he just spoke to me, the thing he just did, *it didn't feel right,* and I have to listen to that feeling and act on it by bringing it up with him. It's never fun to bring anything up with him because he gets so defensive and fights back so hard and ridiculously, but I do it anyway, because if I don't, it just gets worse."

So on the path of your husband's change, when you feel that "tiny little feeling," when something in the relationship doesn't feel right to you, some way he just behaved doesn't sit well with you, bring it up with your husband and then stay for the ridiculous fight he's then going to put up.

Because if you don't do that—especially now that you've read *It's (Mostly) His Fault*—you're going to have to ask yourself these questions:

What is it in me that allows me to be in a relationship with a man who does things and says things that I don't like? What is it in me that keeps me in a relationship with a man who does things and says things that scare, hurt, humiliate, degrade, and anger me? Why do I tolerate things that don't feel good to me? Why do I pretend that things are okay when they're not? What is this silence I live in? My fear of my husband? My bad opinion of myself? Self-distrust? Hopelessness? Laziness?

What *is* that?

If you find it and you're able to fix it—to fix the way *you're* broken inside—maybe by going to a therapist or to a group, or maybe on your own through reading, talking with your friends, and thinking about it all, you summon the strength to call your husband on all his behaviors to you that don't feel right to you (remembering, of course, to cut him and you some slack sometimes by not sweating some of the smaller stuff), and because he's on a path of self-awareness and change, you help him fix what's broken inside *him* that allows him to behave in these ways to you.

5. What to Do with Your Anger

On the path of your husband's change there'll be times when you're angry at him and times when you're *very* angry at him. Anger will come up inside you from the past for the way he's been in this marriage and the things he's done, and anger will flare in the present as he makes mistakes with you, has momentary lapses into old behaviors and then defends or denies them, progresses too slowly, or, on bad days, totally forgets all this good-husband stuff and acts like the same big kahuna of cluelessness he always was.

When those things happen, anger's going to come up in you. More than either of you will like.

The question is, *What are you going to do with it?*

The first thing to do with it is to believe in it.

Remember what was said to him in Chapter 17, "Her Anger: Take the Hit"—that a woman's anger arises naturally and appropriately when she's been wronged or hurt in a relationship, and it forcefully informs the person who wronged or hurt her that that behavior wasn't okay and needs to be changed.

So believe in your anger.

Easier said than done for a woman.

In a hierarchical, dominant-submissive culture like the global patriarchy we all live in, it's very important for the dominant group, men, to divest the submissive group, women, of their anger, because then we men are free to dominate you women, basically do whatever we want to you, and not have to worry about your reaction. By taking away your anger, we take away your power.

One way we take away your anger is by demonstrating to you,

through violence or threat, that we can get *a lot* angrier than you, and you better watch out because we can hurt you. But the best and most efficient way to take away your anger, it turns out, is to get you not to believe in it. At a very early age we get inside your heads and psychologically disarm your belief in yourself, your belief that what you see, feel, think, and say is true, and that what you're angry at him about is what you *should* be angry about because what he just did, the way he just treated you, was wrong. We take that away from you. It's an inside job. The hardest foe to fight, says the writer Sally Kempton, is the one who has outposts inside your own head.

And then, if you do get angry at us for the latest outrageous thing we just did in this marriage, we continue the disempowerment of your anger by trying to convince you that you're pathological for feeling it.

"What are you angry about *now*?!" we say. "What the hell is *wrong* with you?!" . . . "You're making a mountain out of a molehill," we say. "It's no big deal!" . . . "You're crazy!" we say. "Do you spend all day thinking up things to be pissed off at me about?" . . . "Jeff Morton's wife doesn't get all over his case when *he's* late for dinner. Get over it!" . . . "No, you're wrong about that. Knock it off! I was *not* flirting with that woman. You're just being jealous. You're so insecure" . . . "Whaddaya *mean* I never spend time with you? I spend plenty of time with you! I don't want to hear it!" . . . "Don't speak to me in that tone of voice. I'm not listening to that" . . . "I'm not interested in your anger" . . . "Stop your nagging!" . . . "Get off my case!" . . . "I don't want to talk about it. Just forget about it, will ya?!" . . . "To tell you the truth, I don't care *what* you say, so don't waste your breath" . . . "You're always a bitch this time of the month" . . . "What happened to you?" we say. "You've turned into a complete bitch."

Lies. All lies. Robbery of your anger.

You want to know the truth? Here's the truth:

You're absolutely *right* to be angry at him. You're *right* to want more from him in this relationship. You're *right* to hold him to a higher standard of behavior toward you. You're *right* to be fed up with the way he neglects you. You're *right* to call him on his double talk, his insensitivity, his immaturity, his pornography. You're *right* to be pissed at his socks on the floor, the dirty dishes on the table, the way he just yelled at the kids, and the fact that he can never have a decent conversation with you. You're *right* to hate his condescension, his wall of silence, his grumpiness, his selfishness. You're *right* to be as pissed off as you are at him. All the feelings you feel that have anger in them—frustration, irritation, indignation, resentment, rage, fury, wrath—they're all *right*.

Just this week I tried to pull a fast one on Jane. I scheduled an extra therapy session with a couple in crisis at a time when Jane had asked me, and I had agreed, not to schedule therapy appointments anymore. Then I went ahead and did it anyway. I'm a guy, a work in progress; I do things like that. She got mad at me. I tried everything to worm my way out of it: "I forgot!" . . . "They're in *crisis,* fa chrissakes! What am I supposed to do?" . . . "You'll be sleeping at that time anyway; I didn't think you'd mind." Blah blah blah, my whole song and dance. But she did mind, and she didn't buy a word of it, and she got really angry at me.

"Say whatever you want, Robert," she said, "use any excuse you want, but in my heart of hearts I know what you did and it was wrong. You broke our agreement, and you knew what you were doing, and you knew it was wrong, and I have every right to be angry at you."

Which she did . . . and I eventually copped to it, apologized, and rescheduled the appointment.

That's the first thing to do with your anger—know that you have a right to it. Believe in it. Trust it. Recover it.

The second thing to do with your anger is to use it. On the path of your husband's change, your anger is *needed*. It's a tool of change. It tells him, *You can't get away with this anymore. You're going to have to face me on this.*

When you get angry at him, get angry at him in the right way—always use your anger for a good purpose, toward a beneficial outcome. Here's a story about how to use your anger for a good purpose:

One morning a spiritual master was giving a discourse about spiritual life to a group of students. Suddenly she burst into a rage at them for their lack of discipline and dedication to the path. She yelled and raged at them for twenty minutes while they sat there in awed silence, and then she got up suddenly and left the room. Back in her quarters her attendant said to her, "I don't understand. You're a person of the highest wisdom and peace and holiness. How can you get angry like that!"

"My anger," said the master, "is like a dog that I keep on a very tight leash by my knee. When I want it to go out and do a little work for me, I unleash it. When its work is done, I call it back to my knee, and it sits there, leashed, until it's needed again. Like you, like everybody, I have anger, but I'm in control of it, not it of me, and I use it when I need it to help people wake up, to change."

That's the kind of anger I'm talking about.

Whether it's anger from the past or anger in the present, chances are that your anger at your husband is that kind of anger, so you can use it when you need it to try to make a change in him, to do a little work. When the work is done, drop your anger—until you need to use it again.

That's a fine anger, a divine anger, anger put to good use, anger in the service of beneficial change.

When you use your anger like this, it is good for you to remember that on the deepest level of your husband's being, in his *soul*, he married you for many reasons, and one of them was to receive this anger from you because it corrects behaviors of his that are not in harmony with his soul. So you're spiritually okay to direct your anger at him for good use. He needs it, and though he'll put up amazingly strong resistance to it, down in his soul, where it counts, he actually wants and welcomes it.

But remember that there's another anger that's not good use, but abuse. That's when you're not in control of your anger, it's in control of you, and it's pouring out of you uncontrollably for the purpose of hurting, frightening, humiliating, or condemning the person you're angry at. I've seen women with that kind of anger, and I've seen many men with it. I never allow it in my therapy office. Abuse is abuse, and that kind of anger is abuse. In the good-husband work, we're trying to get past *all* abuse.

Don't get me wrong: It's fine to *feel* that kind of anger at your husband—I'm sure he's done things in your marriage that warrant it—you're just not supposed to *get* angry at him like that. What to do with it, then? Here's a third thing you can do with your anger when it comes up inside you on the path of his change.

Some years ago I was seeing a couple in which the husband, a sex addict, had slept with the wife's stepsister, and the wife, both in my therapy office and at home, would somewhat randomly fly into sudden verbal and physical rages at him. This went on for two years. In one session she said, "If I *got* angry at him every time I *felt* angry at him, there'd be no end to it. I'd lose my mind. I'd kill one or both of us."

Over time the husband changed, understood the enormity of

what his addiction and his infidelity had done to his wife, apologized from the bottom of his heart to her, conquered the addiction, and the couple eventually healed and left therapy.

In their last therapy session I said to the wife, "Clare, if you were to give advice to other women who are angry at their husbands like you've been angry at Lawrence, what would you say to them? What most helped you get through all your anger?"

She thought about it for a long time.

"Good girlfriends," she said. "They were totally there for me, all the way through. We'd talk *a lot*. Just speaking to them on the phone helped. E-mailing. Especially my friend Barb. She's never been through something like this, but we'd take long walks and she basically just listened to me rant and rave. Total empathy. I could really let loose with her and with all my friends. When I would tell them about what Lawrence had done, as I did repeatedly—I couldn't seem to stop telling it—they'd get angrier than I was at him, and that was so validating to me that it gave me great strength. Strength in numbers, I guess. And I learned that I wasn't alone in being angry at my husband. Actually it seems universal—every one of my friends I've ever spoken to has to deal with anger at her husband. The more I saw that they were angry too, it helped me to believe in *my* anger. I think we all strengthened each other. One Saturday night we all got together and rented the movie *9 to 5* and also *The First Wives Club* and watched those women find their anger and strength together." She paused. "Good girlfriends, Robert—they helped the most."

6. Keep This Book Out

For all the time that your husband is looking at how he's (mostly) at fault for the problems in your marriage, correcting his faults, doing the good-husband work, and changing, keep this book *out*—cover up—in some well-trafficked and conspicuous place in the house, like on the coffee table in the living room or the kitchen table or his night table. The message of that is, "This is in your life, darlin'!" You might think of putting copies in both bathrooms and the garage too, and perhaps strapping a copy to his forehead while he's sleeping.

7. Do You Need Marital Therapy?

If your husband is willing to read this book, acknowledge his faults, do the program, and, with your help, change, the good-husband work can be done without therapy.

But sometimes not.

Sometimes a third party needs to be brought in, a skilled professional who can look at your marital relationship from outside the relationship and see more clearly than the two of you what's going on in it and what's wrong with it, and say what needs to be said to both of you so you'll both get to work on it.

Sometimes, too, with a man, a therapist is needed because the man just can't hear correction from his wife—he just can't—so another voice needs to be brought in, maybe a male voice, that he *will* listen to . . . until he learns to listen to you.

Remember the rule of thumb in trying to determine whether or not you and your husband need to go see a therapist: If you *think you need to go to therapy, you need to go to therapy, so go.*

If it's difficult to get through to your husband, if he has a hard time trusting what you see and what you say, if you need confirmation and reinforcement and support on his path of change, or if for whatever reason you think a therapist might help, bring in a therapist. If your husband refuses to see a marriage therapist, you could find an individual therapist for yourself and get the support you need there.*

8. See the Best in Him

On the path of your husband's change try to see the best in him. The same great heart that lives in you lives in him too, so try to speak from the best part of you to the best part of him. Speak to who your husband already is deep inside him, the great man, the heroic man who wants to do what's right and who has the courage and strength to do it. The path of change, the road to his greatness, will be hard for your husband, but it'll be a lot easier if he knows that he already has greatness in him, that he's just got to go in there and find it. For you, his wife, to already see that greatness in him, and to tell him you see it, and to hold him to its standard is very important.

- "I know the good man you are, Jason. I know the sweet guy who likes to get in his truck and go over to his aunt's house and spend

---

*To find a marriage counselor in your area, ask around among your friends for a few names. You can also ask your family physician or your gynecologist for a referral. If you can't get a referral from a friend or a health professional, you can go to your local phonebook and look under "Mental Health," "Psychotherapists," or "Marriage Counselors" and make some calls. To find a **psychiatrist** in your area, call 1-888-35-PSYCH. To find a **mental health counselor**, go online at www.counseling.org/AM/consumers.htm or www.Personalsolutions.com or call the American Counseling Association (1-800-347-6647). To find a **clinical social worker**, contact the National Association of Social Workers online at www. NASWdc.org. To find a **marriage and family therapist**, go to the American Association for Marriage and Family Therapy at www.aamft.org. To find a **pastoral counselor**, go to the American Association of Pastoral Counselors at www.aapc.org. To find a **clinical psychologist**, go to the American Psychological Association, found online at www.apahelpcenter.org, or you can call their therapist locator number (1-800-964-2000).

all day fixing her porch. I know you can't feel good about the way you brushed me aside this morning, and I'd like you to apologize."

- "You're the best man I've ever known, Hank. That's why I married you. And I know you adore me. And I adore you. And right now I want you to turn off the TV and come over here and sit next to me and talk to me."

See the best and highest in your husband. Even when he doesn't see it in himself. *Especially* if he doesn't see it in himself. He needs *some*body to be seeing him truly.

"We never know how high we are till we are called to rise," says Emily Dickinson.

We're your husbands, we rise to what you expect of us—what you already see in us—so on the path of our change see the truth in us even as we're becoming that truth.

9. You Are the Goal of His Journey

On the journey of your husband's change always remember that you are the goal of it and the achievement of his manhood. You are the harbor and haven at the end of all his sailing. You are where he's going and where the world is going.

Here's a little story about where the world is going. It's a true story.

It was the summer of 1970. Jane and I, twenty-one and twenty-four, not yet married but living together for a few months, were in the kitchen of our rented Victorian house on a pond in Belmont, Massachusetts. Jane was standing at the stove stirring vegetables in a wok, and I was sitting at the table putting a new ribbon in my typewriter. Our old college friend from Cornell, Mary, was hanging out with us, cutting carrots. The three of us were talking about the sixties. Crosby, Stills, and Nash were playing on the stereo in the living room . . .

Wooden ships
on the water
very free and easy
Easy
you know the way
it's supposed to be . . .

"What do you think was the most important thing to come out of the sixties, Robert?" Mary asked.

"The women's liberation movement," I said instantly.

To this day I don't know where that answer came from. I had never even *thought* about the women's liberation movement before that moment.

"Why do you say that?" Jane said, sounding surprised and pleased.

"Because for the women's liberation movement to really succeed, it has to carry the men's liberation movement along with it, so it's really the leading edge of the *human* liberation movement, which is the salvation of the world."

I *really* have no idea where *that* came from.

Go
take a sister then
by the hand . . .
Lead her away
from this foreign land . . .
Far away
where we might laugh again . . .

"So where's the men's liberation movement, Robert?" Mary said, laughing.

From across the kitchen she and Jane were both looking at me, smiling. I thought for a moment.

"I don't know," I said. "I guess right here."

At the end of the path of your husband's change he finally gets it, he *really* changes, he sees the truth, the work is done (except for a few dribs and drabs), and inside him he's saying, *Right! This is the way I now behave to my wife because it's the truth of how I really feel about her. I know who she is to me: the person helping me to be the best person I can be by bringing these truths into my life—the saving grace of my life, the love of my life—so for the rest of my life I will treat her with all the love, respect, honor, and reverence that she deserves.*

That's the endgame. That's when your husband *totally gets it*. That's where he's going.

And there's really nothing for you to do when he gets it like this except to welcome it, enjoy it, know you deserve it, and return it.

Because now he's a good husband, and now he deserves it.

III. IF YOUR HUSBAND REFUSES TO CHANGE

1. Try One More Time: Get the Two of You to Therapy!

If you finish *It's (Mostly) His Fault* and ask your husband to read it, and he refuses to read it outright, or starts reading it but stops somewhere in the middle because he's angry at it, or if he finishes reading it and gives it back to you saying some version of "This guy has his head up his ass," it may mean that your husband isn't going to change.

"Change? Nope. Not me. I won't change, you're the one who needs to change, I don't need to change, I don't want to even hear the word 'change' anymore, I am who I am, just deal with it, and where's dinner?"

If this is his response, go make dinner, but at some point in the middle of dinner put down your knife and fork, look him straight in the eye, and say this:

"Lanny, I'm asking you one last time to see how you need to change in this marriage. If you can't see it on your own, I'm asking you to please read this book on husbanding that I've been reading. It'll help you see it, and it'll help you change."

If he says no again, continue looking him straight in the eye and tell him that the time has come for the two of you to get some marriage counseling. If he agrees to try out a marriage counselor, he'll want you to be the one to find the counselor, to find out if your health insurance covers it, and to make the first appointment. Do so. In my own therapy practice 95 percent of the time wives make the initial phone call to me and arrange the first meeting. That's okay. Most men just don't reach out for help toward therapy, so you have to do it. Whatever you need to do to get him into therapy, do.

Ask your husband if he'd prefer a male or a female therapist. Many men prefer a male therapist because they tend to feel ganged up on in the presence of two females. That's okay. Find out the names of a few therapists of the gender your husband prefers,* then make the calls to them and ask questions: *Do you work with couples? Do you work with men? Do you work with difficult men like my husband? Do you work with depressingly difficult men like my husband? Can you get through to a man to whom there's no getting through? How long does your therapy take? Does your therapy work?*

Based on the answers you get and on whatever other factors are important to you, choose a therapist, arrange a time, and then get you and your husband there for the first session. From that point on it's the therapist's job to build a relationship with your

---

*For help in finding a good therapist, see the previous footnotes on pages 209–210 and 323.

husband (and of course with you), help the two of you identify the problems in your marriage, somehow stay in relationship with your husband while telling him that most of those problems are (mostly) his fault, and help the two of you learn a way of communicating so that you can solve them. If it's good therapy and the two of you stay to the end of it, you'll have a changed husband, a marriage that feels good to you, a way of communicating that feels good to you, and a good reason to go out and have a romantic dinner at an expensive restaurant.

2. It's Your Choice

What if your husband absolutely refuses to go into therapy, to read this book, to look at himself, to own his faults, to change himself? What if he proves to be immovable? What to do?

You make a choice.

You learn to live with him as he is and just *deal* with it, which many women do; or you leave him, which many women do.

Pain both ways.

Hard choice.

If you choose to stay with him and just deal with him as best you can, you'll feel the pain of your children's pain living in the long gloom of their parents' bad marriage, and you'll feel the pain of your own hurt and sadness and anger in a bad marriage, and you'll feel the heartsick pain of lifelong loneliness. You're married, yes, but you're not *really* married, because you don't really have a husband, a true partner and lover and companion and friend for life's great journey. "That was the loneliest it got for me," a woman once said in my office. "Being without the one you're with."

In my experience a woman chooses to stay with a husband who isn't going to change for many reasons: She can't bear the prospect of divorce, the ripping away from family and friends, the amputation of what she perceives is herself from herself; it's more convenient for her to stay married and in the house and not have to go through the tremendous hassle of one or both of them moving out; she is economically dependent on her husband, who is the primary breadwinner, and she likes the lifestyle that her husband's income provides; she doesn't want her children to go through the long emotional pain of their parents' separation and divorce; she wants her children to grow up in one household with a live-in dad; the prospect of single-parenting is too daunting for her; she doesn't want to deal with lawyers and courts and judges and even the remote possibility of losing her children in a child-custody battle; she's afraid her husband will retaliate against her physically, economically, or by speaking badly of her among family and friends, who will then turn against her; she's afraid her children will be turned against her; she's afraid that if she loses this man, she won't find another and she'll be alone for the rest of her life; despite her husband's behavior to her, she still feels love for the guy, or loyalty, or pity; or she may feel morally or religiously bound by her marriage vows.

I think these are all understandable reasons for a woman to choose to stay married to a low-quality husband who isn't going to change. They may not be the best reasons to stay, because there's subordination, fear, oppression, and various degrees of physical, economic, or psychological captivity built into all of them, but remember: Our culture builds all of them into marriage so that a woman will have a hard time getting out.

Sometimes I look at a couple and I wonder, what in God's name is this woman doing with this man? "The men that women marry, and why they marry them, will always be a marvel and a mystery to the world," wrote Henry Wadsworth Longfellow. I'll say. Sometimes I just don't get it. But then I think, *Who really understands the mystery of why two people get together in marriage and what keeps them together?* There is inevitability and destiny in each soul's journey that we cannot see.

Who can say?

I once worked with an older couple who had had forty-seven years of a combative marriage with a lot of quarreling in it. They'd spend entire therapy sessions squabbling and bickering about stuff so trivial I couldn't believe it. It looked really bad between them, and I didn't understand how they could have stayed together all these years. Then one day I had a dream about them in which I saw below the surface of their relationship down to the deepest level, way under the fighting, where they *weren't* fighting; they were *fine*; as a matter of fact, they were perfect for each other, for I saw that their souls had come here to abrade and smooth and polish each other like precious stones; way down at that level they were at peace with each other, and all was perfection between them. I saw all of that in the dream.

So who can say?

Marriage is a mystery. Who can really say?

So when a woman says to me, "My husband has had his chance to do this work, and he's not doing it, and he's not going to do it, and now I have to decide what I'm going to do, if I'm going to stay with him or leave him, and I want to know what you think," I will definitely tell her what I think, but I will always stop short of telling her what to do.

3. How to Tell If He's Changing

"How do you know whether or not your husband is actually changing?" I asked my client Gwen, a very perceptive forty-three-year-old, married for fourteen years. "You said Stanley has to be changing for you to stay with him, so how do you know if change is really going on with him?"

"I am looking for what is moving and what isn't moving in him," she said. "The whole thing divides along that line. If it's moving, it's fine. If it's not moving, I become an enabler. I have been an enabler of his behavior for all my marriage, and I'm not going to do that anymore. I have to be watching it all from moment to moment. Is he going to allow me to be naming it as we go along so that he'll be looking at it and changing it, or will he just keep re-forming it and re-forming it, and it will never end? It divides along the line of, is he or is he not working on it? That's my line in the sand. As long as he's working on it, as long as he's moving, I can stick with it. If he's not working on it, if he stops working on it, I'm going to divorce him."

4. For the Children's Sake

If you choose to stay for the sake of your children, I get it. I understand your love for them and your self-sacrifice for them. As their mother you go through the long pain of childbirth to give them life, and you are willing to go through the longer pain of marriage to the unsatisfactory husband who is their father in order to give them a family. I think there are millions of women who make that choice, and I think it's a noble choice.

I'm just not sure it's always the right choice—for your children.

I made this point to him in Chapter 35, "A Good Father," and I'll make it again here to you: In a healthy family—the way I think God intended family—the children are supposed to look up from their play or their books or their homework or their iPods and see their two parents being warm and affectionate with each other, talking in soft tones in the kitchen, holding hands on the couch, laughing and giggling with each other, *liking* each other, generally having a good time together. When children look up and see that, they feel all warm and secure and cuddly inside—like all is well with their parents, all's well in the adult world around them—and they can then go safely back into their world and resume doing the extremely important, developmental things, like coloring their coloring books or instant messaging their friends, that they were doing before they left to check out the adult world.

But when they look up from their world and see their parents fighting and hear arguing and feel coldness and hear silence, the children don't go back to their world feeling warm and secure, they go back feeling worried and agitated and wary, which means they don't really even go back but have to stay out, their eyes and ears cocked for the next sign of trouble in their family—*What's the next bad thing that's going to happen around here?*—and so their normal child development process gets disrupted and they start to slip into the anxiety and depression and addiction disorders that will plague them for the rest of their lives.

In some cases, I'm sure, a woman's decision to stay in a bad marriage for the sake of her children is a good one. In some cases I think it's not.

One woman client, Annie, who was nearing a decision whether or not to stay married to her husband for the sake of her children, told me this story. She had a friend who had been in a similar situation some years before, a woman with two young children in a really unhappy marriage with a real lout of a guy, and she agonized for years over what to do. She tried repeatedly to get her husband to talk to her about their problems, but he refused, and he absolutely refused to go for marriage counseling. Dead end. No hope for this guy, no love for him left, no reason to stay married to him except for the children. Should she leave him, or should she stay for their sake? Back and forth, back and forth—nothing solid she could stand on to make that decision. Then one day she was talking on the telephone to her elderly mother in Iowa and decided to ask her point-blank what she should do.

"I can't live your life for you, honey," her mother said, "but I'll tell you this. I'm at an age now where I've realized that the criterion I want to base all my decisions on—little decisions, big decisions, decisions about what to do with my time, what to do with my friends, what to ask of your father—is my own happiness. My *own* happiness. The way I'm living my life now is I'm choosing my happiness over everything, and trusting that that's the way to go, that's what the good Lord wants for me. And I guess I've come to believe that in the end that's best for everybody, like there's something about me being happy that's not only okay but it's really important for everybody. Our minister gave one of his sermons on family a couple of years ago, and he quoted something that's always stuck with me: *If Mama ain't happy, ain't nobody happy.* So if you're not happy, dear, can the children be happy? For me, I've gotten to the point where I'm just letting my happiness be my guide and leaving the rest to the Lord."

Annie's friend left her husband. Annie left hers too.

5. The In-House Divorce

If you choose, for whatever reason, to stay with a husband who isn't going to change, remember that there is a staying with him that is really a kind of leaving him—the in-house kind of leaving—and it might be the right choice for you.

That's the kind of leaving him where you don't separate into two different households, and you don't legally divorce him, but there's an inner divorce from him, even while you remain living with him.

Here's how one of my clients, a woman in her late forties with three teenage children, described it:

"I can't expect him to ever change and be less difficult. He can't really. He's got too much undealt-with material inside him from his childhood, and he doesn't want to introspect or reflect or think about any of it, so he can't really grow beyond where he is. He's like a little boy, with psychological problems that seriously affect his ability to be in a good relationship with me or any adult, and he's not even coming close to addressing them. I looked in on him yelling at someone on the phone the other night, and I realized that's who he is and will always be. He's an angry man. Irritable. *Irritating.* He's just an irritating person. He treats me like I have nothing else to do in my life but serve him. I can't wait on his change any longer.

"So I've gotten to a place inside myself where he doesn't get to me anymore. I don't inwardly react anymore. I'm tired of all that. I no longer let him affect me. I'm on my own. I feel better. My happiness—my*self*—means more to me than it ever has, so I no longer allow myself to get disturbed by him. I get some good stuff from him—he's a good provider, and I get to live in this nice house with the kids, and he's a pretty good dad—and I'm grateful for those aspects of him, I'm his beneficiary there, but I am no longer his victim, I am no longer living at the effect of him. To tell you the truth, there's very little of me that feels married to him.

"I'm making a choice here. When I was growing up, in that first mistreatment of me in my life, I didn't have a choice, but now, in this second one, I do. I'm a grown-up now. My choice is that I can stick it out in this marriage for some time, with the understanding that he's not meeting and cannot meet my deeper needs, and I can bide my time, and I will choose the time—which could be three years from now, when the kids are off to college, or eight or nine or ten years from now. *I* will choose the time when I am out of here."

6. The Question of Sex

For women who choose to stay living with a husband whom they no longer feel emotionally close to, the question arises, *What to do about sex?*

There are four things to do, four options. Three of them, in my opinion, are okay, and one, in my opinion, is not.

If the sexual relationship with your husband has been an enjoyable one, if he's a pretty good lover and gives you sexual pleasure, and if sex is a way that the two of you do manage to connect and feel close for a time, even if there's major disconnection in the other parts of your relationship, then by all means continue having sex with your husband, and enjoy it.

The second option is to forget it. No more sex from me, buddy boy. If your husband doesn't want to learn how to be emotionally intimate with you, you can choose not to be physically intimate with him. You have that right. Bye-bye, sex. Enjoy your swimsuit issue, buddy boy, knock yourself out.

There's a third option. If you're the kind of woman who sincerely believes that being sexual with your husband is part of the marriage contract, part of a wife's obligation to her husband, even though you don't really enjoy it and could easily live without it, you could follow the example of the Victorian baroness Lady Alice Hillingdon, who writes in her journal: "I am happy now that Charles calls on my bedchamber less frequently than of old. As it is, I endure but two calls a week, and when I hear his steps outside my door, I lie down on my bed, close my eyes, open my legs, and think of England."

One thing *not* to do with your sexuality if you stay in the marriage is to bring it outside the marriage to an extramarital affair. I never recommend an affair for either partner in a marriage, for any reason. In my experience working with married couples where there have been extramarital affairs, women usually have them because they're lonely, men have them because they're stupid, but in my opinion nobody should be having them because they wreak havoc in the marriage and in the family and, I think, in all the universe.

7. Pray for a Miracle

If you choose to remain living with your husband for whatever good reason you have, remember that strange and wondrous things do sometimes happen on God's green earth; that lightning does sometimes knock an ignorant and arrogant man unconscious off his horse, and he wakes up a saint; and that we're in the middle of a huge planetwide paradigm shift, a transmutation of consciousness across the globe that on some level is affecting each and every one of us, men and women, even—hard as it may be to believe—your husband.

So who knows? Will he always be difficult? Will he always be impossible to get through to? Will he never face his faults? Will he *never* change?

I don't know.

But I know that seeds get planted, and if it's not stony or thorny or arid ground, but good ground, with time seeds grow; and I know that the times they are a-changing; and I know that in all times and in all places, including in marriages, and maybe in yours, there are sometimes miracles, and we can pray for them.

8. To Leave or Not to Leave

"Associations formed on this earth are not necessarily for the duration of the lifespan," says one spiritual teacher. With separations and divorces, she says, "not only is there no spiritual injury, but spiritual progress may actually be helped."

In other words, if he's not going to change, if the thickness of his head is stronger than the power of your truth, if he's not even going to *try* to become the good husband you want, you can leave him. Stop trying to persuade, debate, appease, or adapt to him. Instead, declare the present state of the relationship unacceptable to you and walk out or kick him out.

"I am strong enough now not to have him in my life," said one of my clients recently. "I don't need him anymore. I'm on my own. There isn't anything I can't handle—by myself," and she made the call to a divorce lawyer.

Divorce.

It happens. It's not pleasant when it happens; and everybody involved in it—you, your husband, your children, family, and friends—feels pain when it happens; and I think angels in heaven shed a few tears when it happens . . . but it happens.

My daughter is in a very happy marriage with a great husband, but if she wasn't, if she was in an unhappy marriage with a man who didn't know how to connect with her or relate to her or take care of her or truly love her, and if that man showed no signs of changing or wanting to change, and if my daughter asked me for advice about what to do, I'd tell her to get out. In a heartbeat.

"It's probably not going to be easy to get out," I'd say, "but get out. You don't have to put up with that stuff, honey. You don't have to stay for that. You don't have to be unhappy for the rest of your life. Not *my* daughter. There are a lot of really good men out there for good women like yourself, so go find one."

One woman I worked with many years ago, Bethany, did not leave her husband even though he treated her with disrespect bordering on contempt, berated her in front of the children, threatened to "screw other women," and was driving the family to the brink of financial ruin with a series of stupid, reckless business ventures. She came into individual therapy to talk about all this, brought him once, he never came back, and she stopped soon after.

In her last session she told me she wasn't going to leave him, that some inner force she didn't understand was keeping her there, and she was going to "ride it out" with him. Did I have any advice?

"When you're living in an unsatisfying relationship with a man," I said, "and you choose to stay, you want to stay in the healthiest way possible, a way that preserves your power and dignity and self-respect, and the people who have figured out how to do that the best, in my opinion, are the people at Al-Anon. Their focus is on living with a partner who's an alcoholic, it's true, but the principles that underlie their program are relevant to all people living with partners who don't know how to have an intimate, connected relationship, and most meetings are open to all comers. So I'd start there. Find an Al-Anon meeting. Listen to other people's stories and tell yours. That may lead you to other kinds of meetings more specific to your situation—women living with flaming assholes, for example—or maybe not, maybe you'll stay with Al-Anon, but the important thing here is to find a fellowship or sisterhood, to not be alone, to learn how to focus on you and nurture you, and not be angry and depressed all the time, and live your life."*

Another woman, Estella, brought her husband into marital counseling with me, but within a few weeks he stopped, left therapy, and refused all change. So she left him, walked right out of the house with her baby one morning, moved to an apartment, got a good lawyer, and initiated divorce proceedings. It was a difficult and contentious divorce, including a child-custody battle, and Estella got no support from her own family—the best they

---

*Al-Anon's Web site is al-anon.alateen.org. Their national phone number is 1-888-4AL-ANON (1-888-425-2666). Another organization that addresses the issues of people living in relationship with addicted and/or abusive partners is Codependents Anonymous (CoDA); their Web site is codependents.org.

could do was warn her grimly of the fiscal realities facing her, and her mother actually took the husband's side, blaming Estella for being too inflexible and demanding of him—but Estella pushed on through the process, faced her legion of fears as they came up, got the support she needed from her woman friends and her therapy, and eventually won the divorce on the terms she wanted.

At one point in the process, after a court appearance in which Estella had had to argue her case before a judge, she said to me in session, "I'm so grounded and centered in my knowledge of this—that I have to be rid of this man—that I don't care what my family thinks, I don't care what anybody thinks, I don't care if life's going to be harder for me now, and I don't care how long or how hard I have to fight him in this divorce. I don't want him anymore, I just don't want him anymore."

Divorce.

The power to walk away from your husband when he doesn't meet your needs and you don't want him anymore.

Power.

IV. THE INNER POWER

It's (Mostly) His Fault is about the big change your husband needs to make in order to be a good husband to you. It's also about your big change. Your big change in the good-husband work is that you experience your power.

Actually this whole book is about your power.

The power that I'm talking about is an inner power, and it exists in you, in all women, and in all human beings. It is a power that does not fluctuate with the fluctuations of other people, how they act and react, what they do or don't do, or with situations and circumstances. This power is in you if your husband reads every word of this book in one sitting, gets it immediately and completely, and before your very eyes undergoes a radiant transfiguration into the world's best and dearest husband; and this power is in you if your husband starts to read it but rips it to shreds in a fit of fury one night, or doesn't read a single word of it and doesn't change a single thing about himself. This power knows that ultimately he's a variable you're not in control of, but *you're* not a variable you're not in control of—you're a constant, your self-respect and dignity are a constant, and your standards of how you want to be treated by your husband are constant. This power is in you if your marriage becomes a great marriage, if you decide to stay in your not-so-great marriage for whatever good reason you have, or if you decide to leave your marriage and look for a better man, or a woman, or go it alone.

The way to get to this inner power is to do psychological and spiritual work on yourself. Following the wise guidance of teachers, counselors, self-help groups and programs, books, and the sisterhood of women, you walk that long and winding road down into yourself until you come to the truth about yourself.

The truth about yourself is that you have this power, and the deepest truth about yourself is that you *are* this power.

Here, in this man's opinion, is what I think your power is in your marriage:

A Woman's Proclamation of Power

- It's the power to believe in yourself—that you are connected to truth, that what you think and feel and say is true, and that you know the difference between truth and untruth.
- It is the power to know what you want and what you don't want from your husband, to know what's okay and what's not okay with you in his behavior to you.

- It's a teaching power, and it teaches your husband *right* behavior toward you, and it derives its authority from universal laws of right behavior which you read about in your books of wisdom and which you know in your heart to be true.
- It's the power to say yes to whatever you want to say yes to, and to say no to whatever you want to say no to, and the right to change your mind when you want to.
- It is the power to say yes or no to sex, depending on how you're feeling at that moment and how you're feeling about him.
- It is the power to set boundaries with him—times and spaces and possessions that are yours, not his—and to draw behavioral lines he may not cross.
- It's the power to tell him all this and keep telling him all this until he *gets* it that you mean what you're saying—and what you're most deeply saying is that he must change in the ways you're telling him to change.
- It's the power to know what's the appropriate and correct action to take or the words to say in any and all dealings with him, and to do it and to say it.
- It's the power to say, "It's not okay to talk to me disrespectfully," and to leave the room if he does.
- It is the power to leave the marriage if he treats you disrespectfully.
- It is the power to not take any form of abuse anymore from him or anyone.
- It's the power to want respect and attention and connection and communication from him, and to say, "We have to sit down together and talk about our relationship," when you're not getting those.
- It is the power to ask and expect your husband to live from his greatness, as you are trying to live from your greatness.
- It's a power that brings you and your husband and your whole family and all things together. It is a peaceful, gentle, compassionate,

and benevolent power that seeks the good of all. It's the power of love. It is the most powerful force in the universe, and it's a fighting force. It fights for the good and the true and the right; and it fights hard, well, and long; and in the end it always wins.

So keep going into yourself and find this great power there. When the wife has found this power in herself, and the husband has found this power in himself, the marriage becomes great. The light of love glows in the faces of the husband and wife. There is respect and kindness between them. And more and more love in the world.

In a good marriage between a man and a woman, each is devoted to the other's full attainment of this inner power because each knows that that's the golden opportunity and the spiritual purpose of marriage: to experience this power, to confer power, to share power, and to use power for the benefit and stewardship of our children, our communities, our nations, and the world.

A MOVE

I suggest that you sit down and write your husband a letter in the next couple of days or weeks. Make it a long letter. Write down whatever it is you want to say to him, whatever's in your mind and heart, now that you've read this book. Now that you know it's okay to ask him to change, ask him to change. Tell him what you want him to change about himself. Don't hold back. Say what you want. Say it clear, say it strong, say it once and for all, and sign it "Love."

Then, when the time is right, give or mail it to him, or put it in his briefcase or on his pillow.

Then don't say another word about it.

Afterword

Once there was a little boy who loved picture puzzles, so his father made him one by cutting up a picture of a map of the world that he found in a magazine. As far as the father knew, the boy had never seen a map of the world before, so the father thought the puzzle would be challenging and fun for the boy. He gave it to his son, who ran off into his bedroom to work on it.

In twenty minutes he was back. He had finished it! There it was, laid out on a square of clear plastic, the map of the world, all pieced together—perfect!

"How did you manage to do it so fast?" asked the father with a mixture of pride and bewilderment. "I thought it would take you much longer. You really don't know what the world looks like, do you?"

"Not really," said the boy, "but I looked at that magazine yesterday, and I remembered that on the back of the page where the picture of the world was, there was a picture of a man. So all I had to do was put the man together. I knew that if I got the man right, I'd get the world right."

Author's Note

You say goodbye, and I say hello . . .

The Beatles

Now that you've finished reading the book, I'd like to invite you to our Web site: agoodhusband.com. You can also get there with: itsmostlyhisfault.com. Jane and I set it up as a place where we can meet with the women and men who have read the book and are doing, or thinking about doing, the good-husband work, or any work, in their marriages. It is free, interactive, and designed so that you can communicate with us. You can:

- Make comments about the book
- Share your experiences in your marriage
- Offer insights
- Ask questions (selected ones of which we will answer on the site)

There'll be quotes for contemplation, suggestions for new Moves husbands and wives can make in their marriages, and other features. Let's meet on the Web site and share our wisdom, stories, challenges, tears, and laughter about being husbands and wives.

And who knows? Maybe someday on the site we'll be offering a quality line of designer sportswear, like T-shirts for women that say, "It's (Mostly) His Fault," sweatshirts for men that say, "It's (Mostly) My Fault," and polo shirts and golf jackets and baseball caps and boxer shorts (cotton or silk) that say, "A Good Husband," so when he becomes one, he gets to wear them.

agoodhusband.com or itsmostlyhisfault.com.

We'll say good-bye to you here and hello to you there.

Endnotes

All the ideas in this book are based on my personal experience as a husband, my professional experience as a psychotherapist, and a lifetime reading the words of the world's wisest people in their poems, songs, books, and scripture. They are my authorities, and I am enormously indebted to them for their teachings and for their many quotes which grace this book.

References to the works that are the source of these quotes follow.

(v) Gurumayi Chidvilasananda, in darshan with Jane and Robert, June 1996.

(xiii) *As Good As It Gets*, screenplay by Mark Andrus, 1997.

(xv) India Arie, "Video," *Acoustic Soul*.

(xix) Geoffrey Chaucer, *The Canterbury Tales*, "The Tale of Melibee," *The Works of Geoffrey Chaucer*, 2nd edition, edited by F.N. Robinson, Houghton Mifflin Co., Boston, 1957, 1961.

(xix) Walt Whitman, "Unfolded Out of the Folds," in *Autumn Rivulets*, *Leaves of Grass and Selected Prose*, edited by John Kouwenhoven, Modern Library, New York, 1950.

(xix) William Shakespeare, *Taming of the Shrew* II:1.

(1) Hecaton of Rhodes, in *Wedding Readings: Centuries of Writing and Rituals on Love and Marriage*, selected by Eleanor Munro, Penguin, New York, 1989.

(5) Michael Moore, *Stupid White Men*, ReganBooks, New York, 2001.

(5) Jean Toomer, "The Blue Meridian," in *Wayward Seeking: A Collection of Writings by Jean Toomer*, edited by Darwin T. Turner, Howard University Press, Washington, D.C., 1980.

(8) From "The Sleeping Beauty," in *Grimm's Fairy Tales*, edited by Louis and Bryna Untermeyer, The Heritage Press, New York, 1962.

(17) Augustus Y. Napier, *The Fragile Bond: In Search of an Equal, Intimate, and Enduring Marriage*, Perennial, Harper and Row, New York, 1988.

(17) Roseanne Barr, in *The Quotable Woman*, Running Press, Philadelphia, 1991.

(19) "Talking with a man is like trying to saddle a cow . . ." Gladys Upham, in *Women's Wicked Wisdom*, edited by Michelle Louvric, Chicago Review Press, 2003.

(31) Bob Dylan, "It's Alright, Ma (I'm Only Bleeding)," Warner Bros., 1965.

(37) This is an adaptation of a story from the Japanese tradition, as told by Swami Durgananda in her article "The Way of the Warrior," in *Darshan* 4 (1987), SYDA Foundation.

(39) *Pleasantville*, written by Gary Ross, 1998.

(41) Ralph Waldo Emerson, *The Journals and Miscellaneous Notebooks of Ralph Waldo Emerson*, edited by William H. Gilman et al, Belknap Press, Harvard University Press, Cambridge, Massachusetts, 1834.

(42) Rebecca West, "Mr. Chesterton in Hysterics: A Study in Prejudice" in the socialist weekly *The Clarion*, Nov. 14, 1913, in *The Young Rebecca: Writings of Rebecca West, 1911-1917*, Viking Press, New York, 1982.

(42) Sally Kempton, "Cutting Loose," in *Esquire*, 1970.

(42) Jalaluddin Rumi, *These Branching Moments*, translated by John Moyne and

Coleman Barks, Copper Beech Press, Brown University, Providence, Rhode Island, 1987.

(63) Anne Lamott, *Operating Instructions: A Journal of My Son's First Year*, Ballantine Books, 1993.

(63 Joseph Campbell with Bill Moyers, *The Power of Myth*, Doubleday, New York, 1988.

(64) Paul Simon and Art Garfunkel, "I Am a Rock."

(64) The Beatles, "Get Back."

(64) The Eagles, "Desperado."

(67) Bob Dylan, "You're a Big Girl Now," *Blood on the Tracks*.

(70) Sigmund Freud in Ernest Jones, *Life and Work of Sigmund Freud*, volume II, Basic Books, New York, 1955.

(70) Alicia Keys, "A Woman's Worth."

(70-71) I do not know the source of the "Building a Bridge to Hawaii" story. A friend told it to me.

(71-74) Swami Durgananda tells a version of the Dame Ragnell story, for a different purpose, in her *Heart of Meditation: Pathways to a Deeper Experience*, SYDA Foundation, South Fallsburg, New York, 2002.

(76) Gurumayi Chidvilasananda, *Courage and Contentment*, SYDA Foundation, South Fallsburg, New York, 1999.

(78) Mark 10:8.

(78) Joseph Campbell with Bill Moyers, *The Power of Myth*, Doubleday, New York, 1988.

(78) Swami Muktananda, *I Have Become Alive: Secrets of the Inner Journey*, SYDA Publishing, South Fallsburg, New York, 1992.

(80) Natalie Merchant, "Kind and Generous."

(82) Bob Dylan, "You're Gonna Have to Serve Somebody," *Slow Train*.

(82) Walt Whitman, "Song of Myself," in *Leaves of Grass and Selected Prose*, edited by John Kouwenhoven, Modern Library, New York, 1950.

(87) St. Augustine, *The Confessions*, in *Mysticism: A Study and an Anthology*, edited by F.C. Happold, Penguin Books, Baltimore, 1963.

(87) D.H. Lawrence, *Sea and Sardinia*, in *D.H. Lawrence and Italy: Twilight in Italy, Sea and Sardinia, Etruscan Places*, Viking Press, New York, 1972.

(88) John 15:13.

(93) The Beatles, "A Hard Day's Night."

(94) Kahlil Gibran, "On Work," in *The Prophet*, Alfred A. Knopf, New York, 1964.

(95) See the chapter "Male Standard Time" in Robert M. Alter with Jane Alter, *How Long Till My Soul Gets It Right?* ReganBooks, 2001.

(96) The *I Ching* is an ancient Chinese book of prophecy and wisdom.

(105) Ralph Waldo Emerson, "The Poet," in *Selected Writings of Ralph Waldo Emerson*, edited by William H. Gilman, New American Library, New York, 1965.

(109) Marion Woodman and Elinor Dickson, *Dancing in the Flames: The Dark Goddess in the Transformation of Consciousness*, Shambhala, Boston.

(109) Jimmy Buffett, "Margaritaville."

(111) Ralph Waldo Emerson, "The American Scholar," in *Selected Writings of Ralph Waldo Emerson*, edited by William H. Gilman, New American Library, New York, 1965.

(111) F. Scott Fitzgerald, *The Crack-Up*, 1936.

(114) Exodus 3:14.

(115) *The Wisdom of Confucius*, translated by Lin Yutang, in *The Enlightened Mind*, edited by Stephen Mitchell, HarperCollins, New York, 1993.

(118) Mary Daly, *Beyond God the Father: Toward a Philosophy of Women's Liberation*, Beacon Press, Boston, 1978.

(118) Baroness Edith Summerskill, in a 1960 speech.

(122) D.H. Lawrence, *Lady Chatterly's Lover*, Modern Library, New York, 1993.

(123-124) Friedrich Nietzsche, "Human, All Too Human," in *The Portable Nietzsche*, edited and translated by Walter Kaufman, Viking Portable Library, New York, 1977.

(127) *Don Juan DeMarco*, written by Jeremy Leven, 1995.

(135) Muriel Rukeyser, "Käthe Kollwitz," in *The Collected Poems of Muriel Rukeyser*, University of Pittsburgh Press, 2005. Copyright © 1973 by Muriel Rukeyser. Reprinted with the permission of International Creative Management, Inc.

(135) *When a Man Loves a Woman*, written by Ronald Bass and Al Franken, 1994.

(136) "Poem of the Ute Indians," found in *The Quotable Woman*, Running Press, Philadelphia, 1991.

(140) I am indebted to my neighbor Will Kastner for help in finding and translating the Chinese character for the verb "to listen." Thank you, Will.

(142) Paul David Maloy, Joe Royer, and Dean Rutherford, "We're Supposed to Do That Now and Then." Copyright © 1990 Crazy Cow Music and Songs of Universal, Inc. All rights administered for Crazy Cow Music by Sony/ATV Acuff Rose Music Publishing LLC, 8 Music Square West, Nashville, TN 37203, and Songs of Universal, Inc. All rights reserved. Used by permission.

(150) *A League of Their Own*, screenplay by Lowell Ganz and Babaloo Mandel, 1992.

(150, 156) Billy Joel, "Tell Her About It."

(150-151) Robert Bly, *Iron John: A Book About Men*, Addison-Wesley, Reading, Massachusetts, 1990.

(151-152) This rendering of the word *emotions* is not etymologically correct, but it makes the point.

(158) Gloria Steinem, *Moving Beyond Words*, Simon and Schuster, New York, 1994.

(158) Sylvia Plath, excerpt from "Lady Lazarus" from *Ariel*. Copyright © 1963 and renewed 1991 by Ted Hughes. Reprinted with the permission of HarperCollins Publishers, Inc. and Faber and Faber, Ltd.

(159) Jean Baker Miller and Janet L. Surrey, "Revisioning Women's Anger: The Personal and the Global," Stone Center Working Paper #43, Wellesley Centers for Women, Wellesley College, Wellesley, Massachusetts. See also Dr. Miller's classic book *Toward a New Psychology of Women*, Beacon Press, Boston, 1976, 1986.

(164) Bob Dylan, excerpt from "License to Kill." Copyright © 1983 by Special Rider Music. All rights reserved. International copyright secured. Reprinted by permission.

(167) The idea that men's anger is often their "sense of entitlement or their reaction if this entitlement is not granted" I owe to Jean Baker Miller and Janet Surrey in their Stone Center Working Paper "Revisioning Women's Anger: The Personal and the Global," *op. cit.*

(169) Harriet Schock, "Ain't No Way to Treat a Lady." Copyright © 1975 (Renewed) Colgems EMI Music, Inc. International Copyright Secured. All Rights Reserved.

(169) Theodore Roosevelt, *The Americanism of Theodore Roosevelt*, in *What Is a Man?* edited by Walter R. Newell, ReganBooks, New York, 2000.

(173) King Solomon, *The Apocrypha*.

(173, 176) *Goldfinger*, screenplay by Richard Maibaum, 1965.

(175) *A League of Their Own*, screenplay by Lowell Ganz and Babaloo Mandel, 1992.

(178) M. Scott Peck, *The Road Less Traveled*, Simon and Schuster, New York, 1978.

(180) Joyce Rebeta-Burditt, *The Cracker Factory*, Macmillan Publishing Co., New York, 1977.

(180) Carl Jung, *Memories, Dreams, and Reflections*, recorded and edited by Aniela Jaffe, translated by Richard and Clara Winston, Vintage Books, New York, 1961.

(182) "There's nowhere to go . . ." adapted from Robert M. Alter, *The No-Nibbling Book: 128 Things to Remember or Do at the Refrigerator Door So You Won't Open It*, Putnam, 1981.

(185) Sam Keen, *Fire in the Belly*, Bantam, New York, 1991.

(185) *Moonstruck*, written by John Patrick Shanley, 1987.

(188) Andreas Cappellanus, *The Art of Courtly Love*, in *What Is a Man?: 3000 Years of Wisdom on the Art of Manly Virtue*, edited by Waller R. Newell, ReganBooks, New York, 2000.

(188) The Chiffons, "He's So Fine."

(192) Sheryl Crow, "Strong Enough."

(192) Sir Walter Raleigh, "As You Come Home from the Holy Land."

(198) "Make Love to Me." Words and Music by Bill Norvas, Allan Copeland, Leon Rappolo, Paul Mares, Ben Pollack, George Brunies, Mel Stitzel, and Walter Melrose. Copyright © 1953 (Renewed) Edwin H. Morris & Company, A Division of MPL Communications, Inc. International Copyright Secured. All Rights Reserved.

(201) "Meet Me Half Way" by Beth Chapman, Annie L. Roboff, and Bonnie Raitt. Copyright © 1998 by BNC Songs, Almo Music Corporation. All rights administered by Almo Music Corporation / ASCAP. Used by permission. All rights reserved.

(201) James E. Chambers, "You Can Get It If You Really Want." Words and Music by James E. Chambers. Copyright © by Songs of Universal, Inc. and Universal Songs of Polygram International Inc. All rights reserved.

(203) Sappho, in *The Quotable Woman*, Running Press, Philadelphia, 1971.

(204) William Blake, "The Marriage of Heaven and Hell," in *The Poetry and Prose of William Blake,* edited by David V. Erdman, Doubleday and Co., Garden City, New York, 1970.

(204) "Secret Garden," © 1995 by Bruce Springsteen. Reprinted by permission. International copyright secured. All rights reserved.

(211) I found the Robin Williams quote on the Web.

(211) Walt Whitman, "So Long," *Songs of Parting: Leaves of Grass and Selected Prose*, edited by John Kouwenhoven, Modern Library, New York, 1950.

(213) Jean Baker Miller, "Connections, Disconnections, and Violations," Stone Center Working Paper #33, Wellesley Centers for Women, Wellesley College, Wellesley, Masschusetts.

(217) Judith Viorst, "True Love," in *It's Hard to Be Hip Over Thirty, and Other Tragedies of Married Life*, World Publishing Co., New York, 1968.

(217) *In Good Company*, written by Paul Weitz, 2004.

(218) "Fidelity seems to come harder . . .", Sam Keen, *Fire in the Belly: On Being a Man*, Bantam, New York, 1991.

(222) *Norma Rae*, written by Harriet Frank Jr. and Irving Ravetch, 1979.

(222) Japanese folk song from *I Like Being Married: Treasured Traditions, Rituals, and Stories,* edited by Michael Leach and Therese J. Borchard, Doubleday, New York, 2002.

(223) Gypsy Rose Lee, in Barbara McDowell and Hana Umlouf, *Woman's Almanac*, 1977.

(224) "There is no old age . . .", Carol Matthau, *Among the Porcupines: A Memoir*, Turtle Bay Books, New York, 1992.

(227) Sumerian wedding poem, adapted from the translation by Diane Wolkstein and Samuel Noah Kramer, *Inanna: Queen of Heaven and Earth*, Harper and Row, New York, 1983.

(227) Steve Miller, Memphis E. Curtis, and Ahmet Ertegun, "The Joker." Copyright © BMG Songs, Inc/Jim Rooser Music Co (ASCAP)/Cotillion Music Inc. (ASCAP). Reprinted by permission of Alfred Publishing Co., Inc., Miami, FL 33014. All rights reserved.

(229) Paul "Bear" Bryant, quoted in *Boston Globe*, "Reflection for the Day" (date unknown).

(229) John Lennon, "Woman."

(231) I have not been able to find the source of the Maya Angelou quote.

(237) *The Honeymooners*.

(242) Marcelene Cox, *Ladies Home Journal* (1954), in *The New Beacon Book of Quotations by Women*, edited by Rosalie Maggio, Beacon Press, Boston, 1996.

(242) Paul Simon, "Father and Daughter." Copyright © 2002 by Paul Simon. Reprinted with the permission of the Publisher, Paul Simon Music.

(243) Joseph Chilton Pearce, *The Biology of Transcendence: A Blueprint of the Human Spirit*, Park Street Press, Rochester, Vermont, 2002.

(243) Albert Schweitzer, in *Great Quotes from Great Leaders*, Successories Publishing, Lombard, Illinois, 1990.

(245-246) Leonard Cohen, "Suzanne."

(246) "The most important thing . . ." Theodore M. Hesburgh, *Reader's Digest* (January 1963), in *Simpson's Contemporary Quotations*, compiled by James B. Simpson, Houghton-Mifflin, New York, 1988.

(246) I cannot cite the source, or attest to the veracity, of this research story. It came through on my e-mail.

(248) Mencius, *The Works of Mencius*, translated by James Legge, Volume II.

(248) Davy Crockett, *A Narrative of the Life of David Crockett of the State of Tennessee*, E. L. Carey and A. Hart Publishers, Philadelphia, 1834.

(252) Aretha Franklin, "Respect."

(252) Jeff Lynne, Roy Orbison and Tom Petty, "You Got It." Copyright © 1988 SBK April Music, Inc. (ASCAP) / Orbisongs (BMI) / Gone Gator Music. (ASCAP). International Copyright Secured. All Rights Reserved.

(253) Barry White, "Never Gonna Give You Up."

(253) Al Green, "Let's Stay Together."

(258) *Webster's New Collegiate Dictionary.* These definitions of "connect" are culled from various Webster's dictionaries: *Webster's New Twentieth Century Dictionary, Webster's New World Dictionary of the American Language* (Concise Edition), *Webster's Ninth New Collegiate Dictionary,* and *Webster's New Universal Unabridged Dictionary,* Merriam-Webster Inc., Publishers, Springfield, Massachusetts, 1956, 1964, 1983, 1983.

(258) Bonnie Raitt, "The Thing Called Love."

(260) "and then you start counting": I stole this line from Judith Viorst: "Brevity may be the soul of wit, but not when someone's saying, 'I love you.' When someone's saying 'I love you,' he always ought to give a lot of details: Like, Why does he love you? And, How much does he love you? And, When and where did he first begin to love you? . . . And even though he insists it would take forever to count the ways in which he loves you, let him start counting." *Love and Guilt and the Meaning of Life, Etc.,* Simon and Schuster, New York, 1979. Thank you, Judith.

(264) Terrence Real, *How Can I Get Through To You?: Closing the Intimacy Gap Between Men and Women,* Simon and Schuster, New York, 2002.

(264) Elizabeth Hawes, *Anything But Love* (1948), in *The New Beacon Book of Quotations by Women,* edited by Rosalie Maggio, Beacon Press, Boston, 1996.

(272) Bob Seger, "Like a Rock." Copyright © 1986 by Gear Publishing Company. Reprinted by permission. All rights reserved.

(277) Paul Overstreet and Donald Alan Schlitz, Jr., "The Calm at the Center of My Storm." Copyright © 1989 by New Hayes Music/New Don Songs (ASCAP). (Adm. by Carol Vincent and Associates, LLC.) All Rights Reserved. Reprinted by permission.

(279) Rig Veda Book I, hymn 54, verse 7.

(279) Thomas à Kempis, *The Imitation of Christ*, Doubleday and Co., Inc., Garden City, New York, 1955.

(283) *Analyze This*, screenplay by Peter Tolan, Harold Ramis, and Kenneth Lonergan, 1999.

(283) Paul Valéry, *Monsieur Teste*, Bollingen Series xlv, vol. 6, Princeton University Press, New Jersey, 1973.

(289) Anne Lamott, *Bird by Bird*, Random House, New York, 1994.

(293) Ralph Waldo Emerson, "The Conduct of Life: Wealth."

(293) Marcus Aurelius, *Meditations*.

(293) "Be strong, and do it." 1 Chronicles 28:10.

(295) Oprah Winfrey, February 1, 2005, on her show.

(302) *A League of Their Own*, screenplay by Lowell Ganz and Babaloo Mandel, 1992.

(303) Walt Whitman, "I Sing the Body Electric," stanza 5, *Children of Adam*, in *Leaves of Grass and Selected Prose*, edited by John Kouwenhoven, Modern Library College Editions, Random House, New York, 1950.

(303) Homer, *The Iliad*, book iii, line 199, translated by Alexander Pope, 1715.

(305) Frederique Apffel-Marglin, *The Sacred Grove*, "Manushi," May-June, 1994, p. 28, quoted in Carol Lee Flinders's wonderful book *At the Root of This Longing: Reconciling a Spiritual Hunger and a Feminine Thirst*, HarperSanFrancisco, New York, 1998.

(308) Oliver Wendell Holmes, *The Professor at the Breakfast Table*, Houghton Mifflin & Co., Boston, The Riverside Press, 1859.

(308) Chris Williamson, "Sweet Woman," *The Changer and the Changed*, Olivia Records, Inc., 1975.

(312) Marion Woodman, *The Ravaged Bridegroom*, Inner City Books, Toronto, Canada, 1990.

(312-313) "Remember that the expectation of superiority and control over a woman . . ." See Marion Woodman, *ibid.*

(317) "The hardest foe to fight is the one who has outposts inside your own head." This is a paraphrase of Ms. Kempton's *"It is hard to fight an enemy who has outposts inside your head"* ("Cutting Loose," *Esquire*, 1970).

(324) Emily Dickinson, "J1176," in Bradley, Beatty, and Long, editors, *American Tradition in Literature*, vol. 2, revised, W.W. Norton and Co., Inc., New York, 1962.

(325) David Crosby, Steven Stills, and Paul Kantner, "Wooden Ships." Copyright © by Gold Hill Music (BMI)/Icebag Corp (BMI)/Stay Straight Music (BMI). All rights administered by Sony/ATV Acuff Rose Music Publishing LLC, 8 Music Square West, Nashville, TN 37203. All rights reserved.

(325) "Because for the women's liberation movement . . . salvation of the world": Joseph Chilton Pearce makes a similar point in his brilliant book *The Biology of Transcendence* (Park Street Press, Rochester, Vermont, 2002): *"The ball is in Eve's court, and her revolution is the radical break with culture that will save us."* Emmeline Pankhurst (1858-1928), the British suffragist leader, said it too: *"We women suffragists have a great mission—the greatest mission the world has ever known. It is to free half the human race, and through that freedom to save the rest."*

(329) Henry Wadsworth Longfellow, *Michael Angelo*, Part First, V, "Vittoria Colonna."

(335) I found the Lady Hillingdon quotation in Terrence Real's excellent book *How Can I Get Through to You?: Closing the Intimacy Gap Between Men and Women*.

(336) *Peace Pilgrim: Her Life and Work in Her Own Words*, An Ocean Tree Book, Friends of Peace Pilgrim, 1982.

(343) John Denver, "What One Man Can Do." Copyright © 1980 by Cherry Lane Music Publishing Co. International copyright secured. All rights reserved.

(345) The Beatles, "Hello Goodbye."